On the *Revival of the Religious Sciences* (*Iḥyāʾ ʿulūm al-dīn*)

"The *Iḥyāʾ ʿulūm al-dīn* is the most valuable and most beautiful of books."

—Ibn Khallikān (d. 681/1282)

"The *Iḥyāʾ ʿulūm al-dīn* is one of al-Ghazālī's best works."

—Aḥmad b. ʿAbd al-Ḥalīm (d. 728/1328)

"Any seeker of [felicity of] the hereafter cannot do without the *Iḥyāʾ ʿulūm al-dīn*"

—Tāj al-Dīn al-Subkī (d. 771/1370)

"The *Iḥyāʾ ʿulūm al-dīn* is a marvelous book containing a wide variety of Islamic sciences intermixed with many subtle accounts of Sufism and matters of the heart."

—Ibn Kathīr (d. 774/1373)

"The *Iḥyāʾ ʿulūm al-dīn* is one of best and greatest books on admonition, it was said concerning it, 'if all the books of Islam were lost except for the *Iḥyāʾ* it would suffice what was lost.'"

—Ḥājjī Khalīfa Kātib Čelebī (d. 1067/1657)

"The *Iḥyāʾ* [*ʿulūm al-dīn*] is one of [Imām al-Ghazālī's] most noble works, his most famous work, and by far his greatest work'"

—Muḥammad Murtaḍā l-Zabīdī (d. 1205/1791)

On Imām al-Ghazālī

"Al-Ghazālī is [like] a deep ocean [of knowledge]."

—Imām al-Ḥaramayn al-Juwaynī (d. 478/1085)

"Al-Ghazālī is the second [Imām] Shāfiʿī."

—Muḥammad b. Yaḥyā l-Janzī (d. 549/1154)

"Abū Ḥāmid al-Ghazālī, the Proof of Islam (Ḥujjat al-Islām) and the Muslims, the Imām of the *imām*s of religion, [is a man] whose like eyes have not seen in eloquence and elucidation, and speech and thought, and acumen and natural ability."

—ʿAbd al-Ghāfir b. Ismāʿīl al-Fārisī (d. 529/1134)

"[He was] the Proof of Islam and Muslims, Imām of the imāms of religious sciences, one of vast knowledge, the wonder of the ages, the author of many works, and [a man] of extreme intelligence and the best of the sincere."

—Imām al-Dhahabī (d. 748/1347)

"Al-Ghazālī is without doubt the most remarkable figure in all Islam."

—T.J. DeBoer

". . . A man who stands on a level with Augustine and Luther in religious insight and intellectual vigor."

—H.A.R. Gibb

"I have to some extent found, and I believe others can find, in the words and example of al-Ghazālī a true *iḥyāʾ* . . ."

—Richard J. McCarthy, S.J.

مَّا يَلْفِظُ مِن قَوْلٍ إِلَّا لَدَيْهِ رَقِيبٌ عَتِيدٌ ﴿١٨﴾

[A human being] utters no word except that with him is an observer prepared [to record]....

Sūrat Qaf

50:18

The Forty Books of the Revival of the Religious Sciences (*Iḥyāʾ ʿulūm al-dīn*)

The Quarter of Worship

1 The Book of Knowledge
2 The Principles of the Creed
3 The Mysteries of Purification
4 The Mysteries of the Prayer
5 The Mysteries of Charity
6 The Mysteries of Fasting
7 The Mysteries of the Pilgrimage
8 The Etiquette of the Recitation of the Qurʾān
9 Invocations and Supplications
10 The Arrangement of the Litanies and the Exposition of the Night Vigil

The Quarter of Customs

11 The Proprieties of Eating
12 The Proprieties of Marriage
13 The Proprieties of Acquisition and Earning a Living
14 The Lawful and the Unlawful
15 The Proprieties of Friendship and Brotherhood
16 The Proprieties of Retreat
17 The Proprieties of Travel
18 The Proprieties of the Audition and Ecstasy
19 The Commanding of Right and the Forbidding of Wrong
20 The Proprieties of Living and the Prophetic Mannerisms

The Quarter of Perils

21 The Exposition of the Wonders of the Heart
22 Training the Soul, Refining the Character, and Treating the Ailments of the Heart
23 Overcoming the Two Desires
24 **The Banes of the Tongue**
25 The Banes of Anger, Malice, and Envy
26 The Censure of This World
27 The Censure of Greed and the Love of Wealth
28 The Censure of Fame and Hypocritical Ostentation
29 The Censure of Pride and Vanity
30 The Censure of Deceit

The Quarter of Deliverance

31 On Repentance
32 On Patience and Thankfulness
33 On Fear and Hope
34 On Poverty and Abstinence
35 On Unity and Trust
36 On Love, Longing, Intimacy, and Contentment
37 On Intention, Sincerity, and Truthfulness
38 On Vigilance and Accounting
39 On Contemplation
40 On the Remembrance of Death and the Hereafter

THE BANES OF THE TONGUE

Kitāb āfāt al-lisān

Book 24 of the

Iḥyāʾ ʿulūm al-dīn

The Revival of the Religious Sciences

بِسْمِ ٱللَّهِ ٱلرَّحْمَٰنِ ٱلرَّحِيمِ

AL-GHAZĀLĪ

Kitāb āfāt al-lisān

THE BANES OF THE TONGUE

Book 24 of the *Iḥyāʾ ʿulūm al-dīn*

THE REVIVAL OF THE RELIGIOUS SCIENCES

Translated *from the* Arabic *with an* Introduction *and* Notes *by*

M. Abdurrahman Fitzgerald and M. Fouad Aresmouk

Fons Vitae
2024

The Banes of The Tongue, Book 24 of the *Revival of the Religious Sciences* first published in 2024 by

Fons Vitae
49 Mockingbird Valley Drive
Louisville, KY 40207 USA

www.fonsvitae.com

The Fons Vitae Ghazali Series
Library of Congress Control Number: 2023949804
ISBN 978-1-94-1610-68-8

Copyediting and indexing: Valerie Joy Turner
Book design and typesetting: www.scholarlytype.com
Text typeface: Adobe Minion Pro 11/13.5

Cover art courtesy of National Library of Egypt in Cairo.
Qurʾānic frontispiece to part 19. Written and illuminated by ʿAbdallāh b. Muḥammad al-Ḥamadānī for Sultan Ūljāytū (Muḥammad Khudābanda Öljeytü) 713/1313. Hamadan.

Printed in Canada

Contents

Editor's Note

THIS is the complete translation of *Kitāb āfāt al-lisān* (*The Banes of the Tongue*) book 24 of the *Iḥyāʾ ʿulūm al-dīn* of Abū Ḥāmid Muḥammad al-Ghazālī. It is a translation of the published Arabic text of volume 5 (pages 387–581), edited by Dār al-Minhāj (Jedda, 2011); the Dār al-Minhāj editors utilized manuscripts and early printed editions, as mentioned on pages 51–111 of the introductory volume.

Arabic terms and names follow the transliteration system of the *International Journal of Middle East Studies*. Common era (CE) dates have been added and follow Hijri dates. The blessings on prophets and others, as used by Imām al-Ghazālī, are represented in the original Arabic, as listed below.

Arabic	English	Usage
عَزَّوَجَلَّ	Mighty and majestic is He	On mention of God
سُبْحَانَهُ وَتَعَالَىٰ	Exalted and most high is He	Used together or separately
صَلَّى ٱللَّهُ عَلَيْهِ وَسَلَّمَ	Blessings and peace of God be upon him	On mention of the Prophet Muḥammad
عَلَيْهِ ٱلسَّلَامُ عَلَيْهِمُ ٱلسَّلَامُ	Peace be upon him Peace be upon them	On mention of one or more prophets
رَضِيَ ٱللَّهُ عَنْهُ رَضِيَ ٱللَّهُ عَنْهُمْ	God be pleased with him God be pleased with them	On mention of one or more Companions of the Prophet
رَضِيَ ٱللَّهُ عَنْهَا	God be pleased with her	On mention of a female Companion of the Prophet
رَحِمَهُ ٱللَّهُ	God have mercy on him	On mention of someone who is deceased

The majority of sources in the notes are from the Dār al-Minhāj editors. Other explanatory information is provided by translators (preceded by Trans.), the reviewer of the translation (preceded by FC for Faris Casewit), and the editors (preceded by Eds.).

In addition, we have compiled a short biography of Imām al-Ghazālī with a chronology of important events in his life. This is followed by an extract from Imām al-Ghazālī's introduction to the *Iḥyāʾ ʿulūm al-dīn;* it serves as a guide to the *Revival of the Religious Sciences* for those reading Imām al-Ghazālī for the first time. For this edition we included the page numbers of this book in volume 5 of the Arabic edition; these appear in the margins after the vertical line mark |.

Biography of Imām al-Ghazālī

He is Abū Ḥāmid Muḥammad b. Muḥammad b. Muḥammad b. Aḥmad al-Ghazālī l-Ṭūsī; he was born in 450/1058 in the village of Ṭābarān near Ṭūs (in northeast Iran) and he died there, at the age of fifty-five, in 505/1111. Muḥammad's father died when he and his younger brother Aḥmad were still young; their father left a little money for their education in the care of a Sufi friend of limited means. When the money ran out, their caretaker suggested that they enroll in a *madrasa*. The *madrasa* system meant they had a stipend, room, and board. Al-Ghazālī studied *fiqh* in his hometown under a Sufi named Aḥmad al-Rādhakānī; he then traveled to Jurjān and studied under Ismāʿīl b. Masʿada al-Ismāʿīlī (d. 477/1084).

On his journey home his caravan was overtaken by highway robbers who took all of their possessions. Al-Ghazālī went to the leader of the bandits and demanded his notebooks. The leader asked, what are these notebooks? Al-Ghazālī answered: "This is the knowledge that I traveled far to acquire," the leader acquiesced to al-Ghazālī's demands after stating: "If you claim that it is knowledge that you have, how can we take it away from you?" This incident left a lasting impression on the young scholar. Thereafter, he returned to Ṭūs for three years, where he committed to memory all that he had learned thus far.

In 469/1077 he traveled to Nīshāpūr to study with the leading scholar of his time, Imām al-Ḥaramayn al-Juwaynī (d. 478/1085), at the Niẓāmiyya College; al-Ghazālī remained his student for approximately eight years, until al-Juwaynī died. Al-Ghazālī was one of his most illustrious students, and al-Juwaynī referred to him as "a deep ocean [of knowledge]." As one of al-Juwaynī's star pupils, al-Ghazālī used to fill in as a substitute lecturer in his teacher's absence. He also tutored his fellow students in the subjects that al-Juwaynī taught at the Niẓāmiyya. Al-Ghazālī wrote his first book, on the founding principles of legal theory (*uṣūl al-fiqh*), while studying with al-Juwaynī.

Very little is known about al-Ghazālī's family, though some biographers mention that he married while in Nīshāpūr; others note that he had married in Ṭūs prior to leaving for Nīshāpūr. Some accounts state that he had five children, a son who died early and four daughters. Accounts also indicate that his mother lived to see her son rise to fame and fortune.

After the death of al-Juwaynī, al-Ghazālī went to the camp (*al-muʿaskar*) of the Saljūq *wazīr* Niẓām al-Mulk (d. 485/1192). He stayed at the camp, which was a gathering place for scholars, and quickly distinguished himself among their illustrious company. Niẓām al-Mulk recognized al-Ghazālī's genius and appointed him professor at the famed Niẓāmiyya College of Baghdad.

Al-Ghazālī left for Baghdad in 484/1091 and stayed there four years—it was a very exciting time to be in the heart of the Islamic empire. At the Niẓāmiyya College he had many students, by some estimates as many as three hundred. In terms of his scholarly output, this was also a prolific period in which he wrote *Maqāṣid al-falāsifa, Tahāfut al-falāsifa, al-Mustaẓhirī,* and other works.

Al-Ghazālī was well-connected politically and socially; we have evidence that he settled disputes related to the legitimacy of the rule of the ʿAbbāsid caliph, al-Mustaẓhir (r. 487–512/1094–1118) who assumed his role as the caliph when he was just fifteen years old, after the death of his father al-Muqtadī (d. 487/1094). Al-Ghazālī issued a *fatwā* of approval of the appointment of al-Mustaẓhir and was present at the oath-taking ceremony.

In Baghdad, al-Ghazālī underwent a spiritual crisis, during which he was overcome by fear of the punishment of the hellfire. He became convinced that he was destined for the hellfire if he did not change his ways; he feared that he had become too engrossed in worldly affairs, to the detriment of his spiritual being. He began to question his true intentions: was he writing and teaching to serve God, or because he enjoyed the fame and fortune that resulted from his lectures. He experienced much suffering, both inward and outward; one day as he stood before his students to present a lecture, he found himself unable to speak. The physicians were unable to diagnose any physical malady. Al-Ghazālī remained in Baghdad for a time, then left his teaching post for the pilgrimage. He left behind fortune, fame, and influence. He was beloved by his numerous students and had many admirers, including the sultan; he was also envied by many. The presumption is that he left in the manner he did—ostensibly to undertake the pilgrimage—because if he had made public his intentions to leave permanently, those around him would have tried to convince him to remain and the temptation might have been too strong to resist.

After leaving Baghdad, he changed direction and headed toward Damascus; according to his autobiography he disappeared from the intellectual scene for ten years. This does not mean that he did not teach, but that he did not want to return to public life and be paid for teaching. This ten-year period can be divided into two phases. First, he spent two years in the East—in greater Syria and on the pilgrimage. We have evidence that while on his return to Ṭūs he appeared at a Sufi lodge opposite the Niẓāmiyya College in Baghdad. He spent the second phase of the ten-year period (the remaining eight years) in Ṭūs, where he wrote the famed *Iḥyāʾ ʿulūm al-dīn*, a work that was inspired by the change in his outlook that resulted from his spiritual crisis.

When he arrived back in his hometown in 490/1097, he established a school and a Sufi lodge, in order to continue teaching and learning. In 499/1106, Niẓām al-Mulk's son, Fakhr al-Mulk, requested that al-Ghazālī accept a teaching position at his old school, the Niẓāmiyya of Nīshāpūr. He accepted and taught for a time, but left this position in 500/1106 after Fakhr al-Mulk was assassinated by Ismāʿīlīs. He then returned to Ṭūs and divided his time between teaching and worship. He died in 505/1111 and was buried in a cemetery near the citadel of Ṭābarān.

Legacy and Contributions of al-Ghazālī

Al-Ghazālī's two hundred seventy-three works span many disciplines and can be grouped under the following headings.

1. Jurisprudence and legal theory. Al-Ghazālī made foundational contributions to Shāfiʿī jurisprudence; his book *al-Wajīz* is a major handbook that has been used in teaching institutions around the world; many commentaries have been written on it, most notably by Abū l-Qāsim ʿAbd al-Karīm al-Rāfiʿī (d. 623/1226). In legal theory, *al-Mustaṣfa min ʿilm al-uṣūl* is considered one of five foundational texts in the discipline.
2. Logic and philosophy. Al-Ghazālī introduced logic in Islamic terms that jurists could understand and utilize. His works on philosophy include the *Tahāfut al-falāsifa*, which has been studied far beyond the Muslim world and has been the subject of numerous commentaries, discussions, and refutations.
3. Theology, including works on heresiography in refutation of Bāṭinī doctrines. He also expounded on the theory of occasionalism.
4. Ethics and educational theory. The *Mīzān al-ʿamal* and other works such as the *Iḥyāʾ ʿulūm al-dīn* mention a great deal on education.
5. Spirituality and Sufism. His magnum opus, the *Iḥyāʾ ʿulūm al-dīn* is a pioneering work in the field of spirituality, in terms of its organization and its comprehensive scope.
6. Various fields. Al-Ghazālī also wrote shorter works in a variety of disciplines, including his autobiography (*al-Munqidh min al-ḍalāl*), works on Qurʾānic studies (*Jawāhir al-Qurʾān*), and political statecraft (*Naṣiḥat al-mūluk*).

Chronology of al-Ghazālī's Life

450/1058	Birth of al-Ghazālī at Ṭūs
c. 461/1069	Began studies at Ṭūs
c. 465/1073	Traveled to Jurjān to study
466–469/1074–1077	Studied at Ṭūs
469/1077	Studied with al-Jūwaynī at the Niẓāmiyya college in Nīshāpūr
473/1080	al-Ghazālī composed his first book, *al-Mankhūl fī l-uṣūl*
477/1084	Death of al-Fāramdhī, one of al-Ghazālī's teachers
25 Rabīᶜ II 478/ 20 August 1085	Death of al-Jūwaynī; al-Ghazālī left Nīshāpūr
Jumāda I 484/ July 1091	Appointed to teach at the Niẓāmiyya college in Baghdad
10 Ramaḍān 485/ 14 October 1092	Niẓām-al-Mulk was assassinated
484–487/1091–1094	Studied philosophy
Muḥarrām 487/ February 1094	Attended the oath-taking of the new caliph, al-Mustaẓhir
487/1094	Finished *Maqāṣid al-falāsifa*
5 Muḥarrām 488/ 21 January 1095	Finished *Tahāfut al-falāsifa*
Rajab 488/ July 1095	Experienced a spiritual crisis
Dhū l-Qaᶜda 488/ November 1095	Left Baghdad for Damascus
Dhū l-Qaᶜda 489/ November – December 1096	Made pilgrimage and worked on the *Iḥyāʾ ᶜulūm al-dīn*
Jumāda II 490/ May 1097	Taught from the *Iḥyāʾ ᶜulūm al-dīn* during a brief stop in Baghdad
Rajab 490/June 1097	Seen in Baghdad by Abū Bakr b. al-ᶜArabī
Fall 490/1097	Returned to Ṭūs

Dhū l-Ḥijja 490/ November 1097	Established a *madrasa* and a *khānqāh* in Ṭūs
Dhū l-Qaʿda 499/ July 1106	Taught at the Niẓāmiyya college in Nīshāpūr
500/1106	Wrote *al-Munqidh min al-ḍalāl*
500/1106	Returned to Ṭūs
28 Dhū l-Ḥijja 502/ 5 August 1109	Finished *al-Mustaṣfā min ʿilm al-uṣūl*
Jumada I 505/ December 1111	Finished *Iljām al-ʿawām ʿan ʿilm al-kalām*
14 Jumada II 505/ 18 December 1111	Imām al-Ghazālī died in Ṭūs

Eulogies in Verse

Because of him the lame walked briskly,
And the songless through him burst into melody.

On the death of Imām al-Ghazālī, Abū l-Muẓaffar Muḥammad al-Abiwardī said of his loss:

He is gone! and the greatest loss which ever afflicted me,
was that of a man who left no one like him among mankind.

About the *Revival of the Religious Sciences*

THE present work is book 24 of Imām al-Ghazālī's forty-volume masterpiece. Below is an excerpt from al-Ghazālī's introduction that explains the arrangement and purpose of the *Iḥyāʾ ʿulūm al-dīn*.

People have composed books concerning some of these ideas, but this book [the *Iḥyāʾ*] differs from them in five ways, by

1. clarifying what they have obscured and elucidating what they have treated casually;
2. arranging what they scattered and putting in order what they separated;
3. abbreviating what they made lengthy and proving what they reported;
4. omitting what they have repeated; and
5. establishing the truth of certain obscure matters that are difficult to understand and which have not been presented in books at all.

For although all the scholars follow one course, there is no reason one should not proceed independently and bring to light something unknown, paying special attention to something his colleagues have forgotten. Or they are not heedless about calling attention to it, but they neglect to mention it in books. Or they do not overlook it, but something prevents them from exposing it [and making it clear].

So these are the special properties of this book, besides its inclusion of all these various kinds of knowledge.

Two things induced me to arrange this book in four parts. The first and fundamental motive is that this arrangement in establishing what is true and in making it understandable is, as it were, inevitable because the branch of knowledge by which one approaches the hereafter is divided into the knowledge of [proper] conduct and the knowledge of [spiritual] unveiling.

By the knowledge of [spiritual] unveiling I mean knowledge and only knowledge. By the science of [proper] conduct I mean knowledge as well as action in accordance with that knowledge. This work will deal only with the science of [proper] conduct, and not with [spiritual] unveiling, which one is not permitted to record in writing, although it is the ultimate aim of saints and the ultimate aim of the sincere. The science of [proper] conduct is merely a path that leads to unveiling and only through that path did the prophets of God communicate with the people and lead them to Him. Concerning [spiritual] unveiling, the prophets عَلَيْهِمُ السَّلَامُ spoke only figuratively and briefly through signs and symbols, because they realized the inability of people's minds to comprehend. Therefore since the scholars are heirs of the prophets, they cannot but follow in their footsteps and emulate their way.

The knowledge of [proper] conduct is divided into (1) outward knowledge, by which I mean knowledge of the senses and (2) inward knowledge, by which I mean knowledge of the functions of the heart.

The physical members either perform acts of prescribed worship, or acts that are in accordance with custom, while the heart, because it is removed from the senses and belongs to the world of dominion, is subject to either praiseworthy or blameworthy [influences]. Therefore it is necessary to divide this branch of knowledge into two parts: outward and inward. The outward part, which is connected to the senses, is subdivided into acts of worship and acts that pertain to custom. The inward part, which is connected to the states of the heart and the characteristics of the soul, is subdivided into blameworthy states and praiseworthy states. So the total makes four divisions of the sciences of the practice of religion.

The second motive [for this division] is that I have noticed the sincere interest of students in jurisprudence, which has become popular among those who do not fear God تَعَالَىٰ but who seek to boast and exploit its influence and prestige in arguments. It [jurisprudence] is also divided into four quarters, and he who follows the style of one who is beloved becomes beloved.

Translator's Introduction

The *Banes of the Tongue* (*Āfāt al-lisān*) is the fourth book in the Quarter of Perils (*Rubʿ al-muhlikāt*) of the *Revival of the Religious Sciences.* In this book, al-Ghazālī continues his exposition of the misuses and sins related to the organs of the body, a topic which he began in the third book of the quarter, *On Overcoming the Two Desires,* which deals with gluttony and lust. In this exposition of the banes of the tongue, al-Ghazālī relies on Ibn Abī l-Dunyā's *ḥadīth* compilation,[1] in addition to the works of numerous other scholars, as he makes clear in his introduction, and as the editors of this edition specify in the footnotes. Al-Ghazālī defines each bane, gives examples of what these mean in practice, analyzes what leads people to commit the faults he discusses, and finally, he recommends how these faults can be overcome.

It may seem surpising that in the architecture of the *Iḥyāʾ*, al-Ghazālī put the sins of the tongue next to the sins of the stomach, the eyes, and the private parts, but we need only consider the exalted place Islam accords to the faculty of speech, which in the Qurʾān is described as the first gift bestowed on human beings after creation: *The Most Compassionate taught the Qurʾān, created humanity,* [*and*] *taught them speech* (*bayān*) [55:1–4]. Here speech (*bayān*, sometimes translated as eloquence) may also be understood as the ability to communicate what is in the heart and mind to another by means of language.

Speech is described as the last faculty of Adam's creation: *And He taught Adam the names—all of them* [Q 2:31], and with this he and his spouse repented of their first act of disobedience: *Then Adam received from his Lord words* [Q 2:37], and they prayed, *Our Lord!*

---

1 His full name was ʿAbdallāh b. Muḥammad b. ʿUbayd b. Sufyān Ibn Abī l-Dunyā l-Baghdādī (823–894/208–281). He is said to have written 164 works.

We have wronged ourselves, and if You do not forgive us and have mercy on us, we will surely be among the losers [Q 7:23].

In fact, the very name of the revelation, "al-Qurʾān," means "the recitation," reminding us that the preferred way to read the Qurʾān is by reciting it aloud in a beautiful voice. Moreover, the practice of *dhikr* (remembrance, invocation, or mentioning God or His words aloud) is prescribed in scores of *ḥadīth*s as a means of salvation, realization, and as a treatment for spiritual and even physical maladies. Pronouncing aloud the testimony of faith, *Lā ilāha illa Allāh, Muḥammad Rasūl Allāh*, with conviction and before witnesses, makes a person legally a Muslim, and the faithful pray that this testimony is the last they utter before death. A *ḥadīth* states that one who dies reciting these words will enter paradise. Language could be described as a divine gift bestowed on human beings before their earthly life and as the last gift they use at its end. Thus, it is easy to understand how al-Ghazālī and others of his time considered the misuse of this gift a serious fault, or even a deadly sin that can lead to suffering in this world and punishment in the next world.

In the *Banes of the Tongue*, al-Ghazālī emphasizes that the sins of the tongue involve others—this is particularly true of backbiting (*ghība*) and gossip (*namīma*); it harms, and can even sever the bonds of friendship between people. Yet, he could not have imagined the situation we face today. With the widespread use of (one could even say addiction to) online social networks, which like the tongue and speech that can be used for good or bad, people are able to broadcast (in writing, speech, and images) insults, lies, and gossip, reaching countless people and potentially harming the very fabric of human societies. The twenty banes about which al-Ghazālī wrote over nine hundred years ago remain a major danger, not just to interpersonal relations between friends, family, and acquaintances, but also to the social contract by which human beings are able live together and overcome their differences for the greater good. Thus, the *Banes of the Tongue* is very much a book for our time.

Acknowledgments

We would like to express our appreciation to Gray Henry, the director of Fons Vitae, who—over ten years ago—shared with us her vision of publishing editions of al-Ghazālī's *Iḥyāʾ ʿulūm al-dīn* designed for children. These, she explained, would need to be based on new translations of the first seven books of the *Iḥyāʾ ʿulūm al-dīn*, five of which we were blessed to translate, a journey that we began in 2012 and completed in 2018. Recently a generous grant made it possible for the present work to be translated. We would also like to thank Valerie Joy Turner and Muhammad Hozien for their editorial work, which has seen us through this process from the first book to the present. In addition, we thank our colleagues and friends at the Center for Language and Culture in Marrakesh, Brahim Zoubairi and Hamza Weinman. Last, but not least, no project such as this could have been undertaken, let alone completed, without the patience and support of our families, starting with our loving spouses, *ḥāfiẓhum Allāh*!

Mohamed Fouad Aresmouk
Abdurrahman Fitzgerald
Marrakesh, Morocco, 4 Jumāda II 1443 (8 January 2022)

Editors' Note on the Translation

As the editors of the English translation that follows we aimed to be true to Imām al-Ghazālī's words, in particular by ensuring the accuracy and consistency of each and every word. This aspect is critical because the book is solely focused on speech and words, peoples' motives for "unleashing their tongues" (to use al-Ghazālī's phrase), and the consequences of these choices in this world and the hereafter. For example, when al-Ghazālī cited a *ḥadīth*, then discussed and defined a specific word from that *ḥadīth*, it is imperative that the same word be used in his discussion. In this, our goal was consistency and accuracy over eloquence. Al-Ghazālī divided the book into twenty banes; thus these terms and his definitions of them absolutely had to be referred to consistently. This led to long discussions of the nuances of words, such as the differences between slander, libel, gossip, and backbiting, as well as the questions he addressed, such as, how can one truly determine whether lying is permissible or not?

We thank those involved in the multiple reviews of this translation: Faris Casewit, who reviewed a major part of the translation, and Shaykh Mahmud Khaylani (contacted through our nephew studying in Iraqi Kurdistan), who helped in several instances where passages of the *Iḥyāʾ* needed explanations that could not be found in the commentary of al-Zabīdī.

Finally, it is our pleasure to thank the indefatigable Gray Henry, the director of Fons Vitae who entrusted us with this series shortly after working on *Marvels of the Heart* in 2010. We especially thank Neville Blakemore and Mustafa Gouverneur for their endless support and aid. We also thank their stalwart team at Fons Vitae who bore our many requests and entreaties with kindness and grace. We thank our cover designer Steve Stivers; the office staff, Ms. Lucy Jones; our printer Friesens, and their wonderful staff, namely, Ms. Brandie Herrel and Ms. Editha Del Moral. Thanks are also due to the proofreading team: Juan Thompson, Mustafa Gouverneur, Elena Lloyd-Sidle, and Gray Henry. In closing we are grateful to Ikbal and Ercument Tokat whose generosity made this work possible.

THE BOOK ON THE BANES OF THE TONGUE

Kitāb āfāt al-lisān
the fourth book of
the Quarter of
Perils
Book 24
of the *Revival of the Religious Sciences*

[al-Ghazālī's Preface] 389

The Book on the Banes of the Tongue

In the Name of God, the Merciful and Compassionate

PRAISE be to God who created humankind with excellence and symmetry, who inspired them with the light of faith by which He adorned and beautified them, who taught them [the ability to] express [themselves], favored them, placed them at the forefront [of creation], flooded their hearts with treasuries of knowledge, and thus perfected them. Then He sent down and draped over them the covering of His mercy, and extended to them a tongue to expound on what their hearts and minds contained, and with which to pull back the covering He sent them, and then loosed [their tongues] with praise to articulate gratitude for what they were entrusted and granted of acquired knowledge and speech, which was made easy for them.

I bear witness that there is no god except God, alone, without partner, and I bear witness that Muḥammad is His servant and Messenger whom He [bestowed with] honor and reverence, and His Prophet who was sent with a revealed book, and signs that He set forth in detail, and a *dīn* that He made easy for him [to understand]. May God bless him, his family, and his Companions, and those before him, [with blessings as numerous as all the times] any servant magnifies God and His oneness.[1]

1 Trans.: Literally, "all the times any servant says the phrase *Allāhu akbar* (God is greater) and *Lā ilāha illā Allāh* (there is no god but God)."

To proceed: Truly, the tongue is one of God's greatest graces and
390 most wondrous and delicate of His creations. It is small |in size but great in its obedience and its crimes; disbelief or faith is not clear except by the testimony of the tongue. And these are the ultimate obedience and disobedience. Moreover, there is nothing that exists or is nonexistent, [no] creator or created [thing], [nothing] illusory or real, supposed or imagined, except that the tongue can reach it and expose it, either through affirmation or negation. Anything that knowledge can reach, the tongue can articulate as true or false, and there is nothing that knowledge cannot reach. This special quality cannot be found in any other organ. The eye, [for example], only senses colors and shapes; the ear [only] senses sounds; the hand [only] senses bodies, and such [is the case] for all other organs.

The tongue's domain is vast. Nothing can resist it, and it has neither limit nor end. In goodness it can reach a broad expanse and in evil it has a long tail. Thus, someone who unleashes his delicate tongue and gives it free rein is led by Satan, in every domain he drives him to the edge of a precipice and compels him to a wasteland [that is, hell], for nothing casts people nose first into the fire as much as what their tongues reap, and no one escapes the evil of the tongue except the one who ties it with the bridle of the law, who does not release it except in what will benefit him in [this] world and the hereafter, and who is able to hold it [back] from all that is feared of its calamity in the short term and the long term.

Knowledge of what is praised or censured [with regard to] unleashing the tongue (*iṭlāq al-lisān*) is obscure (*ghāmiḍ*) and difficult, and putting into practice what that knowledge entails is heavy and demanding, for [the tongue] is the most rebellious organ for humans, inasmuch as unleashing it takes no effort and moving it
391 takes no energy, creation is negligent in guarding | against its banes and calamities, and being wary of its traps and snares, and it is the greatest tool of Satan to ensnare humankind.

With God's success and His good facilitation, we will explain all the banes of the tongue, and mention them one by one, along with their definitions, their causes, and their calamities. We will explain the way to [exercise] caution against them, and what is related in the reports (*akhbār*) and traditions (*athār*) that censure them.

We begin by speaking of the merits of silence (*ṣamt*),[2] and following that, we mention [1] the bane of speaking about what does not concern us (*al-kalām fīmā lā yuʿnīk*); then [2] the bane of needless speech (*fuḍūl al-kalām*); then [3] the bane of delving into baseless (*bāṭil*) [talk]; then [4] the bane of arguing (*mirāʾ*) and debate (*jadāl*); then [5] the bane of disputation (*khuṣūma*).

Then [we speak of] [6] the bane of pretentiousness (*taqʿurr*) in speech, pomposity (*tashadduq*), [of using] affectation (*takalluf*) in rhymed prose (*sajʿ*), then of eloquence (*faṣāḥa*) and artificiality (*taṣannuʿ*) in it, and others that are common to those who claim to be eloquent (*mutafāṣiḥīn*) orators; then [7] the bane of obscenity (*fuḥush*), insult (*sabb*), and vulgarity of the tongue (*bidhāʾat al-lisān*).

Then [we speak of] [8] the bane of cursing (*laʿn*), whether people, animals, or things; then [9] the bane of singing (*ghināʾ*) and poetry (*shiʿr*), and since we have already spoken of what kind of singing is unlawful and what kind is lawful in the *Book on Audition*,[3] we shall not repeat that here; then [10] the bane of joking (*mizāḥ*).

Then [we speak of] [11] the bane of ridicule (*sukhriyya*) and mockery (*istihizāʾ*); [12] the bane of divulging secrets (*ifshāʾ al-sirr*); then [13] the bane of false promises (*waʿd al-kādhib*); then [14] the bane of lying (*kadhib*) either in speech or oaths; and [15] the bane of backbiting (*ghība*).

Then [we speak of] [16] the bane of gossip (*namīma*); then [17] the bane of speaking with two tongues (*lisānayn*), that is, of saying to each of two adversaries what they would agree with; then [18] the bane of praise (*madḥ*); then [19] the bane of heedlessness (*ghafla*) in regard to offenses (*khaṭāʾ*) made in general speech, not to mention what relates to God عَزَّوَجَلَّ, His attributes, and matters of *dīn*; and then [20] the bane of the questions of laymen (*suʾāl al-ʿawāmm*) about God's عَزَّوَجَلَّ attributes, about His speech, and the letters and [whether they are] eternal or created, and it is the last bane and what is related to it.

---

2 Eds.: *Ṣamt* (from the root ṣ-m-t) refers to silence over a period of time and in relation to false or unnecessary speech; it does not include silence when the truth should be spoken.

3 Book 18 of the *Revival of the Religious Sciences: The Proprieties of Audition and Ecstasy* (*Kitāb al-samāʿ wa-l-wajad*).

In all, these are twenty banes, and we ask God for His good success (*ḥusn al-tawfīq*), His benevolence and magnanimity.

[al-Ghazālī's Introduction] 392

An Elucidation of the Great Danger (*Khaṭar*) of the Tongue and the Merit of Silence (*Ṣamt*)

KNOW that the danger (*khaṭar*) of the tongue is great and there is no salvation from its danger except in silence (*ṣamt*). For this, the law extols silence and urges [God's servants] to observe it.

Thus, [the Prophet] صَلَّى ٱللَّهُ عَلَيْهِ وَسَلَّمَ said, "Whoever is silent (*ṣamt*) is saved (*najā*)."[1]

And [the Prophet] صَلَّى ٱللَّهُ عَلَيْهِ وَسَلَّمَ said, "Silence is wisdom but few practice it; that is, it is wisdom and resoluteness."[2]

ʿAbdallāh b. Sufyān related that his father said,

> I said, "O Messenger of God, inform me of something about Islam [such] that I will not need to ask anyone else after you," and he answered, "Say, 'I believe in God,' and then be upright."
>
> [Sufyān then] said, "And what should I shield myself from?"
>
> And [the Messenger] pointed with his hand to his tongue.[3]

ʿUqba b. ʿĀmir said, "I said, 'O Messenger of God, what is salvation?' He said, 'Control your tongue, stay in your house,[4] and weep over your offenses.'"[5] |

---

1 Al-Tirmidhī, *Sunan*, 2501.

2 Ibn ʿAdī, *al-Kāmil*, 5:169; al-Quḍāʿī, *Musnad al-shihāb*, 240; and al-Bayhaqī, *Shuʿab al-īmān*, 4672, conveyed by Anas from the words of Luqmān the Wise عَلَيْهِ ٱلسَّلَامُ.

3 Al-Tirmidhī, *Sunan*, 2410; Ibn Mājah, *Sunan*, 3972; and Muslim, *Ṣaḥīḥ*, 38, without mention of the tongue.

4 Trans.: Literally, "let your house be wide enough to contain you."

5 Al-Tirmidhī, *Sunan*, 2406.

393 And Sahl b. Saʿd al-Sāʿidī said, "The Messenger of God ﷺ said, 'Whoever guarantees what is between the two [sides of] his beard and [what is between] his legs, I guarantee him heaven.'"[6]

And [the Prophet] ﷺ said, "Whoever shields [himself against] the evil of his *qabqab*, his *dhabdhab*, and his *laqlaq* has shielded [himself against] all evil."[7] The *qabqab* is the stomach, the *dhabdhab* are the private parts, the *laqlaq* is the tongue. Indeed, it is these three desires that destroy most of creation, and for this we occupy [ourselves] with citing the banes of the tongue after we completed citing the bane of the two desires of the stomach [lit., mouth] and private parts.[8]

When the Messenger of God ﷺ was asked about what [causes] most people to enter heaven, he replied, "Fear (*taqwa*) of God and good character (*ḥusn al-khuluq*)," and when asked about what [causes] most [people] to enter the fire, he answered, "The two hollow [places]: the mouth and the private parts (*faraj*)."[9]

It is possible that by mouth he meant the banes of the tongue, because [the mouth is] the place [of the tongue], and it is possible that he meant the stomach, because [the mouth] is the entrance [to the stomach]. Muʿādh b. Jabal said, "I said, 'O Messenger of God, are we taken to account for what we say?' He said, 'O Ibn Jabal! May
394 your mother be bereft of you![10] | Are people cast nose first into hell for anything other than the consequences [lit., yield or harvest] of their tongues?'"[11]

6 Al-Bukhārī, *Ṣaḥīḥ*, 6474, 7807; and al-Tirmidhī, *Sunan*, 2408.

7 Al-Bayhaqī, *Shuʿab al-īmān*, 5026; and al-Daylamī, *Musnad al-firdaws*, 5978.

8 Trans.: Book 23 of the *Revival of the Religious Sciences: Overcoming the Two Desires* (*Kitāb āfāt kasr al-shahwatayn* (*shahwat al-baṭan wa-shahwat al-faraj*).

9 Al-Tirmidhī, *Sunan*, 2004; and Ibn Mājah, *Sunan*, 4246. Eds.: That is, it is important to be use polite language and not refer to these topics using vulgar or coarse language.

10 Eds.: Lane (*An Arabic-English Lexicon*, 345) defines *thakala* as an imprecation against the addressee, not with a desire to have it happen, but in the case of intense love.

11 Al-Tirmidhī, *Sunan*, 2616; and Ibn Mājah, *Sunan*, 3973. This wording, however, is from Ibn Abī l-Dunyā, *al-Ṣamt wa-ādāb al-lisān*, 6. Lane has "words that their tongues utter" (*An Arabic-English Lexicon*, 582).

And ʿAbdallāh al-Thaqafī said,

> I said, "O Messenger of God! Tell me a matter that I can take refuge in."
>
> He said, "Say: 'My Lord is God, and be upright.'"
>
> Then I said, "O Messenger of God! What do you fear most for me?"
>
> And he took hold of his own tongue and said, "This."

It is reported that Muʿādh said, "O Messenger of God, what practice is best?" And the Messenger of God صَلَّىٱللَّهُعَلَيْهِوَسَلَّمَ stuck out his tongue and placed it [between] his two fingers.[12]

And Anas b. Mālik said, the Messenger صَلَّىٱللَّهُعَلَيْهِوَسَلَّمَ said, "The faith of the servant will not be upright until his heart is upright, and his heart will not be upright until his tongue is upright, and no man will enter heaven whose neighbor is not secure from [the man's] misfortune."[13]

And [the Prophet] صَلَّىٱللَّهُعَلَيْهِوَسَلَّمَ said, "Whoever is happy to be safe must be silent (*ṣamt*)."[14] |

[We learned] from Saʿīd b. Jubayr in a [*ḥadīth*] *marfuʿ*, that 395
the Messenger of God صَلَّىٱللَّهُعَلَيْهِوَسَلَّمَ said, "When the child of Adam wakes up in the morning, all his limbs begin to accuse [lit., call it a disbeliever] [his] tongue, saying, 'Fear God for our sake. If you are upright, we will be upright, and if you are crooked, we will be crooked.'"[15]

It was related that ʿUmar b. al-Khaṭṭāb came to Abū Bakr رَضِيَٱللَّهُعَنْهُ, who was extending his tongue, and said, "What are you doing, O caliph of the Messenger of God?" He said, "This leads me to [perilous] places. Verily the Messenger of God صَلَّىٱللَّهُعَلَيْهِوَسَلَّمَ said,

---

12 Ibn Abī l-Dunyā, *al-Ṣamt wa-ādāb al-lisān*, 8; and al-Ṭabarānī, *al-Muʿjam al-kabīr*, 20:64.

13 Ibn Ḥanbal, *Musnad*, 3:198; and Ibn Abī l-Dunyā, *al-Ṣamt wa-ādāb al-lisān*, 9. Trans.: That is, no man will enter heaven unless his neighbor is secure from him.

14 Ibn Abī l-Dunyā, *al-Ṣamt wa-ādāb al-lisān*, 11; and al-Ṭabarānī, *al-Muʿjam al-awsaṭ*, 1955.

15 Al-Tirmidhī, *Sunan*, 2407. Eds.: A *ḥadīth marfuʿ* is one that is attributed to the Prophet, and may be narrated by one of the Followers (Tābiʿīn), who does not mention the Companion (Ṣaḥāba) who related it.

'There is nothing in the body that does not complain to God about the tongue [because of] its sharpness.'"[16]

[We learned] from Ibn Masʿūd رضي الله عنه that he was on [the hill of] Ṣafā [repeating the pilgrim's] entreaty, and saying,

> O my tongue! Speak goodness and [you will] benefit or listen and be safe. Submit before you regret!
>
> And when it was said to him, "O Abū ʿAbd al-Raḥmān, is this something you say or something you heard?"
>
> 396 He said, "No. | I heard the Messenger of God صلى الله عليه وسلم say, 'Most of the offenses of the son of Adam are from his tongue.'"[17]

Ibn ʿUmar رضي الله عنهما said, "The Messenger of God صلى الله عليه وسلم said, 'For the one who holds his tongue, God covers his faults. [For] the one who masters his anger, God protects him from His punishment. For the one who asks God to excuse him, God accepts his excuse.'"[18]

It was related that Muʿādh b. Jabal رضي الله عنه said, "O Messenger of God, advise me!" He said, "Worship God as if you see Him, count your soul among the dead, and if you so wish, I will inform you about something that will help you master all that." And then he pointed to his tongue with his hand.[19]

[We learned] from Ṣafwān b. Sulaym that the Messenger of God صلى الله عليه وسلم said, "Shall I not inform you of the easiest worship and the one that is most effortless for the body? Silence (*ṣamt*) and good character (*ḥusn al-khuluq*)."[20]

And Abū Hurayra said, "The Messenger of God صلى الله عليه وسلم said, 'Whoever believes in God and the last day should say what is good or say nothing (*yasukut*).'"[21] |

---

16 Ibn Abī l-Dunyā, *al-Ṣamt wa-ādāb al-lisān*, 13; and in Ibn Abī l-Dunyā, *al-Warʿa*, 91; and Abū Yaʿlā, *Musnad*, 5.

17 Ibn Abī l-Dunyā, *al-Ṣamt wa-ādāb al-lisān*, 18; al-Ṭabarānī, *al-Muʿjam al-kabīr*, 10:197; and al-Bayhaqī, *Shuʿab al-īmān*, 4584.

18 Ibn Abī l-Dunyā, *al-Ṣamt wa-ādāb al-lisān*, 21.

19 Ibn Abī l-Dunyā, *al-Ṣamt wa-ādāb al-lisān*, 22.

20 Ibn Abī l-Dunyā, *al-Ṣamt wa-ādāb al-lisān*, 27.

21 Al-Bukhārī, *Ṣaḥīḥ*, 6018; Muslim, *Ṣaḥīḥ*, 47; and Ibn Abī l-Dunyā, *al-Ṣamt wa-ādāb al-lisān*, 40. Eds.: The word *sakata* (*yasukut* is the present tense verb) is almost synonymous with the word *ṣamat* with the following difference: *sakata* is for a shorter duration and its always voluntary, whereas *ṣamat* is more intense, of a longer

Ḥasan[22] said, "It was mentioned to us that the Prophet ﷺ 397
said, 'May God bestow His mercy on the servant who speaks and benefits, or says nothing (*sakata*) and is safe (*salama*).'"[23]

And Sufyān said, "They said to Jesus عَلَيْهِ ٱلسَّلَامُ, 'Direct us to a practice by which we will enter heaven.' He said, 'Do not ever speak.' They said, 'We cannot do that.' He said, 'Then do not speak except what is good.'"[24]

Solomon, son of David, عَلَيْهِمَا ٱلسَّلَامُ, said, "If speech is silver, then silence (*ṣamt*) is gold."[25]

[We learned] from al-Barāʾ b. ʿĀzib, who said that a Bedouin came to the Prophet ﷺ and said, "Direct me to a practice by which I will enter heaven." He said, "Feed the hungry, give water to the thirsty, command what is right, and forbid what is wrong. And if you cannot, then hold your tongue from anything except [saying] what is good."[26]

[The Prophet] ﷺ also said, "Guard (*ikhzun*) your tongue, except from good, for by doing that you will defeat Satan."[27] |

And [the Prophet] ﷺ said, "God عَزَّ وَجَلَّ is present at the 398
tongue of every speaker, so let a person who knows what he is saying fear God."[28]

And [the Prophet] عَلَيْهِ ٱلصَّلَاةُ وَٱلسَّلَامُ said, "When you see a believer who is silent and dignified, draw near him, for he has been endowed with wisdom."[29]

The Messenger of God ﷺ said, "People are of three [sorts]: the [one who] benefits, the [one who] is sound, and the [one who] is destroyed. The [one who] benefits is he who remembers (*dhikr*) God تَعَالَىٰ, the [one who] is sound (*sālim*) is he [who] says

---

duration, and not always voluntary; see al-Zabīdī, *Tāj al-ʿarūs*, for s-k-t (4:558) and ṣ-m-t (4:590).

22 Trans.: All references to Ḥasan are to Ḥasan al-Baṣrī (d. 110/728 or 729), a Follower (Tābiʿīn) known for his piety and erudition.

23 Hannād, *al-Zuhd*, 1106; Ibn Abī l-Dunyā, *al-Ṣamt wa-ādāb al-lisān*, 41, 46.

24 Ibn Abī l-Dunyā, *al-Ṣamt wa-ādāb al-lisān*, 46.

25 Ibn Abī l-Dunyā, *al-Ṣamt wa-ādāb al-lisān*, 47.

26 Ibn Abī l-Dunyā, *al-Ṣamt wa-ādāb al-lisān*, 67.

27 Ibn al-Ḍarīs, *Faḍāʾil al-Qurʾān*, 68; and al-Ṭabarānī, *al-Muʿjam al-ṣaghīr*, 2:66. Eds.: For guard (*ikhzun*), see Lane, *An Arabic-English Lexicon*, 734, under kh-z-n.

28 Ibn Wahhab, *al-Jāmiʿ*, 334; and Abū Nuʿaym, *Ḥilya*, 8:160.

29 Ibn Mājah, *Sunan*, 4101.

nothing (*sukut*), and the [one who] is destroyed is he who delves into baseless [talk]."[30]

And [the Prophet] عَلَيْهِ الصَّلَاةُ وَالسَّلَامُ said, "The tongue of the believer is behind his heart. When he wishes to speak about something, he contemplates it with his heart and then carries it out with his tongue. The tongue of the hypocrite, however, is in front of his heart. When he is concerned about something, he carries it out with his tongue and does not contemplate it with his heart."[31] |

399 Jesus عَلَيْهِ السَّلَامُ said, "Worship has ten parts, nine of which are in silence and one of which is in fleeing from people."[32]

And our Prophet صَلَّى ٱللَّٰهُ عَلَيْهِ وَسَلَّمَ said, "Whoever speaks much slips much, and whoever slips much transgresses much, and whoever transgresses much, the fire is most fitting."[33]

❁ ❁ ❁

Traditions (*Āthār*)

Abū Bakr al-Ṣiddīq رَضِيَ ٱللَّٰهُ عَنْهُ put a pebble in his mouth to keep himself from speaking and always pointed to his tongue and said, "This leads me to [perilous] places!"

ʿAbdallāh b. Masʿūd رَضِيَ ٱللَّٰهُ عَنْهُ said, "By God, there is no god but Him, nothing is more in need of a long imprisonment than the tongue."[34]

And Ṭāwūs said, "My tongue is a lion; if I let it loose, it will devour me."[35] |

---

30 Ibn Ḥanbal, *Musnad*, 3:75; Abū Yaʿlā, *Musnad*, 1062; Hannād, *al-Zuhd*, 1231; and al-Bayhaqī, *Shuʿab al-īmān*, 10323.

31 Ibn al-Mubārak, *Zuhd*, 390; and Ibn Abī l-Dunyā, *al-Ṣamt wa-ādāb al-lisān*, 425.

32 Abū Nuʿaym, *Ḥilya*, 8:142; Ibn ʿAdī, *al-Kāmil*, 6:442; and al-Bayhaqī, *al-Zuhd al-kabīr*, 127.

33 Al-Ṭabarānī, *al-Muʿjam al-awsaṭ*, 6537; Ibn ʿAdī, *al-Kāmil*, 5:16; and Abū Nuʿaym, *Ḥilya*, 3:74.

34 Ibn Abī Shayba, *al-Muṣannaf*, 27030; and Ibn Abī l-Dunyā, *al-Ṣamt wa-ādāb al-lisān*, 16.

35 Ibn Abī l-Dunyā, *al-Ṣamt wa-ādāb al-lisān*, 39; and Ibn ʿAsākir, *Tārīkh madīnat Dimashq*, 12:292. Eds.: Here, al-Ghazālī introduces a play on words, the man's name, Ṭāwūs, means a peacock, which a lion would devour.

Wahb b. Munabbih said that in the wisdom of the people of 400
David [it is said], "It is incumbent on the intelligent [person] to be cognizant of his time, to watch over his tongue, and to engage in what concerns him."[36]

And Ḥasan said, "One does not understand his *dīn* [if] he does not guard his tongue."[37]

And al-Awzāʿī said, "ʿUmar b. ʿAbd al-ʿAzīz رحمه الله wrote to us: 'To proceed: whoever frequently remembers death is content with little of this world, and whoever counts his speech [to be part of] his deeds rarely speaks about what does not benefit him [in the hereafter].'"[38]

One of [the wise] said, "Silence brings a man two virtues: safety in his *dīn* and understanding of his interlocutor."[39]

Muḥammad b. Wāsiʿ said to Mālik b. Dīnār, "O Abū Yaḥyā, guarding the tongue is harder for people than guarding dinars and dirhams."[40]

Yūnus b. ʿUbayd said, "There is not a person who is careful concerning his tongue except that I can see its benefit in all his actions."[41] |

And Ḥasan said, 401

> "[People] were speaking to one another in the presence of Muʿāwiya رضي الله عنه and al-Aḥnaf b. Qays said nothing."
>
> They said to him, "O Abū Baḥr, what is wrong with you that you are not speaking?"
>
> He said, "I fear God if I lie, and I fear you if I tell the truth."[42]

Abū Bakr b. ʿIyyāsh said,

> Four kings met: the king of India, the king of China, Khusraw, and Caesar. One of them said, "I regret what I have said but do not regret what I have not said." Another said, "If I speak a word, it masters me and I do not master it, and if I do not speak it, I master it and it does not master me." The third said,

36 Ibn Abī l-Dunyā, *al-Ṣamt wa-ādāb al-lisān*, 31.
37 Ibn Abī l-Dunyā, *al-Ṣamt wa-ādāb al-lisān*, 34.
38 Ibn Abī l-Dunyā, *al-Ṣamt wa-ādāb al-lisān*, 35.
39 Ibn Abī l-Dunyā, *al-Ṣamt wa-ādāb al-lisān*, 55.
40 Ibn Abī l-Dunyā, *al-Ṣamt wa-ādāb al-lisān*, 57.
41 Ibn Abī l-Dunyā, *al-Ṣamt wa-ādāb al-lisān*, 60.
42 Ibn Abī l-Dunyā, *al-Ṣamt wa-ādāb al-lisān*, 62.

> "I am amazed by the speaker! If his speech comes back to him, it harms him, and if it does not come back, it does not benefit him." And the fourth said, "I am more able to take back what I do *not* say than what I *do* say!"[43]

It is said that al-Manṣūr b. al-Muʿtamar did not speak after the final night (*ʿishāʾ*) [prayer] for forty years.[44]

And it is said that al-Rabīʿ b. Khaytham did not speak of worldly things for twenty years. When he awoke in the morning, he would set out an ink well, a clean sheet of paper, and a pen and write everything he said. Then he would [take] account of himself in the evening. |

❁ ❁ ❁

402 So if you were to say, "What is the reason for the great virtue of silence (*ṣamt*)?" Know that the reason [for its virtue] is the many banes of the tongue: erroneous [speech], lying, gossip (*namīma*), backbiting (*ghība*), ostentation, hypocrisy, obscenity, arguing, praising oneself (*tazkiyat al-nafs*), disputation, superfluous [talk], delving into baseless [talk], distortion, augmenting or omitting [facts], injuring others [lit., creation], and exposing the private [parts].

These banes are many and [happen] spontaneously for the tongue—[they are] not onerous for it—and [even produce] a pleasure in the heart; they come about from [human] nature and Satan. Once someone's tongue is involved [in them], he can rarely rein it back to speak only about what he loves and say nothing about what he does not love. These then are among the obscure details of knowledge that will be explained; indeed, delving [into any of these banes] is a danger, while in silence (*ṣamt*) there is safety (*salama*). For this, its virtue is great.

[Silence also allows one] to focus on all of his concerns and maintain his dignity, to be free for reflection (*fikr*), worship, and remembrance (*dhikr*), to be safe from the consequences of following what is said in [this] world, and from its reckoning in the hereafter, for as God تعالى says, [*A human being*] *utters no word except that with him is an observer prepared* [*to record*] [50:18].

43 Ibn Abī l-Dunyā, *al-Ṣamt wa-ādāb al-lisān*, 65.

44 Al-Jurjānī, *Tārīkh Jurjān*, 501.

❁ ❁ ❁

[There is] a matter that indicates the virtues of maintaining silence, and these are the four kinds of speech: the kind that is purely harmful, the kind that is purely beneficial, the kind [in which] there is harm and benefit, and the kind [in which] there is neither harm nor benefit. As for what is purely harmful, [one] must not say anything about it,
and similarly, for what has [both] | harm and benefit, [its benefit] 403
does not negate its harm. As for what has neither benefit nor harm, it is superfluous and occupying [oneself] with it is a waste of time and the essence of loss.

All that is left is the fourth kind. Thus, three-fourths of speech slips [away] and one-fourth is left [that is, the kind that is purely beneficial], and [there is in] this one-fourth a danger that could be sinful if it is mixed with a minute [amount of] ostentation, artificiality, backbiting, praise of oneself, and superfluous speech mixed in ways that are imperceptible and dangerous to people.

Whoever knows the details of the banes of the tongue from what we will mention will know with certitude that what the Messenger of God صَلَّى ٱللَّهُ عَلَيْهِ وَسَلَّمَ said—that "Whoever is silent (*ṣamt*) is saved (*najā*)"[45]—is the definitive statement about this and that God indeed gave him the jewels of wisdom and "the all-inclusive speech."[46] Only elect scholars know the oceans of meaning in each of His select words, and we mention these banes and the difficulty of avoiding them to show their reality, God تَعَالَىٰ willing.

❁ ❁ ❁

At this point, we will enumerate the banes of the tongue. We begin with the lightest of them and then proceed, little by little, to the more coarse ones, speaking last about backbiting, gossip, and lying, for the examination of these is lengthy. And there are twenty banes.

---

45 Al-Tirmidhī, *Sunan*, 2501.

46 Trans.: This expression is found in a *ḥadīth* in al-Bukhārī, *Ṣaḥīḥ*, 7013, that quotes the Prophet صَلَّى ٱللَّهُ عَلَيْهِ وَسَلَّمَ as saying, "I have been brought forth with the all-inclusive words (*jawāmiʿ al-kalim*)."

[1]

404

The First Bane: Speaking about What Does Not Concern You (*Fīma lā yuʿanīk*)

Know that the best of your states [involves] guarding your utterances from all the banes we have mentioned: backbiting, gossip, lying, arguing, hypocrisy, and others. [These are] speaking of what is permissible and what does not harm you at all, or [harm] any other Muslim; not speaking about anything of which you have no need and which is not necessary for you, in which case you would be wasting your time; [being] accountable for the movement of your tongue, and not trading what is lower for what is good [lit., higher].[1] So if you used the time it takes to speak about [what does not concern you] for reflection [instead], maybe one of the breezes of God's عَزَّوَجَلَّ mercy[2] would be opened to you. When you reflect [you will receive] what is of great benefit, so it is better for you to repeat the [affirmation] of God's Oneness [*lā ilāha illā Allāh*] سُبْحَانَهُ, and glorify God [lit., saying *subḥān Allāh*] and remember (*dhikr*) Him.

---

1 Trans.: He is referring to the words of Moses عَلَيْهِ السَّلَامُ to the children of Israel in the Qurʾān, *Would you exchange what is better for what is less?* [2:61].

2 Trans.: He is referring to a *ḥadīth* in al-Ṭabarānī, *al-Muʿjam al-kabīr*, 519; Abū Nuʿaym, *Ḥilya*, 3:162; al-Bayhaqī, *Shuʿab al-īmān*, and several other sources with similar wording: "Verily, throughout the days of your life, your Lord has breezes of the spirit. So be open to them that perchance one of them might reach you and you will never be sorrowful again."

How many words lead to palaces built in heaven,[3] and whoever is able to take hold of one of [God's] treasures but instead takes hold of a useless lump of clay, loses [what is] an evident [great] loss.

Such is the example of one who leaves the invocation of God تَعَالَىٰ and busies himself instead with what is permissible but does not concern him. Even though it is not a sin, it is a loss: the loss of the great benefit that [comes from] the remembrance of God تَعَالَىٰ. For "The believer's silence is reflection, his gaze is consideration, and his articulation is remembrance," as the Prophet صَلَّىٱللَّهُعَلَيْهِوَسَلَّمَ said.[4] |

For the servant [of God], his time is his capital, and whenever 405
he spends it on what does not concern him or bring him any reward in the hereafter, he is wasting his capital. The Prophet صَلَّىٱللَّهُعَلَيْهِوَسَلَّمَ said, "Among the [most] excellent [aspects] of a person's Islam is leaving what does not concern him."[5]

Indeed, [a *ḥadīth*] was conveyed that is much harsher than this. Anas said,

> There was a youth among us who was a martyr on the day of Uḥud and it was found that he had tied a stone to his stomach to keep from feeling hunger. His mother brushed the dust from his face and said, "congratulations, my son, on [reaching] heaven!"
>
> The Prophet صَلَّىٱللَّهُعَلَيْهِوَسَلَّمَ said, "How do you know? Perhaps he used to speak about what did not concern him and withheld what would not harm him."[6]

---

3 Eds.: This alludes to supplications, as in the case of Pharaoh's wife who asked for a house/palace in heaven, see Q. 66:11.

4 Trans.: This echoes a *ḥadīth* found in al-Quḍāʿī, *Musnad al-shihāb*, 1159, conveyed by Ibn ʿĀʾisha: "The Messenger God صَلَّىٱللَّهُعَلَيْهِوَسَلَّمَ said in an oration, 'Verily, my Lord commanded that my speech be remembrance, my silence [be] reflection, and looking at someone, a lesson." This *ḥadīth* could be translated more literally as "The believer's silence is not but reflection, his gaze not but consideration, and his speech not but articulation," as the Prophet صَلَّىٱللَّهُعَلَيْهِوَسَلَّمَ said.

5 Al-Tirmidhī, *Sunan*, 2317; Ibn Mājah, *Sunan*, 3976; and Mālik, *al-Muwaṭṭaʾ*, 2:903. Also see al-Nawawī, *an-Nawawī's Forty Hadith*, 54.

6 Ibn Abī l-Dunyā, *al-Ṣamt wa-ādāb al-lisān*, 109; Abū Yaʿlā, *Musnad*, 4017; and in a shorter version in al-Tirmidhī, *Sunan*, 2316. Trans.: Al-Tirmidhī added that he refused to give in charity because he was miserly (*bakhīl*); this included even the smallest amount that would not have been harmful or difficult for him.

In another *ḥadīth*, the Prophet ﷺ could not find Kaʿb, and when he asked about him, they said, [he is] ill. So he set out to visit him, and when he entered, he said,

> "Good tidings, O Kaʿb!"
>
> [Hearing this], his mother said, "Congratulations, O Kaʿb on [reaching] heaven!"
>
> At which [the Prophet] ﷺ said, "Who is this who pronounces sentence [against] God?"[7]
>
> [Kaʿb] said, "She is my mother, O Messenger of God."
>
> [The Prophet] said, "O mother of Kaʿb, how do you know? Perhaps Kaʿb spoke of what did not concern him or withheld what would not make him rich [that is, a small amount]."[8]

[This *ḥadīth*] means that heaven is prepared for those who are not questioned [lit., not held accountable], but if someone speaks about
406 what | does not concern him, it will be accounted against him even if what he said was permissible. Heaven is not prepared for someone who will be interrogated at the reckoning, for that is a kind of punishment [in itself].[9]

From Muḥammad b. Kaʿb [we learned that], the Messenger of God ﷺ said,

> The first [person] who walks through this door will be a man from the people of heaven. Then ʿAbdallāh b. Salām entered and the Companions of the Messenger of God ﷺ rose to meet him and told him [what the Prophet had said].
>
> They said, "Please tell us, which of your deeds gives you the most hope [for salvation]?"
>
> He said, "I am weak, but what gives me most hope with God is that I keep my breast [that is, heart] sound and leave what does not concern me."[10]

---

7 FC: Lane, *An Arabic-English Lexicon*, 86, under *mutʾāl.*

8 Ibn Abī l-Dunyā, *al-Ṣamt wa-ādāb al-lisān*, 110.

9 Eds.: This alludes to the *ḥadīth* that the questioning itself is a punishment.

10 Ibn Abī l-Dunyā, *al-Ṣamt wa-ādāb al-lisān*, 111. That is, does not hold grudges, etc.

And Abū Dharr said, the Messenger of God ﷺ asked me, "Shall I not teach you a practice that is light on the body but heavy in the balance?"[11] I said, "Yes, O Messenger of God!" He said, "Silence (*ṣamt*), good character (*ḥusn al-khuluq*), and leaving what does not concern you."[12]

Mujāhid said, I heard Ibn ʿAbbās say,

> There are five [sayings] more beloved to me than vigorous black [horses].[13] Do not speak about what does not concern you, for truly it is superfluous and does not keep you secure from the burden [on the day of judgment]. Do not speak of what concerns you until you have found the right context [in which to mention] it, for [someone may speak] about a matter that concerns him, but [if he says it] in the wrong context, [it brings him] only distress. Do not argue with a gentle[man] or a fool, for the gentle[man] will diminish you[14] and the fool will injure you. And mention your brother in his absence with what you would like | him to speak of you [in 407
> your absence], pardon him for what you would like him to pardon you [for], treat him how you would like him to treat you, and let your actions be those of a person who sees that he will be recompensed for his goodness and punished for his offenses.[15]

It was said to Luqmān the wise, "What is [the essence of] your wisdom?" He said, "I do not ask about the provision I am given and I do not take upon [myself] what does not concern me."[16]

Muwarriq al-ʿIjlī [or al-ʿAjallī] said, "[There is] a matter that I have been seeking for twenty years and have not achieved, and I still seek it." They said, "What is it?" He said, "Silence about what does not concern me."[17]

---

11 That is, the scale on day of judgment.

12 Ibn Abī l-Dunyā, *al-Ṣamt wa-ādāb al-lisān*, 112.

13 Eds.: For this translation we followed al-Zabīdī who adds, a horse made ready for riding, or valuable and perhaps one given in the way of God; al-Zabīdī, *Itḥāf*, 7:461.

14 Al-Zabīdī, *Itḥāf*, 7:462.

15 Ibn Abī l-Dunyā, *al-Ṣamt wa-ādāb al-lisān* 114.

16 Ibn Abī Shayba, *al-Muṣannaf*, 35436; and Ibn Abī l-Dunyā, *al-Ṣamt wa-ādāb al-lisān*, 115.

17 Ibn Abī Shayba, *al-Muṣannaf*, 36292; and Ibn Abī l-Dunyā, *al-Ṣamt wa-ādāb al-lisān*, 118.

ʿUmar رَضِيَ اللَّهُ عَنْهُ said,

> Do not argue about what does not concern you, avoid your enemy, and be wary of your friend from [among] the group, unless he is trustworthy, and no one is trustworthy except he who fears God تَعَالَىٰ. Do not befriend a profligate lest he teach you his profligacy do not divulge to him your secrets, and seek counsel from those who fear God تَعَالَىٰ.[18]

The definition of what does not concern you is speaking about anything that, if you did not say anything about it, you would not
408 have sinned | nor caused harm now or later.[19]

An example of [this is,] if you were sitting with people and you tell them about your travels—and what you saw of the mountains and rivers, what happened to you, the food and dress you liked, what amazed you about the scholars in the land and what happened to them—these matters—if you had not said them, you would not be sinning nor [causing] harm. Even if you made every effort not to mix into your narrative additions and omissions, and without praising yourself by bragging about what you witnessed of the great events, and did not backbite anyone or find fault with anything that God تَعَالَىٰ has created; even with all that, you would be wasting your time. Who is really safe from the banes we mentioned?

Among these [topics], if you ask someone else about what does not concern you, then with the question you wasted your time and also wasted your companion's [time] requiring him to answer. This is the case if you are asking about something that is not a bane [in itself], but most of the questions [we might pose] contain banes. For example, you ask someone about his worship, saying "Are you fasting?" If his answer is yes, he is displaying his worship, and [this may] lead to [a sort of] ostentation for him, and even if it does not, his worship will no longer be in the domain of what is secret, and worship in secret is superior by many degrees to outward worship. And if he says no, he is lying, and if he says nothing, he will seem to disdain you and you will be hurt by him, and if he tries to avoid answering you, he will struggle and tire [himself]. Thus, your question

18 Ibn Abī Shayba, *al-Muṣannaf*, 26041; and Ibn Abī l-Dunyā, *al-Ṣamt wa-ādāb al-lisān*, 120.

19 That is, only speak about what will bring reward and benefit to you, now or later.

exposes him to ostentation, lying, disdain, or the tiresomeness of strategizing to avoid [answering you].

And similarly, [the same is true about] your questions about any other form of worship. |

And similarly, [this also applies to] your questions about dis- 409
obedience, about anything he hides and is ashamed of, and your questions about what someone else talked about, and your saying, "What did you say? What were you doing?"

And similarly, if you saw someone in the road and asked, "Where are you [coming] from?" Perhaps there is a reason for him not wanting to tell you. If he does tell you, it will hurt him and he will be ashamed, but if he is not honest, he falls into lies and you would be the cause of it.

And similarly, if you ask someone about something of which you have no need, but the one you ask will not let himself say, "I do not know," and so he answers you without insight (*ghayr baṣīra*) [and falls into error].

But I do not mean by speaking about what does not concern [someone], these types [of matters] that could lead to sin or harm. Rather, an example of what does not concern [someone] is what was related about Luqmān the wise. He went to David عَلَيْهِ ٱلسَّلَامُ who was fashioning armor[20] that [Luqmān] had never seen before that day. [Luqmān] was amazed at what he saw and wanted to ask [David] about it, but his wisdom prevented him, so he restrained himself and did not ask. Then, when he finished, David عَلَيْهِ ٱلسَّلَامُ stood up, put it on, and said, "What excellent armor for war!" Luqmān said, "Silence (*ṣamt*) is wisdom and few are they who practice it. I wanted to ask you about it but you saved me [from doing that]." It is said that [Luqmān] refrained from asking for an entire year, and even though he wanted to know, he never asked, and finally he came to know without asking.[21]

These types of questions are not harmful in themselves. They
do not tear off the cover [from something secret], or involve | 410
ostentation and lying, but they are among the [matters] that do

20 That is, a coat of chain mail armor.

21 Al-Bayhaqī, *Shuʿab al-īmān*, 4671.

not really concern [you], and leaving them is "among the [most] excellent [aspects] of [a person's] Islam." Such is their definition.

The causes that lead to [this bane] are a person's desire to know what he does not need to know, or to be sociable in conversation for the sake of friendship, or to pass the time by recounting events that have no benefit.

And the treatment for all this is for him to know that death is ever before him [lit., between his hands], that he is responsible for every word [he utters], that his breaths[22] are his capital, and that his tongue is a net with which he might catch a *ḥūr al-ʿayn*,[23] and so for him to ignore that and waste [his chance] is clearly a loss. Such is the treatment from the standpoint of knowledge.

From the standpoint of action, it is for him to retreat (*ʿuzla*), or to place a pebble in his mouth,[24] and to force himself not to say anything even about some of what *does* concern him, as a way of accustoming his tongue to leave what does *not* concern him. Controlling the tongue in this way, with the exception of those [living in] in retreat, is exceedingly difficult.

22 Trans.: That is, moments, life, one's time on earth.

23 Eds.: *Ḥūr*, from the Arabic noun *ḥūriyya*, is the plural of *ḥawrāʾ* (fem.)/*aḥwar* (masc.), which denotes a general sense of "whiteness." It describes the eye of a gazelle or oryx (the white contrasting with the blackness of its pupil). See Lane, *An Arabic-English Lexicon*, 666. *Ḥūr ʿīn* are mentioned in the Qurʾān specifically by name in 44:54, 52:20, and 56:22–23; additional information on them appears in the context of paradise, but with various wordings (see 37:48–49, 55:72, 56:35–37, and 78:31–33). They are referred to as spouses in 2:25, 3:15, and 4:57. With regard to spouses entering paradise, see 13:22-24, 40:8 and 43:70.

24 In Ibn Abī l-Dunyā, *al-Ṣamt wa-ādāb al-lisān*, 438, it was related that Arṭā b. al-Mundhir said, "A man practiced silence for forty years by putting a stone in his mouth that he would not remove except to eat, drink, or sleep."

[2]

The Second Bane: Superfluous Speech (*Fuḍūl al-kalām*)

[**S**UPERFLUOUS speech] is also censured. It refers to delving into what does not concern [us] or speaking about what concerns [us] but with more words than are needed. If there is a matter that concerns [someone], he may mention it succinctly or he may draw it out and repeat it.

Whenever a single word suffices and someone uses two words instead, the second word is superfluous, that is, unnecessary. So this is also censured [according to] what [we have] said, even if it [the superfluous speech] contains no sin or harm.

ʿAṭāʾ b. Abī Rabāḥ said,

"Those who came before you used to deplore superfluous speech; [that is] what they considered to be anything beyond the Book of God تَعَالَى, or the *sunna* of the Messenger of God صَلَّى ٱللَّهُ عَلَيْهِ وَسَلَّمَ, commanding the right [and forbidding the wrong], or speaking about what they absolutely must in respect to their livelihoods. Do you deny that over you are *keepers, noble and recording* [82:10–11] . . . *seated on the right and on the left, and that a person utters no word except that with him is an observer prepared [to record]* [50:17–18]? And will you not be ashamed if, when your scroll is laid open, what filled the better part of your days had no relation to your *dīn* or your worldly [life] (*dunyā*)?"[1]

---

1   Ibn Abī Shayba, *al-Muṣannaf*, 36618; and Abū Nuʿaym, *Ḥilya*, 3:314.

One of the Companions said, "A man may say something to me
412 and I want to respond to him more than | a thirsty [person] wants a drink of cold water [on a hot day], but I do not do so out of fear that it is superfluous."[2]

Muṭarrif said, "If you wish to keep the majesty of God in your hearts, do not mention Him when you are saying, as to a dog or an donkey, 'may God dishonor you!' or anything like it."[3]

Know that even while superfluous speech is limitless, what is important is limited in the Book of God تعالى by His words, *No good is there in much of their private conversation, except for those who enjoin charity or that which is right or conciliation between people* [Q. 4:114].[4]

The [Prophet] صلى الله عليه وسلم said, "A good state is for whoever holds back the superfluous [speech] of his tongue and spends in charity from the superfluous [part] of his wealth."[5]

So look at how people have turned this upside down so that they hold back superfluous wealth and unleash the superfluous [speech] of [their] tongues!

> From Muṭarrif b. ʿAbdallāh [we learned] that his father said to him,
> I came to the Messenger of God صلى الله عليه وسلم as part of a delegation from the Banī ʿĀmir. They said to him [the Prophet], "You
> 413 are our father, you are our master, | you are the most excellent among us in merit, you are the possessor of abundance, and you are the most magnanimous host [who entertains],[6] you are... you are..."
>
> [The Prophet] صلى الله عليه وسلم said, "Say what you [want to] say and do not let Satan tempt you."[7]

---

2 Ibn Abī l-Dunyā, *al-Ṣamt wa-ādāb al-lisān*, 628.

3 Ibn al-Mubārak, *Zuhd*, 214; and Ibn Abī l-Dunyā, *al-Ṣamt wa-ādāb al-lisān*, 634.

4 Ibn Abī l-Dunyā, *al-Ṣamt wa-ādāb al-lisān*, 14.

5 Ibn Abī ʿĀṣam, *al-Zuhd*, 108; al-Ṭabarānī, *al-Muʿjam al-kabīr*, 5:71; and Ibn ʿAdī, *al-Kāmil*, 1:384.

6 Lane (*An Arabic-English Lexicon*, 434) describes *jafnat al-gharāʾ* as a person who is generous and entertains many guests.

7 Ibn Abī l-Dunyā, *al-Ṣamt wa-ādāb al-lisān*, 73, and with similar wording in Abū Dāwūd, *Sunan*, 4806; and al-Nasāʾī, *al-Sunan al-kubrā*, 10004.

> [This is] an indication that if the tongue is loosed in commendation, even if it is truthful, there is a fear that Satan will tempt someone to add what is not needed.

Ibn Masʿūd said, "I warn you against superfluous speech. It is enough for a person to say [only] what conveys his needs."[8]

And Mujāhid said, "Speech is surely being written. Even when a man quiets his child by saying, 'I will buy you this or that,' it is written as a small lie."[9]

And Ḥasan said, "O child of Adam! A page has been spread out for you and two noble angels write your deeds, so dictate what you wish, be it abundant or sparse."[10]

It was related that Solomon, son of David, عَلَيْهِمَاالسَّلَامُ sent one of his *ʿifrīt*[11] [into the world] and sent a group [of other jinn] to see what he said and report it to him. They told him that [the *ʿifrīt*] passed through the marketplace, lifted his gaze to the sky, then lowered it to the people, and then shook his head. When Solomon asked him about that, he said, "I was marveling at the angels above people's heads and how fast they were writing | and [those] below them and 414
how fast they were dictating."[12]

Ibrāhīm al-Taymī said, "When the believer wants to speak, he first considers [it]: if it is for him, he speaks, and if not, he holds [his tongue], whereas the libertine, his tongue is [always] running loose."[13]

And Ḥasan said, "He who abounds (*kathra*) in speech abounds in lies, and he who abounds in wealth, abounds in transgressions, and he whose character is wicked punishes his soul."[14]

ʿAmr b. Dīnār said, "A man was speaking excessively in the presence of the Prophet صَلَّىٱللَّهُعَلَيْهِوَسَلَّمَ, so [the Prophet] صَلَّىٱللَّهُعَلَيْهِوَسَلَّمَ asked him,

---

8 Ibn Wahhab, *al-Jāmiʿ*, 462; and al-Ṭabarānī, *al-Muʿjam al-kabīr*, 9:93.

9 Ibn Abī l-Dunyā, *al-Ṣamt wa-ādāb al-lisān*, 653.

10 Ibn Abī l-Dunyā, *al-Ṣamt wa-ādāb al-lisān*, 85.

11 Eds.: *ʿifrīt* (from *ʿafara*): Lexicographers say it derives from *ʿafara* ("to roll someone in the dust" and, by extension, "to bring low"). It appears once in the Qurʾān (27:39) as "*a powerful one from among the jinn*" or, in another translation, "*a mighty jinn*." J. Chelhod, "*ʿIfrīt*," in *EI²*, 3:1050–1051; Lane, *An Arabic-English Lexicon*, 2089–2091.

12 Ibn Abī l-Dunyā, *al-Ṣamt wa-ādāb al-lisān*, 86.

13 Ibn Abī l-Dunyā, *al-Ṣamt wa-ādāb al-lisān*, 88.

14 Ibn Abī l-Dunyā, *al-Ṣamt wa-ādāb al-lisān*, 90.

'How many doors are there in front of your tongue?' He answered, 'My lips and my teeth.' [The Prophet] said, 'Are they not enough to hold back your speech?'" In [another] report, [the Prophet] spoke about a man who had praised him and was unrestrained[15] in speech, then said [صَلَّى ٱللَّهُ عَلَيْهِ وَسَلَّمَ] "The most evil [thing] a man can be given is a superfluous tongue."[16]

ʿUmar b. ʿAbd al-ʿAzīz رَحِمَهُ ٱللَّهُ said, "What restrains me from speaking abundantly is the fear of showing off."[17] |

415 One of the sages said, "If a person is sitting [among people] and he is delighted with his own speech, let him be quiet, and if he is quiet, and is delighted by his own quiet, let him speak."[18]

Yazīd b. Abī Ḥabīb said, "One of the temptations for the scholar is to love speaking more than listening even when there is someone [else who can speak] in his place. Verily, in listening there is safety, while in speaking there is embellishment, addition, and omission."[19]

Ibn ʿUmar said, "The most worthy of purification is a man's tongue."[20]

And Abū l-Dardāʾ saw a sharp-tongued woman and said, "If this [woman] were mute, it would be better for her [in the hereafter]."[21]

Ibrāhīm[22] said, "People are destroyed by two things: superfluous wealth and superfluous speech."[23]

So these are the censured [aspects] of superfluous and abundant speech and the causes that lead to it; its treatment is what has been mentioned in respect to speaking about what does not concern us [that is, the first bane].

---

15 Eds.: The Minhāj editors define *istaḥfaza* (from al-Zabīdī, *Itḥāf*, 7:467) as exaggeration, or speaking at length. We believe this is a typo and the text should read *istahtara* (carelessness, recklessness, or as above, unrestrained).

16 That is, a tongue that speaks excessively. Both these were related by Ibn Abī l-Dunyā, *al-Ṣamt wa-ādāb al-lisān*, 93, 94.

17 Ibn al-Mubārak, *Zuhd*, 137; and Ibn Abī l-Dunyā, *al-Ṣamt wa-ādāb al-lisān*, 96.

18 Ibn al-Mubārak, *Zuhd*, 202; and Ibn Abī l-Dunyā, *al-Ṣamt wa-ādāb al-lisān*, 97.

19 Ibn al-Mubārak, *Zuhd*, 48; and Ibn Abī l-Dunyā, *al-Ṣamt wa-ādāb al-lisān*, 98.

20 Ibn Abī l-Dunyā, *al-Ṣamt wa-ādāb al-lisān*, 99.

21 Ibn Abī l-Dunyā, *al-Ṣamt wa-ādāb al-lisān*, 100.

22 Trans.: References to Ibrāhīm, unless otherwise noted, are to Ibrāhīm al-Nakhāʿī (d. ca. 96/714), a devout scholar of Kufa who studied under Ḥasan al-Baṣrī and Anas b. Mālik.

23 Ibn Abī l-Dunyā, *al-Ṣamt wa-ādāb al-lisān*, 103.

[3]

The Third Bane: Delving into Baseless (*Bāṭil*) [Talk] 416

[Delving into baseless talk refers] to talk about disobedience, such as telling stories about women, or about gatherings for wine drinking, places of debauchery, or about the luxuries of the rich, or the tyranny of rulers and their censured ceremonies and their deplorable states. All of these are among [what] it is not lawful to delve into—it is unlawful (*ḥarām*).

As for talking about what does not concern [you], or [talking] excessively about what concerns you, it is better avoided but is not unlawful.

Indeed, whoever talks excessively about what does not concern [him] is not secure from delving into baseless [talk]. Most people sit together to entertain one another with conversation and are not beyond making jokes at the expense of other people's honor or delving into baseless [talk].

The types of baseless [talk] cannot be counted, for they are numerous and varied. So the only way to escape from them is to limit [your speech] to the important [questions] of *dīn* and this world. This category [of *bāṭil*] includes the words that destroy one who utters them thinking they are insignificant. Bilāl b. al-Ḥārith said, the Messenger of God صَلَّى ٱللَّهُ عَلَيْهِ وَسَلَّمَ said,

> A man may say a word pleasing to God, not supposing that it amounts to anything, but by way of it God writes for him His approval | until the day he meets Him, and a man may 417
> say a word that [invokes the] wrath of God, not supposing

> it amounts to anything, and by way of it God writes for him His wrath until the day of resurrection.[1]

[Bilāl said], "ʿAlqama used to say, 'How many words has the *ḥadīth* [narrated by] Bilāl b. al-Ḥārith kept me [lit., barred me] from uttering!"[2]

And the Prophet صَلَّى ٱللَّهُ عَلَيْهِ وَسَلَّمَ said, "A man may say something for the sake of making those he is sitting with laugh, and it casts him deeper [into hell] than [the distance to] the Pleiades."[3]

Abū Hurayra said, "A man may say something he pays no attention to and by it be cast into hell. And a man may say something he pays no attention to and by it God elevates him to heaven."[4]

The Messenger of God صَلَّى ٱللَّهُ عَلَيْهِ وَسَلَّمَ said, "The people with the greatest offenses on the day of resurrection will be those who most often delved into baseless [talk]."[5] And the words of God تَعَالَىٰ refer to this: *And we used to enter into vain discourse with those who engaged* [*in it*] [Q. 74:45] and also, . . . *So do not sit with them until they enter into another conversation. Indeed, you would then be like them* . . . [Q. 4:140]. |

418 Salmān said, "Those who will have the greatest transgressions on the day of resurrection will be those who spoke the most about disobedience to God."[6]

And Ibn Sīrīn said, "One of the Anṣār would pass by people sitting together and say to them, 'Make ablution, for some of what you say is worse than the actions [that invalidate the ablution].'"[7]

This is [what it means] to delve into baseless [talk]. It is behind what will be [discussed] later—backbiting, gossiping, obscenity, and the like. Rather, it is delving into the mention of [acts that are] restricted that have happened or about how they were accomplished, without any religious need to mention it. Also included here is

---

1 Al-Tirmidhī, *Sunan*, 2319; and Ibn Mājah, *Sunan*, 3969.

2 Ibn Abī l-Dunyā, *al-Ṣamt wa-ādāb al-lisān*, 70.

3 Ibn al-Mubārak, *Zuhd*, 948; Ibn Abī l-Dunyā, *al-Ṣamt wa-ādāb al-lisān*, 71; al-Bukhārī, *Ṣaḥīḥ*, 6477; and Muslim, *Ṣaḥīḥ*, 2988.

4 Mālik, *al-Muwaṭṭaʾ*, 2:985; and Ibn Abī l-Dunyā, *al-Ṣamt wa-ādāb al-lisān*, 72.

5 Ibn Abī l-Dunyā, *al-Ṣamt wa-ādāb al-lisān*, 74.

6 Ibn Abī Shayba, *al-Muṣannaf*, 35804; and Ibn Abī l-Dunyā, *al-Ṣamt wa-ādāb al-lisān*, 75.

7 Ibn Wahhab, *al-Jāmiʿ*, 460; and Ibn Abī l-Dunyā, *al-Ṣamt wa-ādāb al-lisān*, 105.

delving into narratives of heresies, false schools [of belief], and narratives about what took place among the Companions [when] they fought [among themselves] in a way that seemed to attack their [integrity].[8] All of this is baseless [talk], and delving into it is delving into futility. We ask God for the goodness of His help with His [infinite] sublimity and magnanimity.

8 Eds.: That is, during the *fitna* (trials, or tribulations) after the death of ʿUthmān in 35/656; the *fitna* lasted until 40/661.

[4]

419 ## The Fourth Bane: Arguments (*Mirāʾ*) and Debates (*Jadāl*)

[ARGUMENTS and debates] are forbidden. [The Prophet] صَلَّى ٱللَّهُ عَلَيْهِ وَسَلَّمَ said, "Do not argue with your brother nor joke with him,[1] and do not make a promise to him and then break it."[2]

And [the Prophet] صَلَّى ٱللَّهُ عَلَيْهِ وَسَلَّمَ, said "Leave aside arguing, for its wisdom is not understood and its tribulations spare no one."[3]

[The Prophet] صَلَّى ٱللَّهُ عَلَيْهِ وَسَلَّمَ also said, "For whoever gives up an argument when he is in the right, a house is built for him in the highest [place] in heaven, and whoever gives up an argument when he is in the wrong, a house is built for him on the outskirts of heaven."[4]

Umm Salama رَضِيَ ٱللَّهُ عَنْهَا said, "The Messenger of God صَلَّى ٱللَّهُ عَلَيْهِ وَسَلَّمَ said, 'The first [thing] my Lord pledged me to and forbade me from, after the worship of idols and drinking wine, was reviling men.'"[5] |

420 And [the Prophet صَلَّى ٱللَّهُ عَلَيْهِ وَسَلَّمَ] also said, "No group goes astray after God has guided them except those given to debate."[6]

---

1 Trans.: That is, excessively, as is explained in chapter 10.

2 Al-Tirmidhī, *Sunan*, 1995.

3 Al-Ṭabarānī, *al-Muʿjam al-kabīr*, 8:152, without the phrase "its wisdom is not understood," Ibn Abī l-Dunyā, *al-Ṣamt wa-ādāb al-lisān*, 127.

4 Al-Tirmidhī, *Sunan*, 1993; Ibn Mājah, *Sunan*, 51.

5 Ibn Abī l-Dunyā, *al-Ṣamt wa-ādāb al-lisān*, 134; al-Ṭabarānī, *al-Muʿjam al-kabīr*, 20:83; al-Bayhaqī, *Shuʿab al-īmān*, 8082; and Ibn Abī Shayba, *al-Muṣannaf*, 24541. Eds.: Reviling (*mulāḥa*) refers to blaming the opponent in an argument with hatred, criticizing him in an insulting or abusive manner.

6 Al-Tirmidhī, *Sunan*, 3253; and Ibn Abī l-Dunyā, *al-Ṣamt wa-ādāb al-lisān*, 135.

And [the Prophet صَلَّى ٱللَّهُ عَلَيْهِ وَسَلَّمَ] also said, "The servant will not reach the reality of faith until he is able to give up arguing even when he is right."[7]

And [the Prophet صَلَّى ٱللَّهُ عَلَيْهِ وَسَلَّمَ] also said,

> Six things show [that a person] has reached the reality of faith: fasting in the summer, striking the enemies of God with a sword, hastening to the prayer on a stormy day, [having] patience in the face of disaster, making the ablution perfectly in difficult circumstances,[8] and leaving an argument even when he is right.[9]

Zubayr said to his son, "Do not debate with people using the Qurʾān—you will not be able [to convince] them—but rather hold fast to the *sunna*."[10]

And ʿUmar b. ʿAbd al-ʿAzīz رَحِمَهُ ٱللَّهُ said, "Whoever makes his *dīn* the object of disputation changes [his view] the most."[11] |

Muslim b. Yasār said, "Beware of arguments, for they [happen] 421
at a time when the scholar is ignorant, and when Satan tries to make him lapse."[12]

And it has been said that a group does not go astray after God has guided them except by debate.

Mālik b. Anas رَحِمَهُ ٱللَّهُ said, "This debate has nothing to do with *dīn*."[13]

And he also said, "Arguing hardens the hearts and leads to grudges."[14]

Luqmān said to his son, "O my son, do not debate with the scholars lest they detest you."[15]

---

7 Ibn Abī l-Dunyā, *al-Ṣamt wa-ādāb al-lisān*, 139.

8 Eds.: For example, when one makes ablutions with cold water on a cold day.

9 Al-Marūzī, *Taʿẓīm qadri al-ṣālat*, 443; and al-Daylamī, *Musnad al-firdaws*, 3484.

10 Al-Khaṭīb al-Baghdādī, *al-Faqīh wa-l-mutafaqqih*, 610.

11 Al-Dārimī, *Sunan*, 312; and Ibn Abī l-Dunyā, *al-Ṣamt wa-ādāb al-lisān*, 161. Trans.: That is, frequently changing one's view in *dīn* is not commendable. Eds.: And bringing up disputed or doubtful issues (whether theological or juristic), in relation to one's *dīn* makes a person more likely to continue questioning and changing his position.

12 Al-Dārimī, *Sunan*, 410; and Ibn Abī l-Dunyā, *al-Ṣamt wa-ādāb al-lisān*, 125.

13 Al-Bayhaqī, *al-Madkhal*, 238.

14 Ibn ʿAsākir, *Tārīkh madīnat Dimashq*, 61:205.

15 Al-Bayhaqī, *al-Zuhd al-kabīr*, 91.

And Bilāl b. Saᶜd said, "If you see a man persistently arguing with others and pleased with his view, [know that] his ruin is complete."[16]

Sufyān [al-Thawrī] said, "If I contradicted my brother about a pomegranate, and he said it is sweet and I said it is sour, he would take me to the sultan."[17] |

422 [Sufyān al-Thawrī] also said, "Be a sincere [companion] to whomever you wish, then anger him by arguing and he will [surely] throw you into such a catastrophe that you are [almost] prevented from living [that is, barely survive it]."

Ibn Abī Laylā said, "I do not argue with my companion because I might [call] him a liar or anger him."[18]

And Abū l-Dardāʾ said, "It is enough of a sin for you to keep arguing."[19]

The [Prophet] صَلَّى ٱللَّهُ عَلَيْهِ وَسَلَّمَ said, "The expiation (*takfīr*) for every invective is two prayer cycles (*rakᶜatān*)."[20]

And ᶜUmar رَضِيَ ٱللَّهُ عَنْهُ said, "Do not acquire knowledge for the sake of three [reasons], and do not leave it because of three [reasons]. Do not acquire it for [the sake of] arguing, for showing off, or for ostentation; and do not leave it [because] you are ashamed to ask, or you underestimate [its value], or you are content to be ignorant."[21]

Jesus عَلَيْهِ ٱلسَّلَامُ said, "Whoever abounds in lying, beauty leaves him; whoever reviles men, valor falls from him; whoever has many worries, sickness [befalls] his body; and whoever has bad manners torments himself [that is, his soul]."[22] |

423 It was said to Maymūn b. Mahrān, "How is it that your brother does not leave you while detesting [you]?" He said, "Because I do not quarrel or argue with him."[23]

Indeed, a great many sayings condemn argument and debate.

---

16 Ibn Ḥibbān, *Rawḍat al-ᶜuqalāʾ*, 79; and Abū Nuᶜaym, *Ḥilya*, 5:228.

17 Ibn Abī l-Dunyā, *Mudārāt al-nās*, 122. Trans.: An argument between brothers, even about such a small matter, is disapproved.

18 Ibn Abī l-Dunyā, *al-Ṣamt wa-ādāb al-lisān*, 124.

19 Ibn Abī l-Dunyā, *al-Ṣamt wa-ādāb al-lisān*, 130.

20 Al-Ṭabarānī, *al-Muᶜjam al-kabīr*, 8:149; Ibn ᶜAsākir, *Tārīkh madīnat Dimashq*, 50:269; and Ibn Abī Shayba, *al-Muṣannaf*, 7731.

21 Ibn Abī l-Dunyā, *al-Ṣamt wa-ādāb al-lisān*, 131.

22 Ibn Abī l-Dunyā, *al-Ṣamt wa-ādāb al-lisān*, 133.

23 Ibn Abī l-Dunyā, *al-Ṣamt wa-ādāb al-lisān*, 146.

The definition of arguing is objecting to the speech of others by pointing out flaws in it, either through expressions, or meanings, or in the aims of the speaker.

And refraining from arguing [means] refraining from denying [someone's statement] or objecting [to it], so for all the speech [one] hears, if it is true, attest to it, but if it is baseless or a lie and not related to matters of *dīn*, be quiet about it.

❁ ❁ ❁

Attacking the speech of others sometimes [takes place] in its expression, [as when someone] points out a flaw in grammar, or word choice, or [his] Arabic, or—in respect to poetry—the rhyme and order [of the verses]. And it is sometimes because of [his] lack of knowledge or sometimes because of the tyranny of the tongue, but however it [the error] occurs, there is no reason to point out his flaw.

As for [attacking] the meaning [of someone's speech, we are referring to] a comment such as, "It is not as you say. You are incorrect concerning it from the point of view of this... and that."

As for [attacking] the aim [of the speaker, we are referring to] a comment such as, "What you say is true, but truth is not your aim, | 424
you have some ulterior motive," and other such things. If this pertains to a scientific inquiry, perhaps it [should be referred to] specifically by the word debate and it, too, is censured. Here it is necessary to be quiet or ask a question to show the usefulness [of what is being said], not in a stubborn or aggravating way, but to gently make it better understood, not for the purpose of opening it to attack.

As for debate, it is an expression of an aim to refute the other, overpower, belittle, and malign his speech and accuse him of deficiency and ignorance about it.

[We find] a sign of that, [for example], when someone else points out the truth, and the debater deplores it. [Rather], he wants to be the one to point out the other's incorrectness to show his own superiority and the deficiency of his companion. There is no salvation from this [peril] except in [remaining] quiet about everything but what it is sinful to remain quiet about.

As for the motivation behind [debate] it is to exalt [the ego] by [1] showing [one's own] knowledge and superiority while attacking the other by [2] showing his deficiencies, and both of these are [among] the hidden and powerful desires of the ego.

As for [1] showing one's superiority, it is a variety of praising oneself, which in turn arises from a servant's wrongful claim to sublimity and grandeur, both of which are attributes of lordship [that is, of God].

As for [2] diminishing the other, it arises from the bestial nature that seeks to rip apart, crush, crash [into], and hurt another.

Both of these are censured and destructive traits that argument and debate reinforce. One who habitually argues and debates,
425 reinforces these destructive traits. And this exceeds | the limit of [what is] reprehensible, rather it is disobedience whenever this hurts someone else.

Argument is almost inseparable from [causing] hurt and arousing anger, and leads an adversary to retreat and seek support for his speech however he can—by truth or falsehood—and to malign the one arguing with him by anything he can imagine about him. This [type of argument] incites a fight between the two opponents just like what incites the aggressive [attack] between two dogs, each one wanting to take a bite from the other in the most injurious [way] and would best [render him] speechless and exhaust him [with arguments].

❁ ❁ ❁

As for the treatment, it is to break the arrogance that motivates him to show his own superiority, and the bestial [nature] that motivates him to diminish another. This will be explained in *The Book on the Censure of Pride and Vanity* and *The Book on the Censure* [sic] *of Anger*,[24] but [in general], the treatment for any malady is to remove its causes. And the cause of arguments and debates is what we have

24 Trans.: Book 29 of the *Revival of the Religious Sciences: The Censure of Pride and Vanity* (*Kitāb dhamm al-kibr wa-l-ʿajab*) and book 25, which al-Ghazālī refers to as the censure of anger is titled *The Banes of Anger, Malice, and Envy* (*Kitāb āfat al-ghaḍab*).

mentioned. So, [for someone who] persists [in doing these], it will become his habit and nature, until it takes hold of his soul and patience in [refraining from it becomes] difficult.

> It was related that Abū Ḥanīfa رَحِمَهُ ٱللَّهُ said to Dāwūd al-Ṭāʾī, "Why have you chosen seclusion?"
>
> [Dāwūd] said, "So that I can struggle against my ego by leaving debating [behind]."
>
> [Abū Ḥanīfa] said, "Attend assemblies, listen to what is said, and do not say [anything]."
>
> [Dāwūd] said, "I did that, and I have not found a struggle more intense for me than that."[25] |

And it is as he said, because for one who hears errors from another 426
and is able to reveal it, patience [and refraining from speaking] is extremely difficult. Thus, [the Prophet] صَلَّى ٱللَّهُ عَلَيْهِ وَسَلَّمَ said, "For whoever gives up an argument when he is in the right, a house is built for him in the highest [level of] heaven,"[26] [because it] is [so] intensely [difficult] for the ego.

[Argumentation is] what most often overcomes [people in regard to] schools [of jurisprudence] and theology. Arguing is part of [human] nature, and if someone believes that there is some reward for it, that will impel him to greater aspirations, so that both his nature and [his understanding of] the law will support him. But this is a clear offense. Rather, a human being should stop his tongue [when speaking to] the people of the *qibla*.[27] If he sees someone [doing something] deviant, he should advise him gently and in private, not by way of debate. Otherwise it will be perceived [by the other] as a ruse to confuse the matter, which the debaters of his school could use if they wished. Thus, deviancy in his heart continues and is reinforced by debate.

And if someone recognizes that [giving] counsel is not beneficial, he should leave it and occupy himself with himself [that is, with his own soul]. The [Prophet] صَلَّى ٱللَّهُ عَلَيْهِ وَسَلَّمَ said, "God is merciful to the one who stops his tongue with the people of the *qibla* to the best of

25 Abū Nuʿaym, *Ḥilya*, 7:341.

26 Eds.: Al-Tirmidhī, *Sunan*, 1995.

27 Eds.: This is a reference to Muslims, who face Mecca in prayer.

his ability." And Hishām b. ʿUrwa said, "The [Prophet] ﷺ repeated this seven times."[28] |

427 Whoever habitually [engages in] debate for a time, and people commend him, will find himself honored and accepted because of it, [and then] these destructive [traits] will be reinforced in him. He will not be able to rid himself of them [that is, the destructive traits] when the power of pride, anger, ostentation, love of high rank, and misuse of merit are combined against him. Struggling against a single one of these traits would be unbearable [for him], so what about the combination of them?

28 Ibn Abī l-Dunyā, *al-Ṣamt wa-ādāb al-lisān*, 137.

[5]

The Fifth Bane: Disputation (*Khuṣūma*) 428

[DISPUTATION] is also censured; it is behind argument (*mirāʾ*) and debate (*jadāl*).

An argument [involves] attacking what someone else said by showing a flaw in it, with the only goal being to disdain the other and show off one's own intelligence.

And debates are an expression of some matter that is attached to schools [of jurisprudence] and their rulings.

Disputation [refers to] speaking insistently about settling in full property [issues] or an intended right. Sometimes they [disputations] arise from initiating [a claim] and sometimes from opposing one, while arguments are only in opposition to what was said.

ʿĀʾisha رَضِيَ ٱللَّهُ عَنْهَا said, "The Messenger of God صَلَّى ٱللَّهُ عَلَيْهِ وَسَلَّمَ said, "The man most loathed to God is the one who is the fiercest disputant."[1]

And Abū Hurayra said, "The Messenger of God صَلَّى ٱللَّهُ عَلَيْهِ وَسَلَّمَ said, 'He who debates in a [legal] disputation without knowledge, God's wrath remains on him until he withdraws.'"[2]

One of them said, "Beware of disputation for it destroys *dīn*."[3] |

1 Al-Bukhārī, *Ṣaḥīḥ*, 2457; and Muslim, *Ṣaḥīḥ*, 2668. Trans.: This is similar to an expression found in Q. 2:204: *And of the people is he whose speech pleases you in worldly life, and he calls God to witness as to what is in his heart, yet he is the fiercest of opponents.*

2 Ibn Abī l-Dunyā, *al-Ṣamt wa-ādāb al-lisān*, 153.

3 Ibn Abī l-Dunyā, *al-Ṣamt wa-ādāb al-lisān*, 154.

429 And it is said, "A person who is scrupulous in *dīn* does not ever [engage in] dispute."[4]

> Ibn Qutayba said, "Bashīr b. ʿUbaydallāh b. Abī Bakra passed by me one day then said, 'Why are you sitting [here]?'"
>
> [Ibn Qutayba] answered, "There is a [legal] dispute between me and one of my [paternal male] cousins."
>
> [Bashīr] said, "Your father helped me and I would like to repay the favor by telling you, by God, that I have never seen anything that takes away [one's commitment to] the *dīn*, diminishes [someone's] valor, deprives [one] of delight, and preoccupies the heart more than [legal] disputes."
>
> [Ibn Qutayba] continued, "Then I stood up and returned to the one who was disputing with me. The [cousin] asked, "What is the matter with you?"
>
> [Ibn Qutayba] said, "I will not dispute with you."
>
> [The cousin] said, "So, you have realized that I am right?"
>
> [Ibn Qutayba] answered, "No, but to keep my honor [I will abstain] from this."
>
> Then [the cousin] said, "[In that case], I seek nothing from you. It is all yours."[5]

❁ ❁ ❁

And if you were to say, "If a person has a right, [then] he must [engage in legal] disputation [to win] his claim or protect [his right] when a wrongdoer wrongs him. How else could there be a judgment and how could [legal] disputation be censured?"

So know that this condemnation refers to someone who disputes a false [claim] or someone who disputes without knowledge, such as a judge's representative. Before [the representative] knows the truth of either side, he represents one side of the dispute, and so he argues without knowledge.

---

4 Ibn Abī l-Dunyā, *al-Ṣamt wa-ādāb al-lisān*, 155. Trans.: Here the verb *khāṣama* refers to a dispute concerning a religious question argued before a judge or scholar.

5 Ibn Abī l-Dunyā, *al-Ṣamt wa-ādāb al-lisān*, 158.

[The dispute] deals with whoever is seeking his right but he does not limit himself to just what he needs, but instead | manifests 430
his vehement dispute for the sake of dominating and hurting [his opponent].

And [the dispute] deals with whoever mixes into the disputation hurtful words that are unnecessary to support his claim or show his right.

And [the dispute] deals with whoever carries out the disputation purely [based on] his stubbornness, in order to overcome his opponent and dissuade him, even though he considers the amount of money [in dispute] insignificant. There are even people who make this clear, saying, "My goal here is only to stubbornly [oppose] him and hinder [him from achieving] his goals. Even if I took this money from him, perhaps I would throw it into a well and not care at all." This [person's] objective is vehemence, disputation, and insistence, [which] are severely condemned.

As for [the one] wronged, who supports his claim legally [by way of the *shar*ʿ] and without vehemence or excess or additional insistence beyond what it warrants, and without the intention of being stubborn or hurtful—such actions are not unlawful, although it would be preferable to forgo [his claim] if he can find a way. Indeed, curbing the tongue in [legal] disputes within the bounds of what is reasonable is next to impossible. [Legal] disputes sour the heart and incite anger, and when anger is incited [the reason for] the contested [issue] is forgotten and there remains so much malice between the two disputants that each would be happy at his opponents' misfortune, and sad at his [opponents' good] fortune, and would be [quick] to unleash his tongue to attack the reputation [of others]. Someone who initiates a [legal] dispute exposes himself to all these hazards, the least of which is that it distracts his thoughts so that even in his prayers, he is preoccupied with quarreling with his disputants. Thus, the matter does not stay within the bounds of what is necessary.

So, [legal] disputation is the beginning of all evil, as are debates and arguments. [Disputation] is a door | that should not be opened 431
except out of necessity, and [even] out of necessity, we should guard

the tongue and the heart from the consequences of disputation, and that is next to impossible.

Whoever limits his [legal] dispute to what is necessary will be safe from sin, and his [legal] dispute is not censured, unless he is not in need of the disputation, because what he has suffices him. So it is preferrable to drop it [the legal dispute], and it is not a sin.

Indeed, the least of what is lost in [legal] disputes, arguments, and debates is pleasant speech and what was transmitted[6] about the reward it brings; the lowest degree of pleasant speech is reaching an agreement. There is no harsher speech than verbal attack and opposition accusing another person of ignorance or lying, for whoever debates, argues, or disputes with another, [makes him out] to be ignorant or a liar, and pleasant speech is lost.

The [Prophet] صَلَّى ٱللَّهُ عَلَيْهِ وَسَلَّمَ said, "pleasant speech and feeding the hungry will enable you to [enter] heaven."[7]

And God تَعَالَىٰ said, *And speak to people good* [*words*] [Q. 2:83].

Ibn ʿAbbās رَضِيَ ٱللَّهُ عَنْهُمَا said, "If any of God's creatures greets you with peace, even if he is a Magian, return [his greeting], for God تَعَالَىٰ says, *And when you are greeted with a greeting, greet* [*in return*] *with one better than it or* [*at least*] *return it* [*in a like manner*] [Q. 4:86].[8] |

432 Ibn ʿAbbās also said, "Even if Pharaoh spoke to me with goodness, I would respond with [the same]."[9]

And Anas said, "The Messenger of God صَلَّى ٱللَّهُ عَلَيْهِ وَسَلَّمَ said, "Verily, in heaven there are rooms, the outsides of which are visible from within and the insides of which [are visible] from without, which God تَعَالَىٰ has prepared for those who feed the hungry and are soothing in their speech."[10]

It was related that a pig passed in front of Jesus عَلَيْهِ ٱلسَّلَامُ and he said, "Pass by in peace!" He was asked, "O spirit of God, do you say that to a pig?" He answered, "I deplore habituating my tongue to evil."[11]

---

6 Trans.: That is, in the Qurʾān and *ḥadīth*.

7 Al-Ṭabarānī, *al-Muʿjam al-awsaṭ*, 1547; and Ibn Abī l-Dunyā, *al-Ṣamt wa-ādāb al-lisān*, 304.

8 Ibn Abī l-Dunyā, *al-Ṣamt wa-ādāb al-lisān*, 309.

9 Ibn Abī l-Dunyā, *al-Ṣamt wa-ādāb al-lisān*, 311.

10 Al-Tirmidhī, *Sunan*, 1984.

11 Ibn Abī l-Dunyā, *al-Ṣamt wa-ādāb al-lisān*, 308.

And our Prophet صَلَّى ٱللَّهُ عَلَيْهِ وَسَلَّمَ said, "A pleasant word is charity."[12]

And [the Prophet] صَلَّى ٱللَّهُ عَلَيْهِ وَسَلَّمَ said, "Protect yourself from the fire even by half a date, and if you do not find that, then with a pleasant word."[13]

ʿUmar رَضِيَ ٱللَّهُ عَنْهُ said, "Goodness is an easy thing: a cheerful face and soothing speech."[14] |

One of the sages said, "Soothing speech washes away the rancor 433
that dwells in the limbs."[15]

And one of the sages said, "All speech to please someone you are sitting with that does not [bring] the wrath of your Lord [is commendable], so do not be miserly with him for it might bring you the reward [equal to the reward] of the charitable."[16]

Such is the merit of pleasant speech. Its opposite is [legal] disputation, argumentation, obstinancy, and debate; and abhorrent, cruel [speech] that is injurious to the heart [makes] life loathesome, incites to anger, and embitters the heart. We ask God for good success by His benevolence and magnanimity.

12 Part of a *ḥadīth* found in the collection of Muslim, *Ṣaḥīḥ*, 1009.

13 Al-Bukhārī, *Ṣaḥīḥ*, 6023; and Muslim, *Ṣaḥīḥ*, 1016.

14 Al-Bayhaqī, *Shuʿab al-īmān*, 7702; and Ibn Abī l-Dunyā, *Mudārāt al-nās*, 109.

15 Ibn Abī l-Dunyā, *al-Ṣamt wa-ādāb al-lisān*, 312.

16 Ibn Abī l-Dunyā, *al-Ṣamt wa-ādāb al-lisān*, 313.

[6]

434 ## The Sixth Bane: Pretentiousness (*Taqʿurr*) in Speech

By [pretentiousness in speech we mean] pomposity (*tashadduq*), affectation (*takalluf*), rhymed prose (*sajʿ*), eloquence (*faṣāḥa*), artificiality (*taṣannuʿ*) in rhapsody (*tashbībāt*), [lengthy] prologues (*muqaddimāt*), and what passes as the customs of those who [claim to be] eloquent (*mutafāṣiḥīn*) orators.

All of this constitutes censured artificiality and detestable affectation [in mannerisms], about which the Messenger of God ﷺ said, "I and the pious ones of my community are free of affectation (*takalluf*) [in mannerisms]."[1]

[The Prophet] ﷺ said, "Those of you who are most loathed to me, the ones seated furthest from me on the day of resurrection, will be the prattlers, the long-winded [people], and those who are pompous in their speech."[2]

Fāṭima رضي الله عنها said, "The Messenger of God ﷺ said, 'The most evil of my community are those who are nurtured in opulence, eat all manner of food, dress in all manner of clothing, and are pompous in their speech.'"[3] |

435 And [the Prophet] ﷺ said, "Truly, the pedants (*mutanaṭṭiʿūn*) are ruined!" And he repeated this three times.[4] The [word] *tanaṭṭaʿ* is one who delves into details [like a pedant].

1 Abū Ṭālib al-Makkī, *Qūt al-qulūb*, 2:229; and al-Daylamī, *Musnad al-firdaws*, 228.
2 Al-Tirmidhī, *Sunan*, 2018.
3 Ibn Abī l-Dunyā, *al-Ṣamt wa-ādāb al-lisān*, 150; and Ibn ʿAdī, *al-Kāmil*, 5:318.
4 Muslim, *Ṣaḥīḥ*, 2670.

And ʿUmar رَضِيَ ٱللَّهُ عَنْهُ said, "haranguing speech is from the harangues of Satan."[5]

ʿUmar b. Saʿd b. Abī Waqqāṣ came to his father Saʿd to ask him for something and spoke for a long time before actually stating his need. So Saʿd said to him, "You have never been further from [fulfilling] your need than today, for I heard the Messenger of God صَلَّى ٱللَّهُ عَلَيْهِ وَسَلَّمَ say, 'There will come a time when people will ruminate on their words like a cow ruminates on her grass.'"[6]

Here he criticized [his son] for introducing his request by rhapsodizing (*tashbīb*) the prologue with affectation and artificiality.

This, too, is one of the banes of the tongue. [This bane] includes affectation, the use of rhymed prose, and similarly the [use of] eloquence beyond the normal limit, and similarly it may apply to affectation in rhymed prose in conversations. The Messenger of God صَلَّى ٱللَّهُ عَلَيْهِ وَسَلَّمَ was asked to judge in the case of the accidental death of a fetus, and someone from the family of the accused said to him, "How do we claim indemnity for one who did not drink, did not eat (*lā akala*), did not cry out, did not open his eyes (*lā ishala*) . . . " and yet [his blood] was spilled (*yaṭilla*).[7] The Messenger of God صَلَّى ٱللَّهُ عَلَيْهِ وَسَلَّمَ said, "[You are speaking] with the rhymed prose | 436
of the Bedouins [lit., al-ʿArāb]?!"[8] He criticized it because the effect of its affectation and artificiality was manifest from him [the speaker]. Indeed, all things should be kept to their aims, and the aim of speech is to explain an issue. What is beyond that is censured artificiality. Using beautiful expressions in an address or a [spiritual] lesson, without exaggeration or [using] unusual [words],[9] is not part of this. The purpose [of these beautiful expressions] is to move hearts, and

---

5 Ibn Abī l-Dunyā, *al-Ṣamt wa-ādāb al-lisān*, 152. FC: Lane (*An Arabic-English Lexicon*, 1579) has "Verily many of the orations or harangues are from the *shaqāshiq* of the Devil" because of the lying introduced into them.

6 Ibn Ḥanbal, *Musnad*, 1:175; Ibn Abī l-Dunyā, *al-Ṣamt wa-ādāb al-lisān*, 149, and in a shortened version in Abū Dāwūd, *Sunan*, 5005; and al-Tirmidhī, *Sunan*, 2853. "Ruminate" here implies taking a long time to say something.

7 Eds.: The verbs used to describe the fetus have a rhyme. Al-Zabīdī, *Itḥāf* (7:477) adds the word blood. An alternative version (in the margin) has "and thus, it [the claim for indemnity] is invalid."

8 Muslim, *Ṣaḥīḥ*, 1682.

9 Trans.: That is, without using rare or strange words for effect.

inspire them through contraction and expansion, with longing [for God]. Skillfulness in expression affects this and so it is appropriate. As for conversations about fulfilling needs, it is inappropriate to use rhymed prose and pompous [speech]. So occupying [oneself] with affected [mannerisms] is censured, and [using it] for no other motive than ostentation, the display [of one's] eloquence, and the distinguishing [of one's] brilliance—all of that is censured and the law [considers it] reprehensible and vehemently [prohibits] it.

[7]

The Seventh Bane: Obscenity (*Fuḥush*), Insult (*Sabb*), and a Vulgar Tongue (*Bidhāʾa al-lisān*) 437

[OBSCENITY, insult, and vulgarity are] censured and forbidden. The source of it is malice and iniquity. The Messenger of God صَلَّى ٱللَّٰهُ عَلَيْهِ وَسَلَّمَ said, "Beware of obscenity. God تَعَالَىٰ does not love obscenity nor the showing of obscenity."[1]

The Messenger of God صَلَّى ٱللَّٰهُ عَلَيْهِ وَسَلَّمَ also forbade people from insulting the polytheists who were slain in [the battle of] Badr, saying, "Do not insult them. Nothing you say is going to reach them now but you will hurt the living [who are related to them]. Vulgar [speech] is surely an iniquity."[2]

[The Prophet] صَلَّى ٱللَّٰهُ عَلَيْهِ وَسَلَّمَ said, "A believer [does] not taunt, nor curse, [is not] obscene, nor vulgar."[3]

And [the Prophet] صَلَّى ٱللَّٰهُ عَلَيْهِ وَسَلَّمَ said, "Entering heaven is unlawful to anyone who is obscene."[4] |

And [the Prophet] صَلَّى ٱللَّٰهُ عَلَيْهِ وَسَلَّمَ said, 438

> Four [acts] will cause more suffering to the people of the fire than what they will [already] have [to endure] as they hasten between boiling water and the inferno crying out from woe

1 Ibn Abī l-Dunyā, *al-Ṣamt wa-ādāb al-lisān*, 319. This forms part of a *ḥadīth* found in Ibn Ḥanbal, *Musnad*, 2:159.

2 Ibn Abī l-Dunyā, *al-Ṣamt wa-ādāb al-lisān*, 323; and al-Kharāʾiṭī, *Masāwiʾ al-akhlāq*, 68.

3 Al-Tirmidhī, *Sunan*, 1977.

4 Ibn Abī l-Dunyā, *al-Ṣamt wa-ādāb al-lisān*, 325; and Abū Nuʿaym, *Ḥilya*, 1:288.

> and doom.[5] [Among them] will be a man from whose mouth will flow pus and blood. It will be asked of him, "What is the matter with [him] that he hurt us even more than the hurt [we already suffered]?" The reply [will be] "[That person] used to see all defamatory, malicious speech [as something] to take pleasure in, like the pleasure of [sexual] foreplay.[6]

[The Prophet] صَلَّى ٱللَّهُ عَلَيْهِ وَسَلَّمَ said to ʿĀʾisha رَضِيَ ٱللَّهُ عَنْهَا, "O ʿĀʾisha, if obscenity were a man, it would be a wicked (*sūʾ*) man."[7]

The Messenger صَلَّى ٱللَّهُ عَلَيْهِ وَسَلَّمَ said, "Vulgarity and elucidation are two prongs of hypocrisy."[8]

[The meaning of the word] elucidation may include disclosing something that [one] is not allowed to disclose, or it may also [mean] going to such lengths to clarify it that [the explanation itself] becomes affectation. [The elucidation] may also refer to [speaking about] matters of *dīn*, such as the attributes of God تَعَالَىٰ. Presenting these in a general way for laymen to hear is preferable to an exaggerated elucidation. The utmost [of detailed] elucidations may incite in them doubts and whisperings. Whereas [when they are left in] general [terms, their] hearts can more readily accept them and they
439 are not | distressed. But [the fact] that [elucidation] is mentioned in conjunction with vulgarity suggests that its intended meaning is making known what a person would be ashamed to have exposed. It is preferable that such matters be obscured and disregarded, rather than disclosing [them] and exposing them [in detail].

The Messenger of God صَلَّى ٱللَّهُ عَلَيْهِ وَسَلَّمَ said, "God does not love one who is obscene [in speech], who shows [lit., makes] obscenity, or shouts in the marketplace."[9]

And Jābir b. Samura said, "I was seated with the Messenger of God صَلَّى ٱللَّهُ عَلَيْهِ وَسَلَّمَ and my father was in front of me when [the Prophet] صَلَّى ٱللَّهُ عَلَيْهِ وَسَلَّمَ said, "Obscenity and making a show of obscenity

---

5 Eds.: For woe (*wayl*) and doom (*thubūr*), Wehr (*A Dictionary of Modern Written Arabic*, 102, under th-b-r) has "bursting into loud laments." See also Lane (*An Arabic-English Lexicon*), 3062 for *wayl* and 330 for *thubūr*.

6 Ibn Abī l-Dunyā, *al-Ṣamt wa-ādāb al-lisān*, 326.

7 Al-Ṭayālisī, *Musnad*, 1495; and Ibn Abī l-Dunyā, *al-Ṣamt wa-ādāb al-lisān*, 331.

8 Al-Tirmidhī, *Sunan*, 2027.

9 Al-Bukhārī, *al-Adab al-mufrad*, 310; and Ibn Abī l-Dunyā, *al-Ṣamt wa-ādāb al-lisān*, 340.

have no place in Islam. The best of people in Islam are those with the best character."[10]

Ibrāhīm b. Maysara said, "It is said that one who is obscene and makes a show of obscenity [will appear on] the day of resurrection in the form of a dog or in the hollow [carcass] of a dog."[11]

Al-Aḥnaf b. Qays said, "Shall I not inform you of the worst illness? A vulgar tongue and an ignoble character."[12]

Such are the censured [aspects] of obscenity (*fuḥush*). |

As for [obscenity's] definition and reality, it refers to expressing 440
repugnant matters in explicit (*ṣarīḥ*) [lit., plain] terms.[13]

Most of this concerns words expressing sexuality and what is related to it. Depraved people use expressions that are explicit and obscene [to refer to sexual matters, whereas], righteous people avoid exposure to [such language]. Instead, they conceal it and allude [to it] and indicate [such meanings] symbolically and by mentioning what is close to or related to it.

Ibn ʿAbbās رَضِيَ ٱللَّهُ عَنْهُمَا said, "Verily God is modest and noble. [When He speaks] of intercourse, He is decent and uses the euphemism, 'touch.'"[14]

[Words like] "touching," "touch," "entering," and "cohabiting" are euphemisms for [sexual] intercourse and are not considered obscene. But there are obscene expressions that are repugnant to mention, used mostly in vilification and upbraiding. These expressions vary [in their degree of] obscenity, some being more obscene than others, and some being used in certain lands and not others. The least [obscene] of these are reprehensible (*makrūh*), the most [obscene] are restricted (*maḥdhūr*), and between these two [extremes] are degrees [of expressions] that one should hesitate to use.

Not all of these concern [sexual] intercourse, rather, euphemisms like relieving [oneself] is preferable to urination, and the call of nature is a term [for] "evacuating the bowels" and preferable to

---

10 Ibn Ḥanbal, *Musnad*, 5:89; and Ibn Abī l-Dunyā, *al-Ṣamt wa-ādāb al-lisān*, 342.

11 Ibn Abī l-Dunyā, *al-Ṣamt wa-ādāb al-lisān*, 329.

12 Ibn Abī l-Dunyā, *al-Ṣamt wa-ādāb al-lisān*, 341.

13 "That is, in respect to the law, or the mind, or our nature, this is something that the mind and our nature finds objectionable, and that the law characterizes as malicious (*khubuth*)." Al-Zabīdī, *Itḥāf*, 7:481.

14 ʿAbd al-Razzāq, *al-Muṣannaf*, 1:134.

441 defecation, and other such terms that | are private and considered embarrassing. Explicit [lit., plain] terms for these are considered obscene and should not be used in speech.

It is also preferable to refer to women euphemistically. Rather than saying, "My wife said this . . ." you would say, "It is said in the home . . ." or "behind the veil . . ." or "the mother of the children . . ." Using delicate [words] in such expressions is praiseworthy while being explicit [can] lead to obscenity.

Likewise, among the [physical] defects that one is embarrassed about, one must not express them explicitly; [these include] leprosy,[15] baldness [alopecia], and hemorrhoids. Rather, one should say the issue at hand, and such similar phrases. So speaking of these matters explicitly borders on obscenity, and thus are included among the banes of the tongue.

Al-ʿAlāʾ b. Hārūn said, "ʿUmar b. ʿAbd al-ʿAzīz was very cautious in his speech. Once he had a growth in his armpit. We said, 'Let us ask him about it to see what he will say.' So we asked him, 'Where did it appear?' and he answered, 'Deep [beyond] the palm of my hand.'"[16]

Obscenity is motivated by a wish to hurt [someone] or it is a habit that arises from frequenting corrupt, malicious, and iniquitous people whose habit is to insult [others].

> A Bedouin said to the Messenger of God, "Advise me."
>
> [The Prophet] answered, "Fear God and if someone upbraids you for something he knows about you, do not upbraid him for something you know about him, for he will bear the con-
> 442 sequences for that | and the recompense [he would have had for desisting] will go to you. Do not swear (*sabb*) at anything."
>
> [The Bedouin] said, "After that, I never swore at anything."[17]

---

15 FC: This may refer to vitiligo.

16 Ibn Abī l-Dunyā, *al-Ṣamt wa-ādāb al-lisān*, 590. Eds.: Here ʿUmar was indicating "deep, beyond" the palm of his hand, to mean that if one were to go up his arm, they would reach the armpit.

17 Ibn Ḥanbal, *Musnad*, 5:63; and al-Bukhārī, *al-Adab al-mufrad*, 1182.

And ʿIyād b. Ḥimār said,

> I said, "O Messenger of God, a man from my tribe insulted me and he is of a lower [status]. Is it wrong for me [to insult] him in return?"
>
> [The Prophet Muḥammad] answered, "Two people insulting one another are two devils giving the lie to, and flinging [accusations], at one another."[18]

And [the Prophet] صَلَّى ٱللَّهُ عَلَيْهِ وَسَلَّمَ said, "If two men insult one another, the initiator [bears the blame] for all that was said, unless the one wronged exceeds [the severity of the original insult]."[19]

And [the Prophet] صَلَّى ٱللَّهُ عَلَيْهِ وَسَلَّمَ said, "Insulting a believer is corruption and fighting[20] [him] is disbelief."[21]

> [The Prophet] صَلَّى ٱللَّهُ عَلَيْهِ وَسَلَّمَ said, "Cursed is the one who insults his parents."[22]
>
> In another version [the Prophet صَلَّى ٱللَّهُ عَلَيْهِ وَسَلَّمَ said], "One of the greatest [sins] is for a man to insult his own parents."
>
> They asked, "O Messenger of God, how could a man insult his own parents?"
>
> He said, "By insulting another man's parents who then insults his [in return]."[23]

---

18 Al-Ṭayālisī, *Musnad*, 1080; Ibn Ḥanbal, *Musnad*, 4:162, and with similar wording in al-Bukhārī, *al-Adab al-mufrad*, 428.

19 Muslim, *Ṣaḥīḥ*, 2587.

20 Eds.: That is, fighting with the intent to kill.

21 Al-Bukhārī, *Ṣaḥīḥ*, 48; and Muslim, *Ṣaḥīḥ*, 64.

22 Ibn Ḥanbal, *Musnad*, 1:217.

23 Al-Bukhārī, *Ṣaḥīḥ*, 5973; and Muslim, *Ṣaḥīḥ*, 90.

[8]

443 The Eighth Bane: Cursing (*Laʿn*)

[Cursing] animals, inanimate [things], or human beings is all censured.

The Messenger of God صَلَّىٱللَّهُعَلَيْهِوَسَلَّمَ said, "The believer is not someone who curses [others]."[1]

And [the Prophet] صَلَّىٱللَّهُعَلَيْهِوَسَلَّمَ said, "Do not invoke God's curse on one another, nor His anger, nor hell."[2]

Ḥudhayfa said, "No group curses another without the curse coming true."[3]

ʿImrān b. al-Ḥaṣīn said,

> While the Messenger of God صَلَّىٱللَّهُعَلَيْهِوَسَلَّمَ was on one of his journeys, a woman from the Anṣār who was riding her she-camel became so angry with it that she cursed it. When [the Messenger of God] صَلَّىٱللَّهُعَلَيْهِوَسَلَّمَ [heard this], he said, "Take everything off that camel and set it free, for it has been cursed." And it is as if I [ʿImrān] can still see that camel walking among people, ignored by everyone.[4] |

444 Abū l-Dardāʾ said, "No one utters a curse against the earth without it saying, 'May God curse those who are most disobedient to God.'"[5]

---

1 Al-Tirmidhī, *Sunan*, 2019; Ibn Abī l-Dunyā, *al-Ṣamt wa-ādāb al-lisān*, 386.

2 Abū Dāwūd, *Sunan*, 4906; and al-Tirmidhī, *Sunan*, 1976.

3 ʿAbd al-Razzāq, *al-Muṣannaf*, 10:413; and Ibn Abī Shayba, *al-Muṣannaf*, 38496.

4 Muslim, *Ṣaḥīḥ*, 2595.

5 Ibn Abī l-Dunyā, *al-Ṣamt wa-ādāb al-lisān*, 585.

And ʿĀʾisha رَضِيَٱللَّهُعَنْهَا said,

> The Messenger of God صَلَّىٱللَّهُعَلَيْهِوَسَلَّمَ heard Abū Bakr رَضِيَٱللَّهُعَنْهُ curse one of his slaves. [The Prophet صَلَّىٱللَّهُعَلَيْهِوَسَلَّمَ] turned to him and said, "O Abū Bakr! Can the veracious (*ṣiddīq*)[6] be cursers? By the Lord of the Kaʿba, no!" and he repeated this two or three times. That same day Abū Bakr freed a number of his slaves and then went to the Prophet صَلَّىٱللَّهُعَلَيْهِوَسَلَّمَ and said, "I [will] not [do that] again."[7]

The Messenger of God صَلَّىٱللَّهُعَلَيْهِوَسَلَّمَ said, "Those who curse [others] will not be intercessors nor witnesses on the day of resurrection."[8]

Anas said, "There was a man traveling with the Messenger of God صَلَّىٱللَّهُعَلَيْهِوَسَلَّمَ riding a camel and he uttered a curse against it. The Prophet صَلَّىٱللَّهُعَلَيْهِوَسَلَّمَ said to him, 'O servant of God! Do not travel with us on a cursed camel,'" and he said that disapprovingly.[9]

A curse is an expression of banishment and exile from God تَعَالَىٰ. It is not [legally] allowable except toward someone who already has the traits that distance him from God عَزَّوَجَلَّ, namely, disbelief and wrongdoing, for it is said, "God's curse is on the wrongdoers and disbelievers." |

[In this sense] the exact words of the law should be followed[10] 445
because there is a danger in cursing [someone] inasmuch as it is a judgment that God عَزَّوَجَلَّ has distanced the accursed [from His presence]. And that is [part of] the hidden [realm] that none but God shows. The Messenger of God صَلَّىٱللَّهُعَلَيْهِوَسَلَّمَ was shown [these matters] only when God showed him.

The traits that warrant [God's] curse are three—disbelief (*kufr*), deviancy (*bidʿa*), and corruption (*fisq*)—and the curse for each them may be of three degrees.

The first is cursing in its most general form, as when someone says, "The curse of God is on the disbelievers, the deviants, and the corrupt."

---

6 Trans.: The honorary title of Abū Bakr رَضِيَٱللَّهُعَنْهُ was "al-Ṣiddīq" (the veracious one).

7 Ibn Abī l-Dunyā, *al-Ṣamt wa-ādāb al-lisān*, 693; and al-Bayhaqī, *Shuʿab al-īmān*, 4791.

8 Muslim, *Ṣaḥīḥ*, 2598.

9 Ibn Abī l-Dunyā, *al-Ṣamt wa-ādāb al-lisān*, 390; and Abū Yaʿlā, *Musnad*, 3622.

10 Trans.: That is, if someone were to utter a curse against another, it would have to be with words found in the Qurʾān and *ḥadīth*.

The second is cursing in a specific form, such as when someone says, "The curse of God is on the Jews, the Christians, the Magians, the Qadiriyya,[11] the Khawārij,[12] the Rāwāfiḍa,[13] on adulterers,[14] oppressors, and those who live from usury."

All of that is allowable [to say], but in cursing types of deviants there is danger, since the [true] knowledge of deviancy is something obscure and no words about it were conveyed,[15] so laymen should be barred from doing it. Indeed, it only attracts [a curse] like it in return and incites people to opposition and depravity.

The third is cursing against a particular person, as when someone says, "Zayd, may God curse him, is a disbeliever, or a corrupt [person], or a deviant." Concerning this there are different views. |

446 And to be specific, any person whose cursing was legally established, cursing him is allowed.

So [it is permissible] to say, "Pharaoh, may God curse him," or "Abū Jahl, may God curse him," because it was established that those [people] died in disbelief and that is known from the law.

[Cursing] a particular person in our time, as when someone says, for example, "Zayd, may God curse him," because he is a Jew, in that, there is danger, for perhaps he might become a Muslim and die in a state of proximity to God. So how can he be judged as cursed?

❁ ❁ ❁

---

11 Eds.: An early theological school that believed that everything was predestined.

12 Eds.: The Khawārij were an early religious sect who identified themselves by their questions on the theory of the caliphate, and by justification by faith or works. In terms of political history, they were involved in the early insurrections; see G. Levi Della Vida, *EI^2*, under "al-Kh̲āridj̲ites," 4:1074–1077.

13 Eds.: The Rāfiḍa (pl. Rāwāfiḍa) were an early Twelver Shīʿa group; see E. Kohlberg, *EI^2*, "al-Rāfiḍa," 8:386–389.

14 Eds.: The word in Arabic for adulterer (*zān*) does not specify the marital status of the person; by contrast, in English, an adulterer is a married person engaged in such actions with someone who is married or single, while a fornicator is an unmarried person doing the same.

15 Trans.: That is, in the Qurʾān or *ḥadīth*.

And if you were to say,

> He is cursed because of his present state of disbelief [it is perilous because he could become a Muslim]. Similarly, it is said of a Muslim, "may God be merciful to him," because of his present state of [being] Muslim [it is perilous because] it is conceivable that he [could become an] apostate.

Know that when we say, "may God be merciful to him," it means, "may God establish him in Islam," which is the means by which mercy reaches him, and [through his] obedience. But it is not possible to say, "may God establish the disbeliever [in disbelief]," which is the reason for being cursed, for that amounts to asking [God for] disbelief, which itself is disbelief. Yes, it is allowable to say, "may God curse him if he dies in disbelief," and "may God not curse him if he dies in Islam," but these pertain to the unseen and are unknowable and making an unconditional statement in either direction is dangerous. There is no danger, [however], in refraining from cursing altogether.

And if you recognize this about a disbeliever, then it is even more important [to recognize] it [when you say] "Zayd is corrupt" or "Zayd is a deviant."

Invoking a curse on individuals is dangerous because people's states change [and so are unknowable] except [for] the Messenger of God صَلَّى ٱللَّٰهُ عَلَيْهِ وَسَلَّمَ. He was allowed to know who would die in disbelief, | and so he cursed specific individuals, as when he said 447
in his supplications against the Quraysh, "O God, on Abū Jahl b. Hishām and ʿUtbah b. Rabīʿa may there be [Your curse]." And he mentioned a number of those who were slain in [the battle of] Badr while in [a state of] disbelief[16] and he cursed some of those whose final ends he did not know, until he was forbidden [by God] from [doing so]. Thus, it was related that [the Prophet صَلَّى ٱللَّٰهُ عَلَيْهِ وَسَلَّمَ invoked God's] curse on those who killed [Muslims] at Biʾr, [the well of] Maʿūna, in his *qunūt* publicly (*shahran*)[17] until [God] تَعَالَىٰ revealed: *Not for you,* [*O Muḥammad, but for God*]*, is the decision whether He should forgive them or punish them, for indeed, they are wrongdoers*

16 Al-Bukhārī, *Ṣaḥīḥ*, 240; and Muslim, *Ṣaḥīḥ*, 1794.

17 Eds.: Alternatively, it could be understood that the Prophet [صَلَّى ٱللَّٰهُ عَلَيْهِ وَسَلَّمَ] invoked the curse while standing in devotion each night (*qunūt*) for a month (*shahran*).

[Q. 3:128].[18] That is, perhaps they will repent, so how can you know that they are cursed?

Similarly, if it is clear to us that someone died in disbelief, it is allowable to curse him or it is allowable to censure him only if it brings no injury to a Muslim, but if it does, it is not allowable. Thus, it was related that when the Messenger of God صَلَّى ٱللَّهُ عَلَيْهِ وَسَلَّمَ asked Abū Bakr رَضِيَ ٱللَّهُ عَنْهُ about a grave they passed on the way to Taif, he answered,

> That is the grave of a man who was insolent toward God and His Messenger, [his name is] Saʿīd b. al-ʿĀṣ," and ʿAmr b. Saʿīd, his son, became angry and said, "O Messenger of God! That is the grave of a man who used to feed people and show more courage in battle than Abū Quḥāfa!"[19]
>
> Then Abū Bakr said, "O Messenger of God! He speaks to me like this?"
>
> To which [the Prophet] صَلَّى ٱللَّهُ عَلَيْهِ وَسَلَّمَ replied, "Desist from speaking against Abū Bakr!" Then he took Abū Bakr aside, turned toward him, and said, "O Abū Bakr, if you speak of the disbelievers, speak of them only in general, for if you specify them, their sons will be angered for the sake of their fathers."
>
> Thereafter, people desisted from doing that.[20] |

448 Nuʿaymān drank wine and was punished a number of times in the presence of the Messenger of God صَلَّى ٱللَّهُ عَلَيْهِ وَسَلَّمَ, and one of the Companions said, "May God curse him! How many times has he been brought [to you] for this?" The [Messenger of God] صَلَّى ٱللَّهُ عَلَيْهِ وَسَلَّمَ said, "Do not help Satan against your brother," and in another version, "Do not say that, for verily he [Nuʿaymān] loves God and His Messenger."[21] [The Prophet] forbade [the companion] from [cursing Nuʿaymān]. This shows that it is not allowed to curse a particular corrupt person.

18 Al-Bukhārī, *Ṣaḥīḥ*, 4070; and Muslim, *Ṣaḥīḥ*, 675.

19 Trans.: The father of Abū Bakr رَضِيَ ٱللَّهُ عَنْهُ.

20 With similar wording in Hannād, *al-Zuhd*, 1168; and Abū Dāwūd, *al-Murāsīl*, 502.

21 Al-Bukhārī, *Ṣaḥīḥ*, 2316.

In general, cursing individuals is dangerous, so it should be avoided, while there is no danger in being quiet even about cursing Iblīs, not to mention others!

❁ ❁ ❁

And if someone asked, "Is it allowable to curse Yazīd, since he is the one who killed Ḥusayn b. ʿAlī رَضِيَ ٱللَّهُ عَنْهُمَا or ordered him [to be slain]?" We would say, this has not been established conclusively, so it is not even allowable to say he killed him or ordered him to be killed if it has not been established, let alone curse him for it. It is not allowable to accuse any Muslim of a major [sin] without verification.

Yes, it is allowable to say that Ibn Muljam killed ʿAlī رَضِيَ ٱللَّهُ عَنْهُ and
that | Abū Luʾluʾa killed ʿUmar رَضِيَ ٱللَّهُ عَنْهُ since both these [events] were 449
established by many sources (*mutawātur*).

So it is not allowable to accuse a Muslim of corruption or disbelief without being able to verify it. [The Messenger of God] صَلَّى ٱللَّهُ عَلَيْهِ وَسَلَّمَ said, "No man accuses another man of disbelief or accuses him of corruption except that the accusation turns back on the accuser if the other [man] is not [guilty]."[22]

And [the Prophet] صَلَّى ٱللَّهُ عَلَيْهِ وَسَلَّمَ said,

> No man testifies that another is a disbeliever except that it will turn back on one of them. If [the one he accuses] is a disbeliever, then he is as the other said, and if he was not a disbeliever, then the one who accused him of disbelief becomes a disbeliever [by his accusation].[23]

This means that he [accuses him] of disbelief while knowing he was a Muslim. If [the accuser] thought he had become a disbeliever because of some deviancy or other such [reason], then it is an offense [on his part, but] not disbelief.

Muʿādh said, "The Messenger of God صَلَّى ٱللَّهُ عَلَيْهِ وَسَلَّمَ said to me, 'I have forbidden you from vilifying a Muslim or disobeying a just leader.'"[24]

---

22 Al-Bukhārī, *Ṣaḥīḥ*, 6045; and Muslim, *Ṣaḥīḥ*, 61, with wording close to this. The wording of the author is found in al-Kharāʾiṭī, *Masāwiʾ al-akhlāq*, 13.

23 Al-Kharāʾiṭī, *Masāwiʾ al-akhlāq*, 18; and al-Daylamī, *Musnad al-firdaws*, 6337.

24 Al-Kharāʾiṭī, *Masāwiʾ al-akhlāq*, 30; Abū Nuʿaym, *Ḥilya*, 1:240, and part of the longer *ḥadīth*.

Subjecting the dead [to cursing] is an even more severe [offense].

> Masrūq said, I came to ʿĀʾisha رَضِيَ ٱللَّهُ عَنْهَا and she asked me, "What did so-and-so do, may God curse him?"
>
> I said, "He died."
>
> She said, "May God be merciful to him."
>
> I said, "How can you say that?"
>
> She said, "The Messenger of God صَلَّى ٱللَّهُ عَلَيْهِ وَسَلَّمَ said, 'Do
> 450 not | insult the dead, for they have reached what they sent forward.'"[25]

And [the Prophet صَلَّى ٱللَّهُ عَلَيْهِ وَسَلَّمَ] also said, "Do not insult the dead lest you hurt the living."[26]

And [the Prophet] صَلَّى ٱللَّهُ عَلَيْهِ وَسَلَّمَ said, "O you people! Protect me in respect to my Companions, my brothers, and my in-laws, and do not insult them. O you people! If someone dies, mention him with goodness."[27]

❁ ❁ ❁

If it were asked, "Is it allowed to say, 'may God curse the one who slew Ḥusayn,' or 'may God curse the one who ordered him to be slain?'" we would say that it would be correct to say of the killer of Ḥusayn, "If he died before seeking repentance, then God curse him" because it may be that he died after repenting. This is because Waḥshī, the killer of Ḥamza, uncle of the Messenger of God صَلَّى ٱللَّهُ عَلَيْهِ وَسَلَّمَ, killed [Ḥamza] when he was a disbeliever, but then he repented of his disbelief and [repented from] all killing, so it is not allowed for him be cursed. Indeed, to slay someone is a major [sin] but it does not reach the level of disbelief. If [the major sin] is not tied to repentence then unleashing [the tongue in cursing someone] is

25 Al-Kharāʾiṭī, *Masāwiʾ al-akhlāq*, 93; and without the introductory sentences in al-Bukhārī, *Ṣaḥīḥ*, 6516.

26 Al-Tirmidhī, *Sunan*, 1982.

27 Al-Kharāʾiṭī, *Masāwiʾ al-akhlāq*, 100; and al-Ṭabarānī, *al-Muʿjam al-kabīr*, 6:104.

dangerous, but in saying nothing about [cursing], there is no danger, and so it is preferable. |

❁ ❁ ❁

We speak of this because of the carelessness of people in respect 451
to cursing and unleashing their tongues for this. And a believer is not someone who curses [others] and the tongue should not be unleashed with curses except toward someone who died in disbelief or toward general types of people known by their traits, not toward specific people. For [the tongue] to be occupied with the remembrance of God is preferable, and in the absence of that, in saying nothing there is safety.

> Makkī b. Ibrāhīm said, "We were with Ibn ʿAwn and they mentioned Bilāl b. Abī Burda and began to curse and disparage him, while Ibn ʿAwn was quiet.
>
> [Finally] they said, 'O Ibn ʿAwn, we are mentioning what he committed against you.'
>
> Ibn ʿAwn said, 'On the day of resurrection, two phrases may stand out on my page—*Lā ilāha illā Allāh* and may God curse so-and-so—and I would love for the one that stands out to be *Lā ilāha illā Allāh* and not, may God curse so-and-so.'"[28]

A man said to the Messenger of God صَلَّى ٱللَّٰهُ عَلَيْهِ وَسَلَّمَ, "Advise me." He said I advise you, "Do not be someone who curses [others]."[29]

And Ibn ʿUmar said, "The most loathesome servants of God are those who [verbally] attack and curse [others]."

One of them said, "Cursing a believer is equivalent to killing
him," and Ḥammād b. Zayd said after | he related this *ḥadīth*, "If it 452
were said to be *marfuʿ*,[30] I would have no objection."[31]

---

28 Ibn Abī l-Dunyā, *al-Ṣamt wa-ādāb al-lisān*, 746.

29 Ibn Ḥanbal, *Musnad*, 5:70; and Ibn Abī l-Dunyā, *al-Ṣamt wa-ādāb al-lisān*, 670.

30 Trans.: A *ḥadīth marfuʿ* is one that is attributed to the Prophet, and may be narrated by one of the Followers (Tābiʿīn), who does not mention the Companion (Ṣaḥāba) who related it.

31 Ibn Abī l-Dunyā, *al-Ṣamt wa-ādāb al-lisān*, 672; and with the wording "Cursing a believer is like slaying him," this is reported as a *ḥadīth* in al-Bukhārī, *Ṣaḥīḥ*; and Muslim, *Ṣaḥīḥ*.

Abū Qatāda said, "It used to be said, 'Cursing a believer is like killing him.'"

This was conveyed as a *ḥadīth marfuʿ*, as [it was said by] the Messenger of God صَلَّى ٱللَّٰهُ عَلَيْهِ وَسَلَّمَ.

Similar to cursing is supplicating [God] to bring a person evil, even if the supplication is on an oppressor. Like the saying of a person, "may God not give health to his body," "may God not keep him safe," or anything of that sort, all of which is censured.

A report [says], "A person who has been wronged may supplicate against his oppressor until it suffices him, but what is superfluous will remain to the credit of his oppressor on the day of resurrection."[32]

32 This meaning is expressed in a *ḥadīth* narrated by ʿĀʾisha [رَضِيَ ٱللَّٰهُ عَنْهَا] in al-Tirmidhī, *Sunan*, 3552.

[9]

The Ninth Bane: Singing (*Ghinā*ʾ) and Poetry (*Shi*ʿ*r*) 453

We have mentioned in *The Book on Audition*[1] what is unlawful in singing and what is lawful, so we will not repeat it.

As for poetry, it is like speech: if [it contains] good [words], it is good and if it [contains] repugnant [words] it is repugnant,[2] but to become wholly taken up with [poetry] is censured.

The Messenger of God ﷺ said, "It is better that your insides fill up with pus until it oozes than for them to fill up with poetry."[3]

And it is said that Masrūq was asked about a verse of poetry and he deplored it. When he was asked about it, he said, "I deplore that poetry be found on my page."[4]

One of them was asked about some poetry and he said, "Put in its place invocation (*dhikr*), for the invocation of God is better than poetry."[5] |

1 Trans.: Book 18 of the *Revival of the Religious Sciences*: *The Proprieties of Audition and Ecstasy* (*Kitāb al-samā*ʿ *wa-l-wajd*).

2 Al-Bukhārī, *al-Adab al-mufrad*, 865, where the wording is, "Poetry is like speech: the good part of it is like good speech and the ugly part of it is like ugly speech."

3 Al-Bukhārī, *Ṣaḥīḥ*, 6155; and Muslim, *Ṣaḥīḥ*, 2257.

4 Ibn Abī l-Dunyā, *al-Ṣamt wa-ādāb al-lisān*, 636. Eds.: That is, the page from one's record of deeds.

5 Ibn Abī l-Dunyā, *al-Ṣamt wa-ādāb al-lisān*, 637. The one who was asked was Ṭalḥa b. Muṣarrif.

454 In general, reciting and composing poetry is not unlawful if it does not contain deplorable language.[6] Indeed, [the Messenger of God] ﷺ said, "In some poetry there is wisdom."[7]

True, the purpose of poetry is to extol, or to censure, or to rhapsodize (*tashbībāt*) about [e.g., someone's beauty], and this may include lies, but the Messenger of God ﷺ ordered Ḥassān b. Thābit al-Anṣārī to satirize the disbelievers.[8]

And talking at length in extolling [someone], even if it is false, is not like the lying that is unlawful. Like the poet said:[9]

> If there were nothing in his hand except his soul
> He would give it, so [let the one who] asks him fear God.

This is a descriptive expression of the epitome of generosity. If
455 the one [it refers to] is not [actually] generous, | it is a lie, and if he is, it is hyperbole (*mubālagha*) crafted by the skill of the poet and not intended to be taken literally. There were lines of poetry chanted in the presence of the Messenger of God ﷺ which, if examined, would be found to contain this kind [of language], and he did not bar [him from] it.[10]

> ʿĀʾisha رَضِيَ ٱللَّهُ عَنْهَا said, "The Messenger of God ﷺ was mending his sandal and I was sitting next to him spinning [wool]. I looked at the Messenger of God ﷺ and saw that his brow was wet with sweat and that the sweat produced a glowing light." She said, I was astonished.
>
> The Messenger of God ﷺ looked at me and said, "What astonished you?"

---

6 In al-Tirmidhī, *Sunan*, 2850, there is a *ḥadīth* related by the Jābir b. Samura رَضِيَ ٱللَّهُ عَنْهُ, "I sat with the Prophet [ﷺ] more than one hundred times, and the Companions used to chant poetry and mention to one another matters from the time of the Jāhiliyya and he remained silent, and perhaps he smiled."

7 Al-Bukhārī, *Ṣaḥīḥ*, 6145.

8 Al-Bukhārī, *Ṣaḥīḥ*, 3213; and Muslim, *Ṣaḥīḥ*, 2486, including the words, "Gabriel is with you."

9 Trans.: There is disagreement about the origin of this verse. The editors of the Minhāj edition list ten possible sources.

10 "For example, Kaʿb b. Zuhayr recited in his presence an ode rhyming in the letter *lām* which contained obvious examples of satire and hyperbole, but he did not object to it." Al-Zabīdī, *Itḥāf*, 7:494.

I said, "O Messenger of God, I looked at you and your brow began to sweat and it produced a light! If Abū Kabīr al-Hudhalī saw you, he would know that you are the most deserving of his poetry."

He said, "And what does Abū Kabīr al-Hudhalī say, O ʿĀʾisha?"

I said, "He recites these two couplets:

> He was born free from all that is impure
> a depleted nursemaid and a deadly sickness[11]
>
> And if you look on the forms of his face
> You see flashes of lightning as from rain-laden clouds |

She said, "Then the Messenger of God صَلَّى ٱللَّهُ عَلَيْهِ وَسَلَّمَ put down 456
what he was holding, stood up before me, kissed me between my eyes, and said, 'May God reward you with goodness, O ʿĀʾisha. You do not find joy from me like the joy I find from you.'"[12]

When the [Messenger of God] صَلَّى ٱللَّهُ عَلَيْهِ وَسَلَّمَ divided the spoils from the day [battle] of Ḥunayn, he ordered that four young camels be given to ʿAbbās b. Mirdās, who began to complain in lines of poetry that ended:

> Badr combined with Ḥābis could not
> prevail over Mirdās,
>
> And I was never lower than any person among them,
> But he who is humbled today shall not be raised up again.

[The Messenger of God] صَلَّى ٱللَّهُ عَلَيْهِ وَسَلَّمَ said, "Stop his tongue against me." So Abū Bakr al-Ṣiddīq رَضِيَ ٱللَّهُ عَنْهُ took [ʿAbbās b. Mirdās] to where he could choose one hundred camels and by the time he returned, he was one of the most satisfied of people. The Messenger of God صَلَّى ٱللَّهُ عَلَيْهِ وَسَلَّمَ asked him, "Do you speak about me in poetry?" And he began to make excuses for himself, saying "By my father,

---

11 According to the beliefs of those during the Jāhiliyya, if someone was conceived while menstruating, or nursed by a woman who was sexually active, or while the nursemaid was ailing, then he would have a defect. Al-Zabīdī, *Itḥāf*, 7:495.

12 Abū Nuʿaym, *Ḥilya*, 2:45; al-Bayhaqī, *al-Sunan al-kubrā*, 7:422; and Ibn ʿAsākir, *Tārīkh madīnat Dimashq*, 3:307.

you, and my mother! Poetry comes to my tongue like a crawling ant and then it stings me and I have to speak it!" The [Prophet] صَلَّى ٱللَّهُ عَلَيْهِ وَسَلَّمَ smiled and said, "The Bedouin cannot give up poetry any more than the camel can give up groaning."[13]

13 Muslim, *Ṣaḥīḥ*, 1060; also see al-Zabīdī, *Itḥāf*, 7:495.

[10]

The Tenth Bane: Joking (*Mizāḥ*) 457

[JOKING] is essentially censured and forbidden except for certain small exceptions. The Messenger of God صَلَّى ٱللَّهُ عَلَيْهِ وَسَلَّمَ said, "Do not argue with your brother nor joke with him."[1]

❁ ❁ ❁

And if you were to say to me, "Arguing can be hurtful because it may include making your brother or friend out to be a liar or ignorant, but joking is just a form of pleasantry, relaxing and pleasant for the heart, so why should it be forbidden?"

Know that the forbidden concerns excessive and habitual [joking].

As for habitual [joking], it busies [the heart] with play and frivolity, and even though play is permissible, to make it a daily habit is censured.

As for excessive [joking] it gives rise to too much laughter, and too much laughter deadens the heart[2] and also, in some circumstances,

---

1 Al-Tirmidhī, *Sunan*, 1995.

2 In a *ḥadīth* found in al-Tirmidhī, *Sunan*, 2305, Abū Hurayra رَضِيَ ٱللَّهُ عَنْهُ said, "The Messenger of God صَلَّى ٱللَّهُ عَلَيْهِ وَسَلَّمَ said, 'Who will take from me these words and act on them or teach them to another to act on?' I said to him, 'I will, O Messenger of God!' Then he took my hand and counted five (with my fingers) saying, "Beware of what is forbidden and you will be the most devout [lit., worshipful] of people. Be content with what God apportions to you and you will be the wealthiest of people. Be good to your neighbor and you will be a believer. Love for other people what you love for yourself, and you will be a Muslim. And do not laugh too much, for too much laughter deadens the heart."'

creates rancor [between people] and [causes] a loss of dignity and stature. |

458 So what is devoid of these matters [that is, excessive or habitual joking] is not censured, as it has been reported that the Prophet صَلَّىٱللَّهُعَلَيْهِوَسَلَّمَ said, "I joke but I speak only the truth."[3] But only one like him is able to joke and speak only the truth. For anyone else, once the door of joking is opened, his only intention will be to make people laugh in whatever way he can, and the Messenger of God صَلَّىٱللَّهُعَلَيْهِوَسَلَّمَ said, "A man may say something for the sake of making those he is sitting with laugh, and it casts him deeper into hell than the distance to the Pleiades."[4]

> ʿUmar رَضِيَٱللَّهُعَنْهُ said, "One who laughs too much, his dignity diminishes; one who jokes [too much] is belittled; one who does anything too much becomes known for it; one who speaks too much slips [that is, errs] too much; one who makes too many slips, his shame diminishes; one whose shame diminishes, his conscientiousness diminishes; and one whose conscientiousness diminishes, his heart dies."[5]

Laughter evinces a heedlessness of the hereafter, as [the Prophet] صَلَّىٱللَّهُعَلَيْهِوَسَلَّمَ said, "If you knew what I know, you would laugh little and weep much."[6] |

459
> A man asked his brother, "O my brother, do you know that you will enter the fire?"[7]
>
> He said, "Yes."
>
> The man then asked, "And do you know that you will be brought out of it?"
>
> He said, "No."

---

3 Ibn Abī l-Dunyā, *al-Ṣamt wa-ādāb al-lisān*, 400; al-Tirmidhī, *Sunan*, 1990; Ibn Ḥanbal, *Musnad*, 2:340.

4 Ibn al-Mubārak, *Zuhd*, 948; Ibn Abī l-Dunyā, *al-Ṣamt wa-ādāb al-lisān*, 71; al-Bukhārī, *Ṣaḥīḥ*, 6477; and Muslim, *Ṣaḥīḥ*, 2988.

5 Al-Ṭabarānī, *al-Muʿjam al-awsaṭ*, 2280.

6 Al-Bukhārī, *Ṣaḥīḥ*, 1044; and Muslim, *Ṣaḥīḥ*, 901.

7 Trans.: This is a reference to what is understood from the verse: *And there is none of you except he will come to it [the fire of hell]. This is upon your Lord an inevitability decreed* (Q. 19:71).

> The man said, "Then what is there to laugh about?" And it is said that he was not seen laughing until he died [that is, at all].[8]

Yūsuf b. Asbāṭ said, "Ḥasan [al-Baṣrī] lived for thirty years without laughing."[9]

And it is said that ʿAṭāʾ al-Salīmī lived for forty years without laughing.[10]

Wahīb b. al-Ward saw some people laughing on the day of ʿĪd al-Fiṭr and said, "If they have been forgiven, this is not the behavior of the thankful, and if they have not been forgiven, this is not the behavior of the fearful."[11]

ʿAbdallāh b. Abī Yaʿlā used to say, "Are you laughing while your shroud is perhaps now on its way from the cloth merchant?"[12]

And Ibn ʿAbbās said, "Whoever transgresses while laughing will enter the fire crying."[13] |

Muḥammad b. Wāsiʿ said, "If you saw a man in heaven weeping, 460
would you not be amazed by his weeping?" They said, "Of course." He said, "The one who laughs in this world and does not know where he is heading is even more amazing."[14]

These are the banes of laughter. What is censured [in this behavior] is becoming engrossed in laughter. And what is praiseworthy is a smile that shows teeth without a sound being heard, as this is how the Messenger of God ﷺ laughed.[15]

> Al-Qāsim, the *mawlā* of Muʿāwiya, said, "A Bedouin rode toward the Prophet ﷺ on an unruly young she-camel. He greeted him [the Prophet] but every time he tried to get nearer so that he could ask him something, [the camel would] take him away, [until some of] the Companions of the Prophet ﷺ started to laugh. This happened three times and then the camel threw the rider off and he was killed.

---

8 Ibn al-Mubārak, *Zuhd*, 311.

9 Abū Nuʿaym, *Ḥilya*, 8:240.

10 Abū Nuʿaym, *Ḥilya*, 6:221.

11 Ibn Abī l-Dunyā, *al-Shukr*, 15.

12 Ibn Abī l-Dunyā, *Qiṣar al-amal*, 85; al-Dīnawarī, *al-Majālisa wa-jawāhir al-ʿilm*, 95; and Abū Nuʿaym, *Ḥilya*, 6:246.

13 Abū Nuʿaym, *Ḥilya*, 4:96, from a *ḥadīth marfuʿ*.

14 This is how it was related by Ibn al-Jawzī, *al-Mudhish*, 1:356.

15 Al-Bukhārī, *Ṣaḥīḥ*, 4829.

> They said, "O Messenger of God! [That she-camel] threw off the Bedouin and killed him!" He said, "Yes, and your mouths are full of his blood."[16]

As for how joking leads to the loss of dignity, ʿUmar [b. al-Khaṭṭāb] رضي الله عنه said, "One who jokes [too much] is belittled [by others]."[17] |

461 Muḥammad b. al-Munkadir said, "My mother said to me, 'O my son, do not joke with children lest they think little of you.'"[18]

And Saʿīd b. al-ʿĀṣ said to his son, "O my son, do not joke with a noble person lest he has malice toward you, nor with the ignoble one lest he becomes brazen toward you."[19]

And ʿUmar b. ʿAbd al-ʿAzīz رحمه الله said, "Fear God and beware of joking for it gives rise to rancor and drags [one] toward repugnance. Sit together and speak to one another about the Qurʾān and if that is too heavy for you, then mention what is best of the words (*ḥadīth*) of the men [*rijāl*, that is, pious or righteous men]."[20]

And ʿUmar b. al-Khaṭṭāb رضي الله عنه said, "Do you know why joking is called *mizāḥ*?" They said no. He said, "Because it is distant[21] from the truth."

And it is said that for everything there is a seed, and the seed of enmity is joking.[22]

And it is said, "Joking steals [one's] intellect and severs friendships."

❁ ❁ ❁

If you were to say, "There are narratives about the joking of the Messenger of God صلى الله عليه وسلم and his Companions, so how can it be forbidden?" |

---

16 According to al-ʿIrāqī, this was related by Ibn al-Mubārak, *Zuhd*. See al-Zabīdī, *Itḥāf*, 7:498.

17 This is part of a longer narrative related in al-Ṭabarānī, *al-Muʿjam al-awsaṭ*, 2280.

18 Ibn Abī l-Dunyā, *al-Ṣamt wa-ādāb al-lisān*, 393.

19 Ibn Abī l-Dunyā, *al-Ṣamt wa-ādāb al-lisān*, 398.

20 Ibn Abī l-Dunyā, *al-Ṣamt wa-ādāb al-lisān*, 397.

21 Ibn Abī l-Dunyā, *al-Ṣamt wa-ādāb al-lisān*, 399. [FC] See *zāḥa*, which can also mean "pass away, or depart from," in Lane, *An Arabic-English Lexicon*, 1275.

22 Ibn Abī l-Dunyā, *al-Ṣamt wa-ādāb al-lisān*, 401.

I would say that if you have the ability, as the Messenger of 462
God صَلَّىٰ ٱللَّٰهُ عَلَيْهِ وَسَلَّمَ and his Companions did, to joke but still speak only the truth, and not injure a heart, nor be excessive in it [joking], and limit [the joking] to rare [occasions], then you are free to [do] it. But it would be a great mistake if a person took joking as a vocation and applied himself to it, did it excessively, and then [claimed] to be following the actions of the Messenger of God صَلَّىٰ ٱللَّٰهُ عَلَيْهِ وَسَلَّمَ. That would be like someone who passes his whole day watching African [acrobats] dancing and then claim he is following the actions of the Messenger of God صَلَّىٰ ٱللَّٰهُ عَلَيْهِ وَسَلَّمَ because he gave permission to ʿĀʾisha رَضِيَ ٱللَّٰهُ عَنْهَا to watch the African (Zanūj) dancing on the day of ʿĪd.[23] This is incorrect. Minor [sins] become major when done persistently and what is permissible becomes a minor [sin] when done persistently. This should not be disregarded.

Yes, Abū Hurayra related that they said, "O Messenger of God, surely you tease us!" He said, "If I tease you, I still say only the truth."[24]

And ʿAṭāʾ said,

> A man asked Ibn ʿAbbās whether the Messenger of God صَلَّىٰ ٱللَّٰهُ عَلَيْهِ وَسَلَّمَ made jokes and Ibn ʿAbbās answered, "Yes."
>
> So the man asked, "What were his jokes like?"
>
> Ibn ʿAbbās said, "One day [the Prophet] صَلَّىٰ ٱللَّٰهُ عَلَيْهِ وَسَلَّمَ asked one of his wives to put on a very large robe and said, 'Put it on, praise God, and let it trail like a bridal train!'"[25] |

And Anas said, "The Prophet صَلَّىٰ ٱللَّٰهُ عَلَيْهِ وَسَلَّمَ was one of the most 463
humorous people with his wives."[26] It was related that he often smiled.[27]

[We learned] from Ḥasan, who said, "An old woman came to the Prophet صَلَّىٰ ٱللَّٰهُ عَلَيْهِ وَسَلَّمَ and he صَلَّىٰ ٱللَّٰهُ عَلَيْهِ وَسَلَّمَ said to her, 'No old women enter heaven,' and she began to weep. He said, 'Because on that

---

23 The Prophet صَلَّىٰ ٱللَّٰهُ عَلَيْهِ وَسَلَّمَ allowed ʿĀʾisha رَضِيَ ٱللَّٰهُ عَنْهَا to watch Abyssinians dancing with spears and shields. Al-Bukhārī, *Ṣaḥīḥ*, 950; and Muslim, *Ṣaḥīḥ*, 892.

24 Al-Tirmidhī, *Sunan*, 1990.

25 Ibn ʿAsākir, *Tārīkh madīnat Dimashq*, 4:41.

26 Ibn Abī l-Dunyā, *Mudārāt al-nās*, 60; and Ibn ʿAsākir, *Tārīkh madīnat Dimashq*, 4:37.

27 In al-Tirmidhī, *Sunan*, 3641, ʿAbdallāh b. al-Ḥārith b. Jazʾ رَضِيَ ٱللَّٰهُ عَنْهُ is reported to have said, "I have never seen anyone who smiled more than the Messenger of God صَلَّىٰ ٱللَّٰهُ عَلَيْهِ وَسَلَّمَ."

day you will not be an old woman.' God تعالى said, *Indeed, We have produced* [that is, *the women of paradise*] *in a* [*new*] *creation and made them virgins* [Q. 56:35–36].[28]

> Zayd b. Aslam related that a woman named Umm Ayman came to the Prophet صلى الله عليه وسلم and said, "My husband has invited you."
>
> He said, "And who is he? Is he the one who has white in his eye?"
>
> She said, "By God, he does not have white in his eye!" [that is, he does not have cataracts]
>
> [The Prophet] insisted, "But he does have white in his eye!"
>
> And she responded to him, "No, by God!"
>
> [The Prophet] صلى الله عليه وسلم said, "There is no one who does not have white in their eyes!"
>
> He meant the white of the eye that surrounds the pupil.[29]

Another woman came and said,

> "O Messenger of God, let me ride on a camel."
>
> He said, "No, we will let you ride on a son of a camel."
>
> She said, "How can I do that? He will not be able to carry me!"
>
> 464 [The Prophet] صلى الله عليه وسلم said | "There is not a camel except that it is the offspring [lit., son of] a camel."[30]
>
> Thus, he was making a joke.

Anas said, "Abū Ṭalḥa had a son named Abū ʿUmayr. The Messenger of God صلى الله عليه وسلم would come to them and say, 'O Abū ʿUmayr, what did the *nughayr* do?'"[31] A *nughayr* is the baby sparrow with which the boy would play.

---

28 Al-Tirmidhī, *al-Shamāʾil al-Muḥammadiyya*, 240.

29 Al-ʿIrāqī says, "This was related by al-Zubayr b. Bakkār in his book, *al-Fukāha wa-l-muzāḥ* and also by Ibn Abī l-Dunyā from a *ḥadīth* of ʿAbdallāh b. Saham al-Fihrī with slight differences." Al-Zabīdī, *Itḥāf*, 7:500.

30 Abū Dāwūd, *Sunan*, 4998; and al-Tirmidhī, *Sunan*, 1991, with similar wording.

31 Al-Bukhārī, *Ṣaḥīḥ*, 6129; and Muslim, *Ṣaḥīḥ*, 2150.

ʿĀʾisha رَضِيَ ٱللَّهُ عَنْهَا said, We went out with the Messenger of God صَلَّى ٱللَّهُ عَلَيْهِ وَسَلَّمَ in the battle of Badr and he صَلَّى ٱللَّهُ عَلَيْهِ وَسَلَّمَ said, "Come so that I can race with you."

So I fastened my armor to my stomach, then we drew a line and both stood on it, and then we raced and he beat me.

He said, "This is for that time at Dhī l-Majāz."

[He said this because] one day we were there when I was still young and my father had given me something [for the Prophet]. [The Prophet] had said, "Give it to me," but I had refused and started walking away quickly, and he also started walking quickly after me but was not able to catch up with me.[32]

She also said, "The Messenger of God صَلَّى ٱللَّهُ عَلَيْهِ وَسَلَّمَ ran a race with me and I beat him. Then, after I had put on weight, we raced again, and he beat me and said, 'This is for that [time]!'"[33]

She also said رَضِيَ ٱللَّهُ عَنْهَا, the Messenger of God صَلَّى ٱللَّهُ عَلَيْهِ وَسَلَّمَ was
with me and | Sawda bt. Zamʿa. I had brought some porridge 465
I made and said to Sawda, "Eat!"

She answered, "I do not like it."

I said, "By God, either you eat some or else I will smear it on your face!"

She answered, "I will not even taste it!"

So I took a bit from the dish and smeared it on her face. The Messenger of God صَلَّى ٱللَّهُ عَلَيْهِ وَسَلَّمَ had been sitting between us but then he lowered his knees so that Sawda could reach the plate and wipe some of it on my face too, and then the Messenger of God صَلَّى ٱللَّهُ عَلَيْهِ وَسَلَّمَ started laughing.[34]

It was related that al-Ḍaḥḥāk b. Sufyān al-Kilābī was an ugly repugnant man. When he [pledged his] allegiance to the Prophet صَلَّى ٱللَّهُ عَلَيْهِ وَسَلَّمَ,[35]

---

32 Ibn Abī l-Dunyā, *al-ʿIyyāl*, 560; Ibn Abī l-Dunyā, *Mudārāt al-nās*, 156; and al-Ṭaḥāwī, *Sharḥ muskhil al-āthār*, 1881.

33 Abū Dāwūd, *Sunan*, 2578; and Ibn Mājah, *Sunan*, 1979.

34 Al-Nasāʾī, *al-Sunan al-kubrā*, 8868.

35 Al-ʿIrāqī says, "This was related by al-Zubayr b. Bakkār in his book, *al-Fukāha wa-l-muzāḥ* from ʿAbdallāh b. Ḥasan b. Ḥasan, and in a similar narration by al-Dāraquṭnī." See al-Zabīdī, *Itḥāf*, 7:501.

he said, "I have two women, both of whom are more beautiful [lit., good] than this red one.[36] Should I give up one of them so you can marry her?" ʿĀʾisha, who was sitting nearby—this was before the verse concerning veiling had been revealed—asked, "Is she more beautiful or [are] you?" He answered, "No, I am more handsome and honorable than she is!" And the Messenger of God صَلَّى ٱللَّهُ عَلَيْهِ وَسَلَّمَ laughed at what she asked him because he was ugly.

And it was related by ʿAlqama that, according to Abū Salama, [the Prophet] صَلَّى ٱللَّهُ عَلَيْهِ وَسَلَّمَ used to stick out his tongue playfully with Ḥusayn b. ʿAlī, and when the child saw his tongue, he became gleeful.
466 ʿUyayna b. Badr | al-Fazārī said, "By God, I have a son whose beard is starting to appear and I have never kissed him." The Messenger of God صَلَّى ٱللَّهُ عَلَيْهِ وَسَلَّمَ said, "Truly, someone who does not show mercy will not be shown mercy."[37]

Many of these narrations of pleasantries [involve] women and children. Such was his صَلَّى ٱللَّهُ عَلَيْهِ وَسَلَّمَ way of treating their gentle hearts [that is, nature], but without tending toward silliness.

[The Prophet] صَلَّى ٱللَّهُ عَلَيْهِ وَسَلَّمَ said to Ṣuhayb who was suffering from conjunctivitis in one eye and was eating a date, "Are you eating a date when you have conjunctivitis in your eye?" He said, "Yes, but I am eating it from the other side, O Messenger of God!" And the Messenger of God صَلَّى ٱللَّهُ عَلَيْهِ وَسَلَّمَ smiled, or other narrators said, "[he smiled] until you could see his molars."[38]

> And it was related that Khawwāt b. Jubayr al-Anṣārī was sitting with women from the Banū Kaʿb on the road to Mecca when the Messenger of God صَلَّى ٱللَّهُ عَلَيْهِ وَسَلَّمَ came on him and said, "O Abū ʿAbdallāh, why are you with the women?"
>
> He said, "They are weaving a hobble for my camel that wanders off."
>
> The Messenger of God صَلَّى ٱللَّهُ عَلَيْهِ وَسَلَّمَ continued on his way and then came back and said to him, "O Abū ʿAbdallāh, has that camel stopped wandering yet?"

---

36 Trans.: By whom he meant ʿĀʾisha رَضِيَ ٱللَّهُ عَنْهَا, who had a reddish complexion.

37 Hannād, *al-Zuhd*, 1330, from a *ḥadīth marfuʿ* related by Abū Hurayra رَضِيَ ٱللَّهُ عَنْهُ.

38 Ibn Mājah, *Sunan*, 3443. Trans.: It was believed that eating dates aggravated conjunctivitis.

> [Khawwāt] said, "I was quiet and ashamed,[39] and after that
> I tried to avoid him [the Prophet] whenever I saw him, out
> of shyness before him, until [one day] I was | in Medina and 467
> he saw me in the mosque praying. He sat down near me and
> I prolonged my prayer.
>
> He said, "Do not make it too long because I am waiting for you."
>
> When I [reached the] salutations [at the end of the prayer], he [the Prophet] said, "O Abū ʿAbdallāh, has that camel stopped wandering yet?"
>
> I was quiet and ashamed. He [the Prophet] stood up to leave and after that, I stayed far from him until one day he met me and he was riding a donkey with his legs on one side.
>
> He said, "O Abū ʿAbdallāh, has that camel stopped wandering yet?"
>
> I answered him, "By the One who sent you with the truth, it has not wandered since I [entered] Islam."
>
> He [the Prophet] said, "God is greater! God is greater! O God, give guidance to Abū ʿAbdallāh." After this his Islam improved and God تَعَالَىٰ guided him.[40]

Nuʿaymān al-Anṣārī was a man who joked a lot and who also used to drink. He was brought to the Prophet صَلَّى ٱللَّهُ عَلَيْهِ وَسَلَّمَ [for drunkenness] and [as punishment] the Prophet صَلَّى ٱللَّهُ عَلَيْهِ وَسَلَّمَ struck him with his sandal and told his Companions to strike him with their sandals.[41] Since this [his drunkenness] happened many times, a man from among the Companions of the Prophet صَلَّى ٱللَّهُ عَلَيْهِ وَسَلَّمَ said [to Nuʿaymān], "May God curse you!"

The Prophet صَلَّى ٱللَّهُ عَلَيْهِ وَسَلَّمَ said to him [the man who cursed Nuʿaymān], "Do not say that, for truly [Nuʿaymān] loves God and His Messenger."[42]

---

39 Eds.: At the time, it was considered unmanly for a man to sit with women at length.

40 Al-Ṭabarānī, *al-Muʿjam al-kabīr*, 4:203; and Abū Nuʿaym, *Ḥilya*, 2:977, with similar wording.

41 Eds.: The punishment for drunkenness was flogging; the Prophet started the punishment and told his Companions to continue.

42 Al-Bukhārī, *Ṣaḥīḥ*, 2316.

Indeed, whenever food or milk arrived in Medina, [Nuʿaymān] would buy some of it. [One day] he came with [some food] to the Messenger of God صلى الله عليه وسلم and said, "O Messenger of God, I bought this for you as a gift."

Then the seller came to Nuʿaymān asking him to pay him for it and [Nuʿaymān] took [the seller] to the Prophet صلى الله عليه وسلم and [Nuʿaymān] said, "O Messenger of God, could you pay him?" |

468 The Messenger of God صلى الله عليه وسلم said [to Nuʿaymān], "Did you not give this to me as gift?"

[Nuʿaymān] said, "O Messenger of God, I wanted you to eat it but I did not have the money to pay for it!"

The Prophet صلى الله عليه وسلم laughed and asked that the seller be given its price.[43]

These pleasantries are permissible if they are rare, not all the time, and [not engaged in] regularly. [Otherwise], they are censured as foolishness and a cause for the laughter that deadens the heart.

43 This is a continuation of the *ḥadīth* above.

[11]

The Eleventh Bane: Ridicule (*Sukhriyya*) and Mockery (*Istihizāʾ*) 469

[Ridicule and mockery] is unlawful whenever it is hurtful. God تَعَالَىٰ said, *O you who have believed, let not a people ridicule (yaskhar)* [*another*] *people; perhaps they may be better than them; nor let women* [*ridicule other*] *women; perhaps they may be better than them* [Q. 49:11].

Here the meaning of ridicule is to disdain and scorn [someone] and point out his defects and deficiencies in order to laugh at him. [Ridicule] can be through imitating [someone's] actions or speech and it can also be by means of gestures or mimicking [them].

If it is in the presence of the one being mocked, it is not called backbiting, but has the connotations of backbiting.

ʿĀʾisha رَضِيَ ٱللَّهُ عَنْهَا said, "I was imitating a person and the Prophet صَلَّى ٱللَّهُ عَلَيْهِ وَسَلَّمَ said, 'I would not like imitating a person even if I were [given] this or that [as a reward].'"[1]

Ibn ʿAbbās said about His تَعَالَىٰ words, *And they will say, "Oh, woe to us! What is this book that leaves nothing small* [a minor sin] (*ṣaghīra*) *or great* [a major sin] (*kabīra*) *except that it has enumerated it?"* [Q. 18:49], "The minor [sin could be a] smile when a believer is being mocked and a major [sin could include] this and laughing out loud."[2] This indicates that laughing at people is a general transgression and a major [sin].

1 Abū Dāwūd, *Sunan*, 4875; and al-Tirmidhī, *Sunan*, 2502.

2 Ibn Abī l-Dunyā, *al-Ṣamt wa-ādāb al-lisān*, 292.

ʿAbdallāh b. Zamʿa said, "I heard the Prophet of God صَلَّى ٱللَّهُ عَلَيْهِ وَسَلَّمَ |
470 orating and he admonished them not to laugh at someone who breaks wind, and he said, "Why would you laugh at what you yourselves do?"[3]

And [the Prophet] صَلَّى ٱللَّهُ عَلَيْهِ وَسَلَّمَ said,

> For one who mocks other people a door to heaven will be opened and it will be said to him, "Come, come!" And he will come to it with his sorrow and distress [but] when he reaches it, it will be closed in his face. Then another door will be opened to him, and it will again be said to him, "Come, come!" And he will come to it with his sorrow and distress and when he reaches it, it will be closed in his face. And this will continue until, when a door is opened to him and it is said to him, "Come, come!" he will not go to it."[4]

Muʿādh b. Jabal said, "The Messenger of God صَلَّى ٱللَّهُ عَلَيْهِ وَسَلَّمَ said, 'Whoever [continually] upbraids his brother for a transgression he repented of will not die until he does it [that is, the one who upbraided his brother commits that transgression].'"[5]

All of this concerns disdaining (*istiḥiqār*) someone, laughing at him, scorning him, and belittling him, and the words of God تَعَالَىٰ refer to this, *Perhaps they may be better than them* [Q. 49:11]; that is, "Do not ridicule or belittle another, for perhaps he is better than you."

This is unlawful [mockery] that is hurtful [to another].

As for whoever makes himself [the object of] ridicule, and is perhaps happy to be ridiculed, this ridicule is a category of joking, and we previously [mentioned, in chapter 10] what is censured and what is extolled. |

471 In fact, the unlawfulness of belittling another [person is because it] hurts the one who is mocked by it, as it is disdainful and scornful. This sometimes comes about when someone is speaking and someone laughs at his words because they are mixed up and not well-arranged; or it may be that his actions are [laughed at] because they are distracting, as in the case of laughing at someone's handwriting, or at something he has fashioned, or at his form and the

3 Al-Bukhārī, *Ṣaḥīḥ*, 4942; and Muslim, *Ṣaḥīḥ*, 2855.

4 Ibn Abī l-Dunyā, *al-Ṣamt wa-ādāb al-lisān*, 287; and al-Bayhaqī, *Shuʿab al-īmān*, 4791, 6333.

5 Al-Tirmidhī, *Sunan*, 2505, without the words "from which he has repented."

way he was created, if he is short or deficient [in terms of] a defect among [the various] defects. Laughing at any of these falls under ridicule, and that is forbidden.

[12]

472 The Twelfth Bane: Divulging Secrets (*Sirr*)

[Divulging secrets] is forbidden because of the injury [inherent] in it and its scorn for the rights of acquaintances and friends.

The Messenger of God صَلَّى ٱللَّٰهُ عَلَيْهِ وَسَلَّمَ said, "If a man says something and then turns aside,[1] it is a trust."

And he said, without exception, "Conversation among you is a trust."[2]

Ḥasan [al-Baṣrī] said, "It is a form of betrayal to speak about your brother's secret."[3]

And it was related that Muʿāwiya رَضِيَ ٱللَّٰهُ عَنْهُ confided a conversation to al-Walīd b. ʿUtba, who then said to his father,

> O my father, the Commander of the Faithful [Muʿāwiya] confided a conversation with me and I do not believe he would conceal [lit., fold] from you what he would reveal [lit., unfold] to another.
>
> [His father] said, "Do not speak to me about it. Whoever keeps a secret, the choice is his, and whoever divulges it, the choice is against him."
>
> [Al-Walīd b. ʿUtba] said, I said, "O my father, does this apply to what is between a man and his father?"

---

1 Abū Dāwūd, *Sunan*, 4868; al-Tirmidhī, *Sunan*, 1959. Trans.: It is said that "turning aside" means checking to see if there is anyone near who could have overheard it.

2 Ibn Abī l-Dunyā, *al-Ṣamt wa-ādāb al-lisān*, 403.

3 Ibn Abī l-Dunyā, *al-Ṣamt wa-ādāb al-lisān*, 404.

[His father] said, "No, by God, my son, but I would not want your tongue | to be humiliated by speaking secrets." 473

[Al-Walīd] said, "Then I went to Muʿāwiya and told him what happened [between me and his father], and he [Muʿāwiya] said, 'O al-Walīd, my brother [that is, your father] has freed you from the slavery of the offense.'"[4]

Thus, divulging a secrets is betrayal. It is unlawful if it causes harm, and [it is] iniquity if it does not cause harm. We have spoken of what is related to keeping secrets in *The Book on the Proprieties of Friendship* [*and Brotherhood*][5] so we will not repeat it.

4 Ibn Abī l-Dunyā, *al-Ṣamt wa-ādāb al-lisān*, 410. Trans.: Walīd's father, ʿUtba b. Abī Sufyān, was Muʿāwiya's brother.

5 Trans.: Book 15 of the *Revival of the Religious Sciences: The Proprieties of Friendship and Brotherhood* (*Kitāb ādāb al-ṣuḥba wa-l-maʿāshara maʿ aṣnāf al-khalaq*).

[13]

474 ## The Thirteenth Bane: False Promises (*Waʿd al-kādhib*)

THE tongue is quick to make a promise, then perhaps the self does not consent to fulfill it and the promise is broken. This is among the signs of hypocrisy.

God تَعَالَىٰ said, *O you who have believed, fulfill* [*all*] *contracts* [Q. 5:1].[1]

And [the Prophet] صَلَّى ٱللَّهُ عَلَيْهِ وَسَلَّمَ said, "A promise is a gift."[2]

And [the Prophet] صَلَّى ٱللَّهُ عَلَيْهِ وَسَلَّمَ said, "A promise (*wāʾī*) is like a debt or more."[3] And *wāʾī* means a promise.

And God تَعَالَىٰ in His noble book commended His Prophet Ishmael (Ismāʿīl) عَلَيْهِ ٱلسَّلَامُ, saying, *He kept true to the promise and was a messenger, a prophet* [Q. 19:54].

It has been said that [Ishmael] promised [to meet] a person at a certain place and the person did not come—indeed he forgot—yet Ishmael remained waiting for twenty-two days.[4]

When ʿAbdallāh b. ʿAmr was near death, he said,

> A man from the Quraysh asked me for the hand of my daughter in marriage and [what I said] to him resembled a
> 475 promise. By God, I do not want to meet God | with one-third

1 Trans.: The term from the Qurʾānic verse, *ʿuqūd*, translated above as "contracts," may also be understood to mean promises, covenants, and agreements.

2 Al-Ṭabarānī, *al-Muʿjam al-awsaṭ*, 1773; and Ibn Abī l-Dunyā, *al-Ṣamt wa-ādāb al-lisān*, 456. Trans.: Meaning, just as when we give a gift, we should not ask for it back, when we give a promise, we should not break it. See al-Zabīdī, *Itḥāf*, 7:505.

3 Ibn Abī l-Dunyā, *al-Ṣamt wa-ādāb al-lisān*, 457.

4 Ibn Abī l-Dunyā, *al-Ṣamt wa-ādāb al-lisān*, 461.

> of hypocrisy,[5] so [bear] witness that I gave him my daughter's hand in marriage.[6]

ʿAbdallāh b. Abī l-Ḥamsāʾ said,

> Before he was sent forth [from God as a Prophet], I bought [something] from the Prophet صَلَّى ٱللَّٰهُ عَلَيْهِ وَسَلَّمَ and had a balance left to pay him. I promised him that I would bring it to that place, but I forgot about it for two days. On the third day I went to that place and found him there. He said, 'O young man, you have [given me] a hardship. I have been waiting for you here for three [days].'"[7]

And it was asked of Ibrāhīm [al-Nakhāʿī], "[What should one do if] a man promises to meet another, but does not come?"[8] [Ibrāhīm] answered, "Let him wait until the next prayer time comes."

When the Messenger of God صَلَّى ٱللَّٰهُ عَلَيْهِ وَسَلَّمَ made a promise, he said, "may it be . . . ."

And Ibn Masʿūd never made a promise without saying, "God willing" (*in shāʾ Allāh*) and this is preferable.[9]

Then, if a promise is understood to be firm, it must be fulfilled unless there is an excuse. And if someone makes a promise intending not to keep it, that is hypocrisy. Abū Hurayra said, "The
Prophet صَلَّى ٱللَّٰهُ عَلَيْهِ وَسَلَّمَ said, 'Three [traits] are in | a hypocrite, even one 476
who fasts and prays and claims to be a Muslim: when he speaks, he lies; when he promises [something], he breaks it; and when he is given a trust, he betrays it.'"[10]

ʿAbdallāh b. ʿAmr رَضِيَ ٱللَّٰهُ عَنْهُمَا said,

> The Messenger of God صَلَّى ٱللَّٰهُ عَلَيْهِ وَسَلَّمَ said, "Four [traits] are in one [who] is a hypocrite, and whoever has one of the traits, has a trait of hypocrisy until he rids himself of it: when he speaks, he lies; when he promises [something], he breaks

---

5 Eds.: That is, if hypocrisy were divided into thirds, he would not want even a bit of it.

6 Ibn Abī l-Dunyā, *al-Ṣamt wa-ādāb al-lisān*, 459.

7 Abū Dāwūd, *Sunan*, 4996; and Ibn Abī l-Dunyā, *al-Ṣamt wa-ādāb al-lisān*, 460.

8 Ibn Abī l-Dunyā, *al-Ṣamt wa-ādāb al-lisān*, 463.

9 Ibn Abī l-Dunyā, *al-Ṣamt wa-ādāb al-lisān*, 467, with similar wording.

10 Al-Bukhārī, *Ṣaḥīḥ*, 33; and Muslim, *Ṣaḥīḥ*, 59, with similar wording.

> it; when he makes a covenant, he breaches it; and when he disputes, he is insolent."[11]

This applies to whoever makes a promise intending to break it or whoever fails to keep it without an excuse. As for the one who intends to keep a promise and is barred from it, then he has an excuse, he is not a hypocrite, even if it appears that he is a hypocrite.

But [one] should avoid the appearance of hypocrisy just as one is cautious [about] its true nature, and he should not makes excuses for himself without a compelling reason. It was related that the Messenger of God ﷺ promised [to send] Abū l-Haytham b. al-Tayyihān a servant. Three captives of battle were brought to him and he gave two of them and kept one. Then Fāṭima, the daughter of the Messenger of God ﷺ, came and requested a servant. She said, "Do you not see, O Messenger of God, the marks left on my hand from [turning] the mill?" But he mentioned the promise to Abū l-Haytham and said, "But what about my promise to Abū l-Haytham?" Thus, because of his promise, he chose him [that is,
477 giving the servant to him] over Fāṭima | even if it meant that she had to turn the mill with her own weak hand.[12]

The Messenger of God ﷺ was sitting dividing the spoils of the Hawāzin [after the battle of] Ḥunayn when a man came to him and said,

> Truly, you promised me [something], O Messenger of God.
>
> [The Prophet] said, "You are right. Claim whatever you want."
>
> [The man] said, "I want eighty lambs and their shepherd."
>
> [The Prophet] said, "They are yours, and in fact, you have demanded little. The woman who showed Moses عَلَيْهِ ٱلسَّلَامُ the bones of Joseph was more demanding and shrewd. When she made her claim to Moses عَلَيْهِ ٱلسَّلَامُ, she said, 'My demand is that you restore my youth and bring me with you into heaven.'"[13]

11 Al-Bukhārī, *Ṣaḥīḥ*, 34; and Muslim, *Ṣaḥīḥ*, 58.

12 Al-Bayhaqī, *Dalāʾil*, 1:360.

13 Al-Ḥākim al-Nīsābūrī, *al-Mustadrak*, 2:404, with similar wording.

It is said that people thought his demand was modest, such that it became an example [and people] would say "[his demand] is more meager than the one [who asked for] eighty [lambs] and a shepherd."[14]

The Messenger of God ﷺ said, "When a man promises [something] to another man and intends to fulfill it [but cannot], it is not reneging."[15]

And in another version, "If a man promises his brother [something] with the intention of fulfilling it but is unable to do so, then there is no sin on him."[16]

14 That is, one should ask for a higher reward in the hereafter.

15 Abū Yaʿlā, *Musnad*, 5363.

16 Abū Dāwūd, *Sunan*, 4995; and al-Tirmidhī, *Sunan*, 2633, with nearly the same wording.

[14]

478 ## The Fourteenth Bane: Lying in Speech (*Qawl*) and Oaths (*Yamīn*)

[LYING in speech and oaths] is one of the most repugnant transgressions and obscene defects.

Ismāʿīl b. Awsaṭ said,

> I heard Abū Bakr al-Ṣiddīq رَضِيَ ٱللَّهُ عَنْهُ orating after the death of the Messenger of God صَلَّى ٱللَّهُ عَلَيْهِ وَسَلَّمَ and he said, "One year ago the Messenger of God صَلَّى ٱللَّهُ عَلَيْهِ وَسَلَّمَ stood among us in this place where I am standing," and [Abū Bakr] wept, and said, "Beware of lying (*kadhib*), for it goes with profligacy (*fujūr*) and [those who do these two acts] are both in the fire."[1]

Abū Umāma said, "The Messenger of God صَلَّى ٱللَّهُ عَلَيْهِ وَسَلَّمَ said, 'Truly, lying is a gate from [among] the gates of hypocrisy.'"[2]

And Ḥasan [al-Baṣrī] said, it was said that "Hypocrisy is dissonance between [one's] innermost [thoughts] and [what one does] overtly, and [it is dissonance] in speech and conduct [between] what is within and what is without. And the foundation on which hypocrisy is built is lying."[3] |

479 [The Prophet] صَلَّى ٱللَّهُ عَلَيْهِ وَسَلَّمَ said, "It is a great betrayal to tell your brother something that he thinks is credible, but you [know] to be a lie."[4]

---

1 Ibn Mājah, *Sunan*, 3849; and Ibn Abī l-Dunyā, *al-Ṣamt wa-ādāb al-lisān*, 469.

2 Al-Kharāʾiṭī, *Masāwiʾ al-akhlāq*, 121; its meaning is as in the *ḥadīth*, "A sign of the hypocrite . . . ."

3 Ibn Abī l-Dunyā, *al-Ṣamt wa-ādāb al-lisān*, 484.

4 Abū Dāwūd, *Sunan*, 4971; and Ibn Ḥanbal, *Musnad*, 4:183.

Ibn Masʿūd said, "The Prophet صَلَّى ٱللَّٰهُ عَلَيْهِ وَسَلَّمَ said, 'The servant who continually lies and is intent on lying will be written, before God, as a liar.'"[5]

The Messenger of God صَلَّى ٱللَّٰهُ عَلَيْهِ وَسَلَّمَ passed two men bargaining over a sheep and swearing oaths as they did so. One of them said,

> By God, I am not going to take less from you than such-and-such [a price]. . . .
>
> And the other said, "By God, I am not going to pay you more than such-and-such [a price]. . . . "
>
> [Later the Prophet] passed by the sheep after one of them had bought it and said, "One of them brought on himself a sin and [must pay] expiation (*kaffāra*)."[6]

And [the Prophet] صَلَّى ٱللَّٰهُ عَلَيْهِ وَسَلَّمَ said, "Lying diminishes one's [predestined] provision (*rizq*)."[7]

And the Messenger of God صَلَّى ٱللَّٰهُ عَلَيْهِ وَسَلَّمَ said, "Verily, merchants are profligates." He was asked, "O Messenger of God, did not God make commerce lawful?" He said, "Yes, but when they make oaths, they sin, and when they speak, they lie."[8]

And [the Prophet] صَلَّى ٱللَّٰهُ عَلَيْهِ وَسَلَّمَ said, "There are three [types of] individuals to whom God will not speak on the day of resurrection |
nor look upon: a [person who] obligates others with his gifts, a 480
merchant who sells his goods [by swearing] oaths recklessly, and [one who] lets his lower garment drag [in pride]."[9]

And [the Prophet] صَلَّى ٱللَّٰهُ عَلَيْهِ وَسَلَّمَ said, "No one swears an oath by God that contains so much as a gnat's wing [of falsehood] except that it leaves a [dark] spot on his heart until the day of resurrection."[10]

---

5 Al-Bukhārī, *Ṣaḥīḥ*, 6094; Muslim, *Ṣaḥīḥ*, 2606; and al-Tirmidhī, *Sunan*, 1971.

6 Al-Kharāʾiṭī, *Masāwiʾ al-akhlāq*, 116.

7 Al-Kharāʾiṭī, *Masāwiʾ al-akhlāq*, 117.

8 Ibn Ḥanbal, *Musnad*, 3:428; and al-Ḥākim al-Nīsābūrī, *al-Mustadrak*, 2:6; where instead of the word "yes" (*naʿm*), "indeed it is" (*balā*) appears.

9 Muslim, *Ṣaḥīḥ*, 106.

10 Al-Tirmidhī, *Sunan*, 3020; as part of a longer *ḥadīth*, and with these words alone in al-Kharāʾiṭī, *Masāwiʾ al-akhlāq*, 124.

Abū Dharr said, the Messenger of God صَلَّى ٱللَّٰهُ عَلَيْهِ وَسَلَّمَ said,

> There are three whom God loves: a man who [fights] in a force, his chest thrust forward, until he is slain or God gives victory to him or his companions; a man who is hurt by a wicked neighbor but bears it until they are separated by death or [when he] moves away; and a man who travels with people on a journey, by day or by night, that has become so long that they are delighted to touch ground, so they dismount [at night] and he goes off to pray, then he wakes up his traveling companions to depart. And there are three whom God hates: the merchant or seller [who swears] oaths, the poor [person who is] deceitful, and [the person who is] miserly and obligates [others with his gifts].[11]

And [the Prophet] صَلَّى ٱللَّٰهُ عَلَيْهِ وَسَلَّمَ said, "Woe to the one who talks to a group, lying to make them laugh. Woe to him, woe to him."[12] |

481 [The Prophet] صَلَّى ٱللَّٰهُ عَلَيْهِ وَسَلَّمَ said,

> I saw [in a dream] a man who came to me and said, "Arise!" So I arose [and went] with him, and behold, there were two men, one of whom was standing and the other was seated. In the hand of the one standing was an iron hook that he inserted into the side of the seated man's mouth and then pulled it until it reached the back of his neck. Then he went to the other side, stretched it, and when he stretched it, [the first side] returned to how it had been. I said to the one who had taken me there, "What is this?"
>
> He said, "This man is a liar being punished in his grave until the day of resurrection."[13]

And from ʿAbdallāh b. Jarrād [we learned] that he asked the Prophet صَلَّى ٱللَّٰهُ عَلَيْهِ وَسَلَّمَ, saying,

> O Messenger of God, does a believer [commit] *zinā*?
>
> He said, "He might do that."

---

11 Ibn Ḥanbal, *Musnad*, 5:151; and al-Kharāʾiṭī, *Masāwiʾ al-akhlāq*, 126.

12 Abū Dāwūd, *Sunan*, 4990; and al-Tirmidhī, *Sunan*, 2315.

13 Al-Kharāʾiṭī, *Masāwiʾ al-akhlāq*, 131, with these words. In al-Bukhārī, *Ṣaḥīḥ*, 1386, this is part of a long *ḥadīth*.

> I said, "O Prophet of God, does a believer lie?"
>
> He said, "No."
>
> Then the Messenger of God صلى الله عليه وسلم followed this [by reciting] the words of God تعالى, *They only invent falsehood (kadhib) who do not believe* [Q. 16:105].[14]

Abū Saʿīd al-Khudrī said, "I heard the Messenger of God صلى الله عليه وسلم supplicating, and saying in his supplication, 'O God, purify my heart of hypocrisy, my loins of [committing] *zinā*, and my tongue of lying.'"[15] |

And [the Prophet] صلى الله عليه وسلم said, "There are three to whom God 482
will not speak, nor look at, nor praise, and theirs will be a painful punishment: an elder who [commits] *zinā*, a ruler who lies, and a poor man who is arrogant."[16]

ʿAbdallāh b. ʿĀmir said,

> The Messenger of God صلى الله عليه وسلم came to our home when I was a little child and I had gone out to play. My mother said, "O ʿAbdallāh, come here so I can give you [something]!"
>
> [The Prophet] صلى الله عليه وسلم said, "What do you want to give him?"
>
> She said, "A date."
>
> He said, "[Know] that if you do not do it, it is written against you as a lie."[17]

And [the Prophet] صلى الله عليه وسلم said, "If God gave me camels as numerous as these thorn bushes, I would divide them among you and [in doing this] you would not find me a miser, or a liar, or a coward."[18]

And [the Prophet] صلى الله عليه وسلم said, as he was reclining, "Shall I not inform you of the gravest of the major [sins]? Associating

---

14 The continuation of the verse is, *in the verses of God and it is those who are the liars*. Al-Kharāʾiṭī, *Masāwiʾ al-akhlāq*, 132, in which the question is also found, "O Messenger of God, does a believer steal?" He answered, "He might." This is also found in Ibn Abī l-Dunyā, *al-Ṣamt wa-ādāb al-lisān*, 477, in which the question is only about lying and the questioner is Abū l-Dardāʾ رضي الله عنه.

15 Al-Kharāʾiṭī, *Masāwiʾ al-akhlāq*, 134.

16 Muslim, *Ṣaḥīḥ*, 107.

17 Abū Dāwūd, *Sunan*, 4991; and al-Kharāʾiṭī, *Masāwiʾ al-akhlāq*, 140.

18 Al-Bukhārī, *Ṣaḥīḥ*, 2821; and al-Kharāʾiṭī, *Masāwiʾ al-akhlāq*, 144.

[partners] with God and ingratitude toward parents." Then he sat up, and said, "And saying deceitful [words]."[19]

And Ibn ʿUmar said, "The Messenger of God ﷺ said, 'A servant tells a lie that drives the angel [recording his good deeds] a mile away from him because of its stench [that is, of the lie]."[20]

And Anas said,

> The Prophet ﷺ said, "Grant me six things and [God
> 483 will] grant | you heaven."
>
> They said, "And what are they?"
>
> [The Prophet] said, "When you speak, do not lie. When you [make a] promise, do not break it. If you are given a trust, do not betray it. Lower your gaze, stop your hands [from harming another], and guard your loins."[21]

And [the Prophet] ﷺ said, "Satan has [his own] kohl (*kuḥl*), syrup, and snuff. His syrup is lying, his snuff is anger, and his kohl is sleep."[22]

ʿUmar b. al-Khaṭṭāb رضي الله عنه gave an oration in al-Jābiyya and said,

> The Messenger of God ﷺ stood among us as I am standing among you and said, "Be good to my Companions, and then to [the generation] that follows them. [Then there will come a time when] lying becomes so widespread that a man will swear oaths [without being asked] to swear and testify [without being asked] to testify."[23]

---

19 Al-Bukhārī, *Ṣaḥīḥ*, 2654; and Muslim, *Ṣaḥīḥ*, 87.

20 Al-Tirmidhī, *Sunan*, 1972; and al-Kharāʾiṭī, *Masāwiʾ al-akhlāq*, 155.

21 Al-Kharāʾiṭī, *Masāwiʾ al-akhlāq*, 157; and al-Ḥākim al-Nīsābūrī, *al-Mustadrak*, 4:359.

22 Al-Bayhaqī, *Shuʿab al-īmān*, 2836; al-Ṭabarānī, *al-Muʿjam al-kabīr*, 7:206; and Ibn ʿAdī, *al-Kāmil*, 3:374, with similar wording. Trans.: Kohl is antimony, a chemical element used by those in the desert and hot climates for beauty and to protect their eyes from the glare of the sun. FC: The meaning suggests that Satan, through various orifices, consumes medicinal substances that vivify him. He lines his eyes with kohl, he licks the syrup with his tongue, and he snorts the snuff through his nostrils. See also *Lisan al-ʿArab* under n-sh-q, where it explains that the *ḥadīth* means that Satan seeks to enter the human being through any orifice available.

23 Al-Tirmidhī, *Sunan*, 2165.

And the Prophet ﷺ said, "Whoever relates a *ḥadīth* knowing that it is a lie, is one of the liars."[24] |

And [the Prophet] ﷺ said "Whoever relates a *ḥadīth* attributed to me knowing it to be a lie is one of the liars."[25] 484

And [the Prophet] ﷺ said, "Whoever swears an oath sinfully in order to take a Muslim's wealth without right will meet God عَزَّوَجَلَّ in His anger."[26]

And it has been related that the Prophet ﷺ refused to accept the testimony of a man because of a lie he told.[27]

And [the Prophet] ﷺ said, "Every trait of a believer can be imprinted on or folded over [that is, hidden], except betrayal and lying."[28]

And ʿĀʾisha رَضِيَ اللَّهُ عَنْهَا said,

> There was no characteristic more intense[29] for the Companions of the Messenger of God ﷺ than lying. If the Messenger of God ﷺ discovered that a man from his Companions had lied, his chest was not lightened until he knew [that the man who had lied] had made repentance to God عَزَّوَجَلَّ.[30]

Moses عَلَيْهِ السَّلَامُ said, "O Lord, who is the best of Your servants in deeds?" He [God] answered, | "The one whose tongue does not lie, whose heart does not act immorally, and whose loins do not fornicate."[31] 485

Luqmān said to his son, "O my son, beware of lying. It is tasty like the meat of a sparrow but the one who [eats it will] soon detest it."[32]

[The Prophet] ﷺ said in extolling truthfulness, "There are four [traits] that, if you have them, anything you lose [e.g., opportunities] in this world will not harm you: truthfulness in

---

24 Ibn Ḥanbal, *Musnad*, 4:252; and al-Kharāʾiṭī, *Masāwiʾ al-akhlāq*, 166.

25 Muslim relates it in the introduction to *Ṣaḥīḥ*, 1:9; and al-Kharāʾiṭī, *Masāwiʾ al-akhlāq*, 168.

26 Al-Bukhārī, *Ṣaḥīḥ*, 2357; and Muslim, *Ṣaḥīḥ*, 138.

27 Ibn Abī l-Dunyā, *al-Ṣamt wa-ādāb al-lisān*, 490.

28 Ibn Ḥanbal, *Musnad*, 5:252; and Ibn Abī l-Dunyā, *al-Ṣamt wa-ādāb al-lisān*, 475.

29 Eds.: That is, more intense for them and the people around them to bear, as their punishment will be more severe.

30 Ibn Ḥanbal, *Musnad*, 6:152; and Ibn Abī l-Dunyā, *al-Ṣamt wa-ādāb al-lisān*, 476.

31 Ibn Abī l-Dunyā, *al-Ṣamt wa-ādāb al-lisān*, 488.

32 Ibn Abī l-Dunyā, *al-Ṣamt wa-ādāb al-lisān*, 542.

speech, safeguarding trusts, good character, and virtuousness [about] food."[33]

And Abū Bakr رَضِيَ اللَّهُ عَنْهُ said in an oration after the passing of the Messenger of God صَلَّى اللَّهُ عَلَيْهِ وَسَلَّمَ, "One year ago, the Messenger of God صَلَّى اللَّهُ عَلَيْهِ وَسَلَّمَ stood among us in this place where I am standing"—and Abū Bakr began to weep—"and said, 'I enjoin on you truthfulness, for verily it [goes along] with kindness and [those with] both of them are in heaven.'"[34]

And Muʿādh said, "The Messenger of God صَلَّى اللَّهُ عَلَيْهِ وَسَلَّمَ said to me, 'I advise you to fear God, be truthful in speech, fulfill trusts, keep promises, spread [greetings of] peace, and lower the wing.'"[35] |

❁ ❁ ❁

486 As for the Traditions (*Āthār*)

ʿAlī رَضِيَ اللَّهُ عَنْهُ said, "The greatest of offenses before God عَزَّ وَجَلَّ are a lying tongue, and the worst regret will be the regret [felt] on the day of resurrection."[36]

ʿUmar b. ʿAbd al-ʿAzīz رَحِمَهُ اللَّهُ said, "I have not told a lie [lit., lied a lie] since I reached puberty."[37]

And ʿUmar رَضِيَ اللَّهُ عَنْهُ said,

> Before I saw you, the most beloved of you to me were those with the best names.[38] Then when I saw you, the most beloved

33 Ibn Ḥanbal, *Musnad*, 4:177; al-Ḥākim al-Nīsābūrī, *al-Mustadrak*, 4:314; and al-Bayhaqī, *Shuʿab al-īmān*, 4463.

34 This is part of a *ḥadīth* related by Ibn Mājah, *Sunan*, 3849; and Ibn Abī l-Dunyā, *al-Ṣamt wa-ādāb al-lisān*, 469.

35 Abū Nuʿaym, *Ḥilya*, 1:240; al-Bayhaqī, *al-Zuhd al-kabīr*, 956; and al-Khaṭīb al-Baghdādī, *Tārīkh Baghdād*, 8:434. Trans.: "Lowering the wing" is mentioned in Qurʾān 26:25 where it means showing kindness.

36 Ibn Abī l-Dunyā, *al-Ṣamt wa-ādāb al-lisān*, 481.

37 Ibn Abī l-Dunyā, *al-Ṣamt wa-ādāb al-lisān*, 486.

38 Eds.: That is, people were thought to embody the meanings of their names, or the best traits from their names; for example, *amīn* is a trustworthy person, *ṣādiq* is a truthful person, etc.

> of you to me were those with the best characteristics. And now that I have tested you, the most beloved of you to me are those [who are] most truthful in their speech and most trustworthy.[39]

Maymūn b. Abū Shabīb [related that],

> I sat down to write a letter and a word came to me which, if I had written it, would embellish my writing, but would have made me a liar. So I decided not to write it and at that very moment I heard a voice call to me from the side of the room, *God keeps firm those who believe, with the firm word* (*al-qawl al-thābit*),[40] *in worldly life and in the hereafter* [Q. 14:27].

Al-Shaʿbī said, "I do not know who will be deeper in the fire—the liar or the miser."[41] |

Ibn al-Sammāk said, "I do not see myself being recompensed 487
for giving up lying, rather I rebuffed it out of pride."[42]

It was said to Khālid b. Ṣubayḥ, "Can whoever lies just once be called corrupt?" He said, "Yes."[43]

Mālik b. Dīnār said, "I read in a certain book that there is no orator except that his oration will be compared to his deeds. If he is truthful, he will be attested to be truthful, and if he is lying, his lips will be clipped by scissors of fire, and every time they are clipped, they will grow back."[44]

Mālik b. Dīnār also said, "Truthfulness and lying battle one another in the heart until one expels the other."[45]

ʿUmar b. ʿAbd al-ʿAzīz spoke to al-Walīd b. ʿAbd al-Malik about something and [al-Walīd b. ʿAbd al-Malik] said to [ʿUmar b. ʿAbd

---

39 Ibn Abī l-Dunyā, *al-Ṣamt wa-ādāb al-lisān*, 487.

40 Ibn Abī l-Dunyā, *al-Ṣamt wa-ādāb al-lisān*, 539. Trans.: "The firm word" (*al-qawl al-thābit*) is generally explained as a reference to the testimony of faith, that is, *Lā ilāha illā Allāh, Muḥammad rasūl Allāh*.

41 Ibn Abī l-Dunyā, *al-Ṣamt wa-ādāb al-lisān*, 543.

42 Ibn Abī l-Dunyā, *al-Ṣamt wa-ādāb al-lisān*, 549.

43 Ibn Abī l-Dunyā, *al-Ṣamt wa-ādāb al-lisān*, 552.

44 Ibn Abī l-Dunyā, *al-Ṣamt wa-ādāb al-lisān*, 501; and Abū Nuʿaym, *Ḥilya*, 2:378.

45 Ibn Abī l-Dunyā, *al-Ṣamt wa-ādāb al-lisān*, 516; and Abū Nuʿaym, *Ḥilya*, 2:360.

al-ʿAzīz], "You lied." ʿUmar replied, "By God, I have not lied since I learned that lying disgraces the one [who does it]."[46] |

❁ ❁ ❁

488 The elucidation of which [kinds of] lies are permissible

Know that lying in itself is not unlawful but rather what [is unlawful is] the harm it does to the one addressed or to others. The lowest level [of its harm] is that the recipient believes something contrary to fact and is thus ignorant, and that involves harming others.

Perhaps ignorance in [the lie one was told] has a benefit and advantage, so the lying leads to that ignorance [and in this case], it is authorized and may even be mandatory.

Maymūn b. Mahrān said,

> A lie in certain circumstances is preferable to the truth. Can you imagine a situation when a man is chasing another one with a sword [to kill him], and [the one being pursued] goes inside a house [to hide], and the pursuer asks you, "Have you seen so-and-so?" What would you say? Would you not say, "I have not seen him" rather than tell the truth?

In such a case, lying is mandatory.[47]

So we say that speech is a means to an end. For every praiseworthy aim that can be achieved either by the truth or by a lie, a lie is unlawful. And if [the praiseworthy aim] can be achieved by a lie but not by the truth, then a lie is permissible if achieving that aim is permissible. And it [lying] is mandatory if that aim is mandatory, as in [the case] of [maintaining] the inviolability of the blood of a Muslim (*ʿaṣmat dam al-Muslim*), [which is] mandatory. When telling the truth would lead to spilling the blood of an individual Muslim hiding from a tyrant, then lying is mandatory, so [the tyrant's] aim of the murder (*ḥarb*) is not fulfilled. Or if reconciliation between |

46 Ibn Abī l-Dunyā, *al-Ṣamt wa-ādāb al-lisān*, 529.

47 Ibn Abī l-Dunyā, *al-Ṣamt wa-ādāb al-lisān*, 506, with wording close to this.

parties [is desired], or when the heart of an aggrieved party can only 489
be won over by means of lying, then lying is permissible. However, the greatest precaution should be taken, because if someone opens the door to lying for himself, there is a fear that he may resort to it even when there is no need, [or in cases] that fall short of the condition of necessity. [In short,] lying is essentially unlawful except for necessity.

What proves these exceptions is what was related by Umm Kulthūm, who said, "I never heard the Messenger of God ﷺ take any license in respect to lying except in three [cases]: when a man says something for the sake of reconciliation, when a man says something in war, and when a man speaks to his wife or a woman speaks to her husband."[48]

She [Umm Kulthūm] also said, "The Messenger of God ﷺ said, he is not a liar if, to reconcile two parties, he says what is good or transmits the good [someone else said]."[49]

And Asmāʾ bt. Yazīd said "The Messenger of God ﷺ said, 'Every lie will be written against the son of Adam except a person's lie to bring about reconciliation between two people.'"[50]

And it was related that Abū Kāhil said,

> Some [harsh] words had passed between two of the Companions of the Prophet ﷺ, to the point that they were estranged. So I met with one of them and said to him, "What is the matter with you and the other? I heard him speaking highly of you." Then I met the other one and said the same thing, until they reconciled. Then I said [to myself], "I tired myself
> and reconciled those two." | So I told the Prophet ﷺ 490
> about this, and he said, "O Abū Kāhil, reconcile people even if . . . " meaning, [even if] by lying.[51]

48 Muslim, *Ṣaḥīḥ*, 2605. Umm Kulthūm رضي الله عنها was the daughter of ʿUqba b. Abū Muʿīṭ and one of the wives of the Prophet. Trans.: That is, to engender love between them. See the *ḥadīth* narrated by al-Nawwās below.

49 Al-Bukhārī, *Ṣaḥīḥ*, 2692; and Muslim, *Ṣaḥīḥ*, 2605.

50 Al-Tirmidhī, *Sunan*, 1939.

51 Al-Ṭabarānī, *al-Muʿjam al-kabīr*, 18:361, ending with the words, "O Abū Kāhil, reconcile people even with this or that" (*bi-kadhā wa-kadhā*).

ʿAṭāʾ b. Yasār said, "A man asked the Prophet صلى الله عليه وسلم, 'May I lie to my family?' He said, 'There is no goodness in lying.' [The man] said, 'I promise her and say [things] to her.'[52] He said, [in that case], 'you are not to blame.'"[53]

It was related that during the caliphate of ʿUmar رضي الله عنه, the women whom Ibn Abī ʿUzra al-Duʾālī married [used to] divorce him [by *khalʿ*].[54] This fact spread quickly among people and he deplored it when he learned about it. So [Ibn Abī ʿUzra al-Duʾālī] brought ʿAbdallāh b. al-Arqam to his house, invited him in, and then [Ibn Abī ʿUzra al-Duʾālī] said to his wife,

> Tell me, by God: do you loathe me?
>
> She said, "Do not make me swear [by God]."
>
> He said, "Truly, I am asking you by God."
>
> She said, "Yes."
>
> Then [Ibn Abī ʿUzra al-Duʾālī] said to Ibn al-Arqam, "Did you hear?"
>
> Then they continued until they came to ʿUmar رضي الله عنه. And [Ibn Abī ʿUzra] said, you say that I oppress women and they divorce me [by *khalʿ*]. So ask Ibn al-Arqam. Then [ʿUmar] asked [Ibn al-Arqam]. Then [Ibn al-Arqam] replied. [Ibn al-Arqam] informed [ʿUmar of what had been said], and [ʿUmar] sent for the wife of Ibn Abī ʿUzra. She came to him along with her paternal aunt, and [ʿUmar] said to her, "Are you the one who is saying to her husband that you loathe him?"
>
> She answered, "I am the first to turn in repentance and return to the command of God تعالى, but he asked me to swear by God and I could not bring myself to lie. Should I lie, O Commander of the Faithful?"
>
> 491 He said, "Yes, lie. If there is one of you women who | does not love one of us [men], do not say that to him. It is rare to

---

52 Eds.: This does not refer to promises he cannot keep, or does not plan to keep; rather, this refers to kind words between spouses.

53 Mālik, *al-Muwaṭṭaʾ*, 2:989; and Ibn ʿAbd al-Barr, *al-Tamhīd*, 16:247. Eds.: The phrase, *lā jināḥ ʿalayka* (lit., there is no sin or misdemeanor against you), means it will not be held against you.

54 Eds.: *Khalʿ* is divorce intiated by the wife.

> find a house built on love, but people live with one another by Islam and goodness."[55]

From al-Nawwās b. Samʿān al-Kilābī [we learned] that the Messenger of God صَلَّىٱللَّهُعَلَيْهِوَسَلَّمَ said,

> Why do I see you attracted to lying like moths are attracted to fire? Every lie is certainly written as a lie, except a lie by a man during war—for war is deception—or between two men at odds, to reconcile them, or what a man says to his wife to please her.[56]

Thawbān said, "All lying is a sin except what benefits a Muslim or shields him from harm."[57]

And ʿAlī رَضِيَٱللَّهُعَنْهُ said, "When I relate something the Messenger of God صَلَّىٱللَّهُعَلَيْهِوَسَلَّمَ said, I would rather fall from the sky than lie about him. But if I relate something that is between me and you, [know that] war is deception."[58]

These three [cases] clearly convey the exceptions [to the unlawfulness of lying] and their meaning includes anything with a sound purpose for the one [who tells the lie] or for the other [he may be protecting].

As for what [concerns] him [personally], for example, if a tyrant were to seize him and ask about [the location or existence
of] his wealth, he may deny it, or if | the sultan were to seize him 492
and ask him whether he had committed an obscene [act] that was between him and God تَعَالَىٰ [that is, that no one knows about], he may deny it and say, "I did not [commit] *zinā* and I did not steal." The Messenger صَلَّىٱللَّهُعَلَيْهِوَسَلَّمَ said, "Whoever commits any of these [moral] defilements should seek the protection of God's veiling,"[59] because disclosing an obscene [act] is [in itself] another obscene [act]. So a

---

55 Al-Kharāʾiṭī, *Masāwiʾ al-akhlāq*, 186. Eds.: Note that this was ʿUmar's view—not a legal reason for lying to one's spouse. He may have had firsthand knowledge of the couple and their situation, and thus given his opinion based on that. Al-Ghazālī is clear that lying should be avoided except in the rare cases he outlines.

56 Al-Kharāʾiṭī, *Masāwiʾ al-akhlāq*, 162.

57 Al-Bazzār, *Musnad al-Bazzār*, 4162.

58 Al-Bukhārī, *Ṣaḥīḥ*, 3611; and Muslim, *Ṣaḥīḥ*, 1066.

59 Mālik, *al-Muwaṭṭaʾ*, 2:825; and al-Ḥākim al-Nīsābūrī, *al-Mustadrak*, 4:383.

man should protect his life and wealth that [a tyrant] seizes unjustly and [protect] his honor verbally, even if [he must] lie.

As for the interests of others, if he is asked about his brother's secret, he may deny it; and if he [lies] to reconcile two people; or if in reconciling co-wives among his women, he assures each of them that she is his most beloved; or if his wife does not obey him unless he [makes a] promise to her that he cannot fulfill and he promises her [something] to please her heart; or if he [makes an] excuse to a person and that person's heart will not be pleased unless he denies a transgression and flatters [him, that is, that person] intensely—there is nothing wrong with any of that.

But the defining [principle] in this is that lying is hazardous. If one told the truth in these [hypothetical] situations, it would engender [something] hazardous. So one must compare one to the other and weigh them with a balanced scale. If one knows that the hazardous [thing] that results from [telling] the truth is a worse occurrence [or offense] in the law (*sharᶜ*) than lying, then he should lie, and if the [hazardous thing] intended in telling the truth [results in] an intended [hazard] that is a lesser [offense in the law], then he must be truthful.[60] And if, in comparing the two matters he is unable to decide, then it is preferable for him to incline toward truthfulness because lying is permissible by necessity or great need, but if he has doubt about whether those conditions [of necessity] exist, then the principle is that [lying] is unlawful and he should return to that [principle]. |

493 Because of the ambiguity of discerning the levels of the aims [for lying], a person must guard against lying as much as possible. So, whenever he has a need, it is preferable for him to leave his interests, and forgo lying [to achieve them].

But as for someone else's interest, it is not allowable to waive the right of another and harm [them] by it.

60 Eds.: That is, in principle, lying is hazardous. Al-Ghazālī also presents a principle of doing the least amount of harm possible. With regard to the hypothetical examples mentioned in the previous two paragraphs, if one is truthful and it will result in a greater harm than if one lied, in those circumstances, one must lie; however, if the opposite is the case and being truthful results in a lesser harm than lying, then one must be truthful.

Most of the lies of people, however, are for their own personal share and to increase [their] wealth and fame, and for cases [in which] losing [an opportunity] is not hazardous. Such as [in the case of] a woman who bragged about her husband by lying in order to make another wife jealous. This is unlawful.

Asmāʾ رَضِيَٱللَّهُعَنْهَا said,

> I heard a woman ask the Messenger of God صَلَّىٱللَّهُعَلَيْهِوَسَلَّمَ, and she said, "I have a co-wife and I [say] that my husband does a lot [when in fact] he does not do [these things], in order to annoy her. Am I doing something [wrong]?"[61]
>
> [The Prophet] صَلَّىٱللَّهُعَلَيْهِوَسَلَّمَ said, "The one [who pretends to be full] of what he was not given is like [one] wearing two garments of duplicity."[62]

And [the Prophet] صَلَّىٱللَّهُعَلَيْهِوَسَلَّمَ said, "Whoever claims to have eaten what he was not [given] to eat, who says, 'I have [this and that]' and he has not, and 'I was given [this and that]' and he was not, will be like someone wearing two garments of duplicity on the day of resurrection."[63]

Included here is the case of a scholar who gives a legal ruling (*fatwā*) about [something] he has not verified (*taḥaqqa*), or relates a *ḥadīth* that | he has not affirmed and his interest is to display his 494
own excellence and he is unwilling to say, "I do not know." This is unlawful.[64]

And as for what concerns girls [lit., "little women"], if a girl will not go to school unless she is falsely promised or threatened, that is permissible.[65]

---

61 Eds.: Lit., is there something against me (that is, a sin) in this.

62 Al-Bukhārī, *Ṣaḥīḥ*, 5219; and Muslim, *Ṣaḥīḥ*, 2129. Asmāʾ was the daughter of Abū Bakr al-Ṣiddīq رَضِيَٱللَّهُعَنْهُ.

63 Al-ʿIrāqī said, "I did not find (this saying) with these words." Al-Zabīdī, *Itḥāf*, 7:526. Abū Nuʿaym, *Ḥilya*, 6:147, from a *ḥadīth* of Jābir رَضِيَٱللَّهُعَنْهُ which says, "He who falsely adorns himself is like someone wearing two garments of falsehood."

64 On the authority of al-Ḥasan, he said: "He who embellishes himself before people by way of something that God knows is untrue will be humiliated by God." Al-Bayhaqī, *Shuʿab al-īmān*, 6547

65 Eds.: The fact that al-Ghazālī includes an example in which he specifically uses the word girls, or "little women," in relation to persuading them to go to school,

True, we have related reports that [permissible] lies will be written [in the book of deeds]. Indeed, a permissible lie is also written and reckoned against [the one who tells it] and he will be asked to show whether his intention in telling it was sound, then be pardoned for it. [Lying] was made permissible for the goal of reconciliation, but may also involve him in great delusion [or danger] since his motivation in doing so may be his own personal share and interests that he has no need of, while outwardly it may appear to be for reconciliation. For that reason, it is recorded [as a lie].

And anyone who tells a lie falls into the dangers [associated with] independent judgment (*ijtihād*) that [involves] determining whether, in respect to the law (*sharᶜ*), his aim in lying is more important than being truthful. Since such [a determination] is extremely obscure, the prudent [choice] is to avoid [lying], except in a situation where it becomes mandatory and not allowable to avoid, such as when [the truth] may lead to spilling blood or the commission of some other disobedience. |

495 Some of those without firm knowledge thought that it is allowable to fabricate *ḥadīth*s on the merits of certain practices (*faḍāʾil ᶜamāl*) or the severity of [certain] disobediences; and they claim that their aim is valid. But this is a absolutely incorrect, for [the Prophet] صَلَّى ٱللَّهُ عَلَيْهِ وَسَلَّمَ said, "Whoever intentionally lies about me has prepared his place in the fire."[66] No one would commit [such a sin] except out of necessity, and [in fact] there is no necessity here, since there is enough leeway in the truth to avoid lying. What has been conveyed in the verses and reports suffices over [the fabricated *ḥadīth*s].

As for someone who says, "These [*ḥadīth*s] have been repeated so often that they have ceased to have any effect, something new will have a greater effect," this is madness. It is not a reason to lie concerning God تَعَالَىٰ and the Messenger of God صَلَّى ٱللَّهُ عَلَيْهِ وَسَلَّمَ, and it leads [one] to open a door that confuses (*tashawwish*) the law (*sharīᶜa*). Certainly, the good it may contain does not outweigh its evil, for a lie concerning the Messenger of God صَلَّى ٱللَّهُ عَلَيْهِ وَسَلَّمَ is one

---

illustrates that in his time, girls went to school and it was so important that there was a discussion of persuading them to go.

66 Al-Bukhārī, *Ṣaḥīḥ*, 110; and Muslim, *Ṣaḥīḥ*, 3.

of the major [sins] that nothing outweighs. We ask God's pardon for ourselves and for all Muslims. |

❁ ❁ ❁

The elucidation of [using] precaution (*ḥadhir*) [against] lying by allusion (*bi-l-maᶜārīḍ*)[67] 496

The Predecessors (Salaf) said allusive [speech] gives [one] freedom to choose (*mandūḥ*)[68] [another word or phrase] instead of lying.

ᶜUmar رَضِيَ ٱللَّهُ عَنْهُ said, "Allusion is sufficient [to enable] a man not to lie." This has been related by Ibn ᶜAbbās and others.[69]

And what [the Salaf] meant by that is [that allusion is permissible] when a person is compelled to lie. But if there is no need or necessity, neither allusive [speech] nor explicit [lying] is allowable, but [using] allusive [speech] is the lesser [of two evils].

An example of allusive [speech] was narrated about Muṭarrif, who kept Ziyād waiting and when he [Muṭarrif] entered [the room] he blamed it on illness, saying, "I have not raised myself [from my bed] since I last saw the *amīr* except for when God raised me."[70]

And Ibrāhīm said, "If something about you reaches a man and you deplore lying, say, 'Verily, God تَعَالَىٰ knows that I did not (*mā*) say anything like that.' [Your] saying *mā*, | [is heard as] a particle 497
of negation by [the addressee, but is intended by the speaker] as ambiguity."[71]

---

67 "*Maᶜārīḍ*, the plural of *miᶜrāḍ*, refers to a phrase that may be understood by the one who hears it in a way that differs from what the speaker means." Al-Zabīdī, *Itḥāf*, 7:528. Trans.: Al-Zabīdī, *Itḥāf* also states that this notion is based on the verse: *There is no blame upon you for that to which you* [*indirectly*] *allude* (*mā ᶜaraḍtum*) *concerning a proposal to women or for what you conceal within yourselves* [Q. 2:235].

68 Al-Zabīdī, *Itḥāf*, 7:528. Eds.: Here we have translated *mandūḥ* according to al-Zabīdī's definition.

69 Al-Bukhārī, *al-Adab al-mufrad*, 884; and al-Bayhaqī, *al-Sunan al-kubrā*, 10:199.

70 Ibn Saᶜd, *Ṭabaqāt*, 9:144.

71 Ibn al-Jawzī, *al-Adhkīyāʾ*, 71. Trans.: The saying in Arabic, *Allāh yaᶜlam mā qultuhu*, may be understood by the listener as "God knows I did not say it," or "God knows

Muʿādh b. Jabal was a governor for ʿUmar رَضِيَ ٱللَّهُ عَنْهُمَا, and when he returned, his wife said to him, "What did you bring me from what governors are given as gifts for their families?"

> He had not brought anything for her, and said [as an excuse], "There was an observer (*ḍāghiṭ*) with me."
>
> She said, "You were a trustee of the Messenger of God صَلَّى ٱللَّهُ عَلَيْهِ وَسَلَّمَ and of Abū Bakr رَضِيَ ٱللَّهُ عَنْهُ, and ʿUmar sent with you an observer!?" Then she spread this to her women [companions], and she complained about ʿUmar, and when [her complaint] reached [ʿUmar], he summoned Muʿādh and said,
>
> "Did I send an observer with you?"
>
> He said, "I found no other excuse to tell her except that."
>
> ʿUmar رَضِيَ ٱللَّهُ عَنْهُ laughed and then gave him something and said, "Make her content with this!"
>
> His statement, *ḍāghiṭ* means observer, and [by this Muʿādh] meant his Lord عَزَّ وَجَلَّ.[72]

Al-Nakhāʿī did not use to say to his daughter, "I will buy you sweets." Rather, he would say, "I will see if I [can] buy you sweets." Because perhaps he would not fulfill that.

And when Ibrāhīm was sought at home by someone whom he
498 deplored going out to see, he would say | to his maidservant, "Tell him 'ask for him in the mosque,' but do not say, 'He is not here,'" so it is not a lie.

When al-Shaʿbī was sought at home by someone whom he deplored, he would draw a circle and tell his maidservant, "Put your finger in it [that is, in the circle] and say [to him], 'He is not here.'"

All this concerns situations [in which there is] some need [not to tell the exact truth]. If [there is] no [need], then no [do not do it], because this is understood to be a lie.

Even if the statement is not a lie, it is nonetheless generally reprehensible. Similarly, it was related that ʿAbdallāh b. ʿUtbah said,

---

what I said." Al-Zabīdī, *Itḥāf*, 7:529.

72 Al-Kharāʾiṭī, *Masāwiʾ al-akhlāq*, 178. Trans.: One of the divine names is al-Raqīb, the One who watches over. Eds.: See Lane, *An Arabic-English Lexicon*, 1794 (under ḍ-gh-ṭ).

> My father and I went to see ʿUmar b. ʿAbd al-ʿAzīz رَحِمَهُ ٱللَّهُ, and when we came out, I was wearing a garment and people began to ask, "Is this what the Commander of the Faithful put on you [as a gift of honor]?"
>
> And I used to say, "May God reward with goodness the Commander of the Faithful!"
>
> My father then said to me, "O my son, beware of lying! Stay clear of lies! and what is similar to it. [His father] forbade him from that [type of lie] because it confirms false suppositions for the sake of boasting (*mufākhura*), and this is an invalid reason, without benefit.

True, allusive (*maʿāriḍ*) [speech] is permissible for light-hearted purposes like delighting the heart of another in joking, as when [the Prophet] صَلَّىٰ ٱللَّهُ عَلَيْهِ وَسَلَّمَ said, "No old women enter heaven," | or 499
like his saying to the other, "Your husband is the one with white in his eye," or to another, "We are going to mount you on a son of a camel," and the like.

As for explicit lying, like what Nuʿaymān al-Anṣārī did with ʿUthmān in the story of the blind man, when he [Nuʿaymān] said to him [the blind man], "It is Nuʿaymān."[73] Or what people regularly [say] to tease simpleminded [people], when they deceive [them, saying] that a woman desires to marry [them]; [such lying] contains harm and can injure the heart, and it is unlawful. And if it [such lying] is only in jest, then the one who does it cannot be characterized as sinful, although it diminishes his degree of faith, [for] the Messenger of God صَلَّىٰ ٱللَّهُ عَلَيْهِ وَسَلَّمَ said, "A servant does not have complete faith until he loves for his brother what he loves | for himself and until 500
he stays clear of lying, [even] in jest."[74]

73 Ibn ʿAbd al-Barr recounts a mean trick that Nuʿaymān played on Makhrama b. Nawfal, an elderly man who was blind, which resulted in Makhrama mistakenly striking ʿUthmān with his cane, thinking he was Nuʿaymān. Ibn ʿAbd al-Barr, *al-Istīʿāb*, 734.

74 This part of the *ḥadīth*, "A servant does not have complete faith until he loves for his brother what he loves for himself," was related by Ibn ʿAbd al-Barr, *al-Istīʿāb*, 859, and with similar words is found in al-Bukhārī, *Ṣaḥīḥ*, 13; Muslim, *Ṣaḥīḥ*, 45; and Ibn Ḥanbal, *Musnad*, 2:352.

And as for [the Prophet's] صَلَّىٱللَّهُعَلَيْهِوَسَلَّمَ saying "A man may say something for the sake of making people laugh, and it casts him deeper into hell than the distance to the Pleiades,"[75] what is meant here is backbiting a Muslim or injuring [someone's] heart, not purely a joke.

Among the lies that are not necessarily [considered] sinful are those that commonly occur in exaggeration, such as one who says, "I looked for you such-and-such number of times," or "I told you so a hundred times!" Here, the intention is not to make clear the number of times but rather to convey an exaggeration. If he looked for him [only] once, he is a liar; and if he looked for him an unusually high number of times, he did not sin [even] if it was not [exactly] one hundred [times], and between these two [scenarios], he who lets loose his tongue in exaggeration exposes [himself] to degrees of danger [associated with] lying.

Among what commonly [involves] lying but which are taken lightly, are [for example], when it is said, "Eat the food!" and he says, "I do not desire it." That is forbidden and unlawful when there is no valid purpose [behind it]. Mujāhid said, |

> 501 Asmāʾ bt. ʿUmays, said, "I was the companion of ʿĀʾisha رَضِيَٱللَّهُعَنْهَا | on the night the other women and I were preparing her and brought her in to Prophet's صَلَّىٱللَّهُعَلَيْهِوَسَلَّمَ [quarters]. And by God, we did not find anything to offer as food except a bowl of milk. He [the Prophet] drank from it and then passed it to ʿĀʾisha رَضِيَٱللَّهُعَنْهَا." She [the narrator] said [ʿĀʾisha] was shy [to drink]. Then [the narrator] said, I said [to her], "Do not refuse [something coming from] the hand of the Messenger of God صَلَّىٱللَّهُعَلَيْهِوَسَلَّمَ. Take some of it [from him]." So she took it shyly and drank from it.
>
> Then he said, "Pass it to your companions,"
>
> and they [رَضِيَٱللَّهُعَنْهُنَّ] said, "We do not desire it."
>
> He said, "Do not combine hunger and lying."

75 Ibn al-Mubārak, *Zuhd*, 948; Ibn Abī l-Dunyā, *al-Ṣamt wa-ādāb al-lisān*, 71; al-Bukhārī, *Ṣaḥīḥ*, 6477; and Muslim, *Ṣaḥīḥ*, 2988.

> [The narrator] said, I said, "O Messenger of God, if one of us says about something we desire, 'I do not desire it,' is that counted as a lie?"
>
> He said, "The lie is written as a lie and even a small lie is [written as] a small lie."[76]

The people of scrupulousness (*ahl al-waraᶜ*) were cautious about excusing this kind of lie. Al-Layth b. Saᶜd said, "Saᶜīd b. al-Musayyib had cloudy eyes that started secreting [fluid] outside his eyes. It was said to him, 'Wipe away this cloudiness [from your eyes].' He said, 'What about the doctor [who] told me "do not touch your eyes."' So I said to him 'I will not do [that].'"[77] |

Such is the vigilance of the people of scrupulousness. And 502
[for] those that abandon [this scrupulousness], their tongues will be unleashed in lies beyond the limit of their choices and will lie without realizing it.

Jawwāb al-Taymī said,

> The sister of al-Rabīᶜ b. Khuthaym visited one of his children [who was] sick. She sat down next to him and said, "How are you, O my son?"
>
> Al-Rabīᶜ sat and said, "Did you nurse him?"
>
> She said, "No."
>
> He said, "Then why not just say, 'O my son of my brother [that is, my nephew]?' and you would be truthful?"[78]

It is also common to say, "God knows . . ." about what one does not know. Jesus عَلَيْهِ ٱلسَّلَامُ said, "One of the greatest transgressions

---

76 Ibn Ḥanbal, *Musnad*, 6:438; and Ibn Abī l-Dunyā, *al-Ṣamt wa-ādāb al-lisān*, 524. Al-Haythamī said in *Majmaᶜ al-zawāʾid*, 4:54, "This was related by Aḥmad [b. Ḥanbal] and also by al-Ṭabarānī in *al-Muᶜjam al-kabīr* (with reliable narrators) except that Asmāʾ bt. ᶜUmays was in Ethiopia with her husband Jaᶜfar when the Prophet صَلَّى ٱللَّهُ عَلَيْهِ وَسَلَّمَ wed ᶜĀʾisha, so the correct name would be Asmāʾ bt. Yazīd. And God knows best." This is how it was reported by Ibn Mājah, *Sunan*, 3298, but without the details of the story. Eds.: The narration indicates that they should use a word or phrase other than "I do not desire it" (because they did desire it), or they could be silent.

77 Ibn Abī l-Dunyā, *al-Ṣamt wa-ādāb al-lisān*, 511.

78 Ibn Abī l-Dunyā, *al-Ṣamt wa-ādāb al-lisān*, 533.

against God is for the servant to say, 'Verily, God knows . . .' about what cannot be known.'"[79]

Perhaps [a person] lies in recounting a dream and that is a great sin, for [the Prophet] صَلَّى ٱللَّٰهُ عَلَيْهِ وَسَلَّمَ said, "Among the greatest of falsehoods is for a man to claim [descent] from someone other than his father, to claim he was shown something in a dream that he was not, or to attribute to me what I did not say."[80]

And [the Prophet] صَلَّى ٱللَّٰهُ عَلَيْهِ وَسَلَّمَ said, "Whoever lies about a dream will be charged on the day of resurrection with tying together two strands of hair [or, two pieces of oat] and he will never [be able to] tie the two together."[81]

79 Ibn Abī l-Dunyā, *al-Ṣamt wa-ādāb al-lisān*, 727. Eds.: That is, the transgression arises if one does not know something and does not want to say "I do not know" out of pride or arrogance, and says instead "God knows."

80 Al-Bukhārī, *Ṣaḥīḥ*, 3509.

81 Al-Bukhārī, *Ṣaḥīḥ*, 7042; and Abū Dāwūd, *Sunan*, 5024.

[15]

The Fifteenth Bane: Backbiting (*Ghība*) 503

THE examination of backbiting (*ghība*) is lengthy. Let us first mention the censure of backbiting and what has been related about it in [textual] evidence from the law (*sharʿ*).

God سُبْحَانَهُ specified its censure in His book and likened the one who does this to someone who eats carrion.

[God] تَعَالَىٰ said, *And do not backbite each other. Would one of you like to eat the flesh of his brother when dead? You would detest it* [Q. 49:12].

And [the Prophet] صَلَّى ٱللَّهُ عَلَيْهِ وَسَلَّمَ said, "All of the Muslim is unlawful to [another] Muslim, [this includes] his life [lit., blood], his wealth, and his reputation,"[1] and backbiting is part of reputation, which God has grouped with life (blood) and wealth.

Abū Hurayra said, "The Messenger of God صَلَّى ٱللَّهُ عَلَيْهِ وَسَلَّمَ said, 'Do not envy one another, do not hate one another, do not deceive (*tanājjush*) one another,[2] do not turn your backs on one another, do not backbite one another, and be worshipers of God in brotherhood.'"[3]

[We learned] from Jābir and Abū Saʿīd, [who] said, "The Messenger of God صَلَّى ٱللَّهُ عَلَيْهِ وَسَلَّمَ said, 'Beware of backbiting. For backbiting is worse than [committing] *zinā*, [indeed] for a man may [commit] *zinā* and then repent and God سُبْحَانَهُ will forgive him. But the one

---

1 Muslim, *Ṣaḥīḥ*, 2564.

2 [FC] Lane (*An Arabic-English Lexicon*, 2771, under n-j-sh), refers specifically to this *ḥadīth*, and defines *tanājjush* as bidding one against another, successively increasing their offers, in a sale, or other case.

3 Ibn Abī l-Dunyā, *al-Ṣamt wa-ādāb al-lisān*, 163.

who backbites is not forgiven until his companion [that is, victim] forgives him.'"[4] |

504 Anas said, "The Messenger of God ﷺ said, 'On the night journey, I passed by people scratching their faces with their fingernails. I said, "O Gabriel, who are these [people]?" He answered, "These people are the backbiters and the ones who attack the reputations of others."'"[5]

Sulaym b. Jābir said,

> I came to the Messenger of God ﷺ and said, "Teach me something virtuous that will benefit me before/with God." He said, "Do not underestimate the value of a charitable deed, even if it is just to pour [some water] from your pail into the cup of a thirsty person, or meet your [Muslim] brother with a cheerful face, and when he turns his back [to leave], do not backbite him."[6]

Al-Barāʾ [b. ʿĀzib b. al-Ḥārith] said,

> The Messenger of God ﷺ orated to us [loudly enough] so that even young girls in their homes heard. He said, "O you who say you are believers with your tongues but do not believe with your hearts, do not backbite [your fellow] Muslims; nor probe their faults, for verily, whoever probes the faults of his [Muslim] brother, God [in turn] probes his faults; and he whose faults God probes will be exposed in the sanctum of his [own] house."[7]

It was said that God تعالى revealed to Moses عليه السلام, "Whoever dies repenting from backbiting will be the last one to enter heaven, and whoever dies persisting in it [backbiting] will be the first to enter the fire."[8] |

4 Ibn Abī l-Dunyā, *al-Ṣamt wa-ādāb al-lisān*, 164.
5 Abū Dāwūd, *Sunan*, 4878; and Ibn Abī l-Dunyā, *al-Ṣamt wa-ādāb al-lisān*, 165.
6 Ibn Abī l-Dunyā, *al-Ṣamt wa-ādāb al-lisān*, 166.
7 Ibn Abī l-Dunyā, *al-Ṣamt wa-ādāb al-lisān*, 167; and Abū Dāwūd, *Sunan*, 4880.
8 Al-Qushayrī, *al-Risāla*, 284.

Anas said, 505

> The Messenger of God ﷺ ordered people to fast one day, saying, "And let no one break his fast until I give him permission."
>
> So the people fasted. Then when evening fell a man came [to him] and said, "O Messenger of God, I fasted. Give me permission to break my fast."
>
> He gave him permission, then another man [came], and another and another [with the same request], and then a man came who said, "O Messenger of God, [there are] two young women from your family who remained fasting [all day], but are too shy to come to you. So give them permission to break their fasts."
>
> [The Prophet] ﷺ turned away from him, so he repeated what he had asked, and [the Prophet] again turned away from him. He repeated his request yet again, and [the Prophet ﷺ] said, "They have not fasted. How could they have fasted when they spent the day eating the flesh of other people? Go back to them and order them, if they were fasting, [to force themselves] to vomit."
>
> So he returned to them and told them what [the Prophet had said] and when they forced themselves to vomit, each of them vomited up a clot of blood. Then [the man] returned to the Prophet ﷺ and told him [what happened], and he [ﷺ] said, "By the One in whose Hand is Muḥammad's soul,[9] if it had remained in their stomachs, the fire would have consumed them [both]."[10]

And [another] narration [of this *ḥadīth*] states that when [the Prophet ﷺ] first turned away from him, he returned and said,

> "O Messenger of God, by God, they died or are on the brink of death!"

---

9 Eds.: Here the Prophet is swearing by God, and speaking about himself in the third person.

10 Ibn Abī l-Dunyā, *al-Ṣamt wa-ādāb al-lisān*, 170.

The Prophet ﷺ said, "Bring them to me," and they came to him and then he asked for a bowl to be brought, and said to one of them, "Vomit," and she vomited enough pus, blood, and [other] matter to fill the bowl. Then he said to the other, "Vomit" and she vomited the same. Then he said [to the people], "These two fasted from what God made lawful for them, but broke their fasts with what God made unlawful for them because one sat next to the other and they began eating people's flesh."[11] |

506 Anas said,

The Messenger of God ﷺ [gave] an oration to us and mentioned usury and how serious [a sin] it was. He said, "The [single] dirham that a man gets from usury is a greater offense before God than his [committing] *zinā* thirty-six times, but [attacking] the reputation of a Muslim is an even greater [offense] than usury."[12]

Jābir said,

We were with the Messenger of God ﷺ on a march and we came to two graves whose occupants were being punished [in their graves]. He said, "These two are being punished, but not for major [sins]. One them used to backbite people and the other did not clean himself after urination." Then he asked that one or two green palm fronds be brought; he broke them into two [pieces] and asked that a piece of each be planted on the graves and said, "Would that their punishments be lessened for as long as these fronds remain green (or "for as long as they do not dry up")."[13]

When the Messenger of God ﷺ [ordered that] Maʿza be stoned for adultery (*zinā*), a man said to his companion,

---

11 Ibn Ḥanbal, *Musnad*, 5:431; and Ibn Abī l-Dunyā, *al-Ṣamt wa-ādāb al-lisān*, 171. Eds.: The physical manifestation of pus is considered one of the miracles of the Prophet ﷺ.

12 Ibn Abī l-Dunyā, *al-Ṣamt wa-ādāb al-lisān*, 175.

13 Al-Bukhārī, *al-Adab al-mufrad*, 735; Ibn Abī l-Dunyā, *al-Ṣamt wa-ādāb al-lisān*, 176; al-Bukhārī, *Ṣaḥīḥ*, 216; and Muslim, *Ṣaḥīḥ*, 292.

"This [one] died quickly like a dog dies!"[14] Later, they passed a corpse and [the Prophet] صَلَّى ٱللَّهُ عَلَيْهِ وَسَلَّمَ said, "Take a bite of it!"

They said, "O Messenger of God, are we to take a bite out of a corpse?"

He said, "What you gained from your brother is more foul than this."[15] |

The Companions رَضِيَ ٱللَّهُ عَنْهُمْ met one another cheerfully and did not 507
backbite someone who was absent. They considered that the most excellent of deeds and saw its contrary as the habit of hypocrites.

Abū Hurayra said, "Whoever eats the flesh of his brother in this world will have that flesh offered to him in the hereafter and it will be said to him, 'Eat it dead as you ate it living.' And so he will eat it [while] wailing and frowning."[16] And it was narrated as *marfuʿ* [as the statement of the Prophet].

And it was related that two men were sitting at the door of the mosque and there passed by them a man who had been [at one time] effeminate but who had given that up. They said, "There is still something of it [effeminate] in him." Then the *iqāma* of the prayer was [called], so they entered and prayed with the people, but what they said stayed in themselves (*anfus*). So [afterward] they went to ʿAṭāʾ and asked him [about it] and he ordered them to repeat the ablution and the prayer, and commanded them, if they were fasting, to make up the fast of that day.[17]

[We learned that] Mujāhid said [about the words of God] *Woe to every scorner and mocker* [104:1], "The scorner (*humaza*) is one who attacks people['s honor] and the mocker (*lumaza*) is one who eats people's flesh."[18]

And Qatāda said, "It was mentioned to us that the punishment of the grave comes from three things: one-third from backbiting, |

---

14 Eds.: That is, a death without honor (Lane, *An Arabic-English Lexicon*, 2549).

15 Al-Ṭayālisī, *Musnad*, 2473; Abū Dāwūd, *Sunan*, 4428; and al-Nasāʾī, *Kitāb al-sunan al-kubrā*, 7128.

16 Ibn Abī l-Dunyā, *al-Ṣamt wa-ādāb al-lisān*, 178. Trans.: ʿAṭāʾ b. Abī Rabāḥ (d. 114/732) was the *muftī* of Mecca at that time.

17 Ibn Abī l-Dunyā, *al-Ṣamt wa-ādāb al-lisān*, 181.

18 Ibn Abī l-Dunyā, *al-Ṣamt wa-ādāb al-lisān*, 185.

508 one-third from [not cleaning after] urination, and one-third from gossip."[19]

Ḥasan said, "By God, backbiting [destroys] the *dīn* of the believer more quickly than gangrene eats away his body."[20]

One of them said, "We met some of the Predecessors (Salaf) and they did not see worship as fasting and praying but rather in abstaining from [speaking about] the reputations of others."[21]

Ibn ʿAbbās said, "When you want to mention the defects of your companion, mention your own defects [instead]."[22]

Abū Hurayra said, "One of you sees the speck of dust in your brother's eye and does not see the tree branch in his own eye."[23]

And Ḥasan used to say,

> Son of Adam, you will not attain true faith until you stop blaming others for a defect that you have and start correcting
> 509 that defect | in yourself. When you do that, your concern will be [completely] with your own defect. The most beloved servants of God are the ones [with such a disposition].[24]

Mālik b. Dīnār said, "Jesus عَلَيْهِ السَّلَام and his disciples passed by the corpse of a dog. The disciples said, 'How foul is the stench of this dog!' And Jesus عَلَيْهِ السَّلَام said, 'How brilliantly white are its teeth!'"[25] It was as if he عَلَيْهِ السَّلَام was forbidding them from backbiting the dog and reminding them not to mention any of the creation of God except by what is best [in its description].

ʿAlī b. Ḥusayn heard one man backbiting another and said to him, "Beware of backbiting, for it is a [savory] sauce for the hounds among people."[26]

---

19 Ibn Abī l-Dunyā, *al-Ṣamt wa-ādāb al-lisān*, 190.
20 Ibn Abī l-Dunyā, *al-Ṣamt wa-ādāb al-lisān*, 192.
21 Ibn Abī l-Dunyā, *al-Ṣamt wa-ādāb al-lisān*, 193.
22 Ibn Abī l-Dunyā, *al-Ṣamt wa-ādāb al-lisān*, 194.
23 Ibn Abī l-Dunyā, *al-Ṣamt wa-ādāb al-lisān*, 195.
24 Ibn Abī l-Dunyā, *al-Ṣamt wa-ādāb al-lisān*, 198.
25 Ibn Abī l-Dunyā, *al-Ṣamt wa-ādāb al-lisān*, 297.
26 Ibn Abī l-Dunyā, *al-Ṣamt wa-ādāb al-lisān*, 299.

And ʿUmar رَضِيَ اللَّهُ عَنْهُ said, "I enjoin on you the remembrance of God تَعَالَى, for verily, it is a cure. And I caution you against the mention of people, for verily, it is a malady."[27]

We ask God for His goodly accord in obeying Him. |

❁ ❁ ❁

An elucidation of the meaning of backbiting (*ghība*) and its definitions 510

Know that the definition of backbiting is speaking about your brother in a way that he would deplore if it were to reach him, whether it be about something lacking in his physical [appearance], or his lineage, his character, his deeds, his speech, his *dīn*, his worldly affairs—even his clothes, his house, or his mount.

As for his physical [appearance], this might be your mentioning [that he has] a watery eye, is cross-eyed, [that he is] bald, short, tall, black, or pale [lit., yellow], all descriptions imaginable that he would deplore, regardless of what it is.

As for lineage, [it is like] saying someone's father was Nabatean, or Indian, or corrupt, or mean, or a cobbler, or a trash collector, or whatever else someone might deplore, regardless of what it is.

As for character, if you say that he has a wicked character, is a miser, or arrogant, or argumentative, quick to anger [lit., has a tremendous anger], [is] cowardly, weak, faint-hearted, rash, or something similar.

And as for his actions regarding the *dīn*, [it is] saying [he is] a thief, or a liar, or [one who] drinks intoxicants, or a traitor, or an oppressor, or [someone who takes] the prayer and *zakāt* lightly, or [who] does not bow and prostrate correctly, or [who] is not careful about avoiding impurities, or is not kind to his parents, or does not pay *zakāt* properly, or divide it properly, or does not guard his fast

27 Ibn Abī l-Dunyā, *al-Ṣamt wa-ādāb al-lisān*, 204.

from sex, backbiting, or [guard himself from] attacking people's reputation.

And as for his actions related to worldly [life], [it is] saying that
511 he is ill-mannered, that he [thinks] little | of others, that he does not see the rights of others [due from] him but sees his right [from them], that he speaks too much, eats too much, is [always] sleepy, sleeps at times not [suitable] for sleep, and sits in the wrong places. As for his clothes, it is saying that his sleeves are too wide, his outer garment is long [and trails on the ground], and his clothes are dirty.

There are group[s] who say,

> There is no backbiting about a person's *dīn*, because it amounts to censuring what God تَعَالَىٰ censured, so mentioning his disobedience and censuring him for it is allowable. [Their contention is] based on a narration in which mention was made to the Messenger of God صَلَّىٱللَّهُعَلَيْهِوَسَلَّمَ of a woman [who was] pious and frequently fasted and prayed but who, with her tongue, [said things that were] injurious to her neighbors, and [the Prophet] said, "She is in the fire."[28] Another woman who was mentioned in his presence was said to be miserly, and [the Prophet] said, "Then what goodness is in her?"[29]

This, however, is a false [analogy], inasmuch as those who mentioned such things to him [the Prophet] did so to know [certain legal] rules (*aḥkām*), not so they could demean [people], and this [need to mention people by name] is unnecessary except [when] consulting the Messenger of God صَلَّىٱللَّهُعَلَيْهِوَسَلَّمَ.

The proof of this is the consensus of the community [of believers], that anyone who mentions something about someone else that he would deplore [to have mentioned] is a backbiter. This is included in what the Messenger of God صَلَّىٱللَّهُعَلَيْهِوَسَلَّمَ mentioned in the definition of backbiting. In all this, even if he is being truthful, he is a backbiter disobeying his Lord, and devouring the flesh of his brother. The proof [of this] is in what was narrated by the Prophet صَلَّىٱللَّهُعَلَيْهِوَسَلَّمَ, [who] said,

> Do you know what backbiting is? |

28 Ibn Ḥanbal, *Musnad*, 2:440.
29 Ibn al-Mubārak, *Zuhd*, 743.

They said, "God and His Messenger know best." 512

He said, "It is mentioning [something] about your brother that he would deplore [to have mentioned]."

Then they asked, "But what if what you say about your brother is true [lit., something that is in him]?" He said, "If it is true [lit., something that is in him], you have backbitten him, and if it is not true, you have falsely accused him."[30]

Muʿādh b. Jabal said,

A man was mentioned in the presence of the Messenger of God صَلَّىٱللَّهُعَلَيْهِوَسَلَّمَ and they said about him, "How weak he is!"

[He] صَلَّىٱللَّهُعَلَيْهِوَسَلَّمَ said, "You are backbiting your brother."

They said, "O Messenger of God, we only said what is true [lit., something that is in him] about him."

He replied, "If what you said were not true, you would be falsely accusing him."[31]

Abū Ḥudhayfa reported that ʿĀʾisha رَضِيَٱللَّهُعَنْهَا said that she mentioned a woman in the presence of the Messenger صَلَّىٱللَّهُعَلَيْهِوَسَلَّمَ and said, "She is very short," and the Prophet صَلَّىٱللَّهُعَلَيْهِوَسَلَّمَ said, "You have backbitten her."[32]

Ḥasan said,

There are three ways of speaking [ill] of someone else—backbiting, falsely accusing [them], and [through] scandal—and all of them are in the Book of God تَعَالَىٰ. Backbiting is saying something about him that is true [lit., "that is in him"], falsely accusing him is saying something about him that is false [lit., "what is not in him"], and scandal is saying whatever you heard.

Ibn Sīrīn mentioned a man and said, "That black man." Then he said, "May God forgive me. I see that I have just backbitten him."[33] |

And Ibn Sīrīn mentioned Ibrāhīm al-Nakhaʿī and put his hand 513
over his eye so as not to say, "The one-eyed."

30 Muslim, *Ṣaḥīḥ*, 2589.

31 Al-Ṭabarānī, *al-Muʿjam al-kabīr*, 20:39; and al-Bayhaqī, *Shuʿab al-īmān*, 6308.

32 Abū Dāwūd, *Sunan*, 4875; al-Tirmidhī, *Sunan*, 2502; and Ibn Abī l-Dunyā, *al-Ṣamt wa-ādāb al-lisān*, 207.

33 Ibn Abī l-Dunyā, *al-Ṣamt wa-ādāb al-lisān*, 214.

ʿĀʾisha رَضِيَ اللَّهُ عَنْهَا said, Do not backbite one another, for once I said to a woman in the presence of the Prophet صَلَّى اللَّهُ عَلَيْهِ وَسَلَّمَ, "This one's robe is trailing (*ṭawīl al-dhayl*) behind her,"[34] and he said to me, "Spit [it out]! Spit [it out]!" And I spit out a morsel of meat.[35] |

❁ ❁ ❁

514 An elucidation that backbiting (*ghība*) is not limited to speech

Know that [backbiting] in speech is unlawful because it consists of alerting others to the deficiencies of your brother and because it identifies him by what he would deplore, [regardless of whether this were done by] alluding through direct [speech], actions or words, gestures, mimicry, [facial] expressions, symbols, writing, or movements, and anything by which the aim [of showing a failing] is understood is considered backbiting and is unlawful.

An example of this is in what ʿĀʾisha رَضِيَ اللَّهُ عَنْهَا said: "A woman came to visit and when she left, I gestured, mimicking, with my hand [to indicate] that she was short, and [the Prophet] صَلَّى اللَّهُ عَلَيْهِ وَسَلَّمَ said, "You have backbitten her."

This also applies to imitation. Walking with a limp [when one does not have a limp] or walking like he [the lame person] does is backbiting; indeed, it is worse than backbiting because it is better in portraying and informing [others about the disability].

Thus, when the Messenger of God صَلَّى اللَّهُ عَلَيْهِ وَسَلَّمَ saw ʿĀʾisha imitate a woman, he said, "I would find no pleasure in imitating a person even if I were [given] this or that [as a reward]."[36]

Likewise, there is backbiting by the written word, for the pen is one of [our] two tongues. If an author mentions a specific person

---

34 FC: Arabic, *ṭawīl al-dhayl* can also mean one is rich, proud, or conceited (see Lane, *An Arabic-English Lexicon*, 991).

35 Ibn Abī l-Dunyā, *al-Ṣamt wa-ādāb al-lisān*, 216; and al-Kharāʾiṭī, *Masāwiʾ al-akhlāq*, 201. Eds.: The physical manifestation of the morsel is considered one of the miracles of the Prophet صَلَّى اللَّهُ عَلَيْهِ وَسَلَّمَ.

36 Abū Dāwūd, *Sunan*, 4875; and al-Tirmidhī, *Sunan*, 2502.

and excoriates that person's words in writing, it is backbiting, unless it is related to a excusable need to mention him; this will be explained in what is to come. |

But if one writes, "Some groups [hold such and such a view] . . . ," 515
that is not backbiting because it is not an affront to the reputation of a specific person, either living or dead.

It is [considered] backbiting for you to say, "A certain person passed by us today" or "someone we saw," if the one to whom you are speaking understands by it a specific person. What must be guarded against is what he understands [from what you say], not how he is made to understand it; so if he does not understand [what you say as referring to] a particular person, it is allowable. This is why if the Messenger of God صَلَّى ٱللَّٰهُ عَلَيْهِ وَسَلَّمَ deplored something someone had done, he would say, "What is the matter with groups (*aqwām*) who do this or that?" without specifying [a particular person].[37]

If you say, "A certain person who has come back from traveling . . . " or "A certain person who claims to have knowledge . . . ," and it is accompanied by a context (*qarīna*)[38] that communicates the identity of the person, then it is backbiting.

The most malicious type of backbiting is done by argumentative scholars (*al-qurrāʾ al-murāʾīn*)[39] who make their aims understood in the fashion of the people of righteousness, to show themselves as abstaining from backbiting, but making their aim [the specific person they are backbiting] understood. In their ignorance they do not see that they are combining two obscenities (*fawaḥish*): ostentation and backbiting. Thus, when a particular person is mentioned in the presence of one of them and he says, "Praise be to God who has not tried us by having to go to the sultan and grovel for crumbs," or, "We seek refuge from God from having little shame . . . we ask God تَعَالَىٰ to protect us from it," his aim is making known the defects

37 Abū Dāwūd, *Sunan*, 4788; relates a *ḥadīth* according to ʿĀʾisha رَضِيَ ٱللَّٰهُ عَنْهَا, "If he learned a certain thing about a man, the Messenger of God صَلَّى ٱللَّٰهُ عَلَيْهِ وَسَلَّمَ would not say, "What is the matter with so-and-so," but rather, "What is the matter with those people who say such and such thing."

38 FC: *Qarīna* refers to the "context, connection, or relation" (see Lane, *An Arabic-English Lexicon*, 2988; and Wehr, *A Dictionary of Modern Written Arabic*, 759–760, under q-r-n).

39 Eds.: Lit., "reciters"; al-Zabīdī (*Itḥāf*, 7:542) defines them as *ʿulamāʾ* (scholars).

of another [who is known to the listener], but it is done in the fashion of a supplication (*duʿāʾ*). |

516 Similarly, when someone begins by praising the one he wants to backbite, saying [for example], "How good are the circumstances of so-and-so. He never used to fall short in worship, but he has become lax, and has been tried the way we all are tried, by having little patience." Thus, while mentioning himself, his aim is to censure someone else—all while [indirectly] extolling himself by emulating the righteous who censure themselves. In doing so, he is backbiting, [being] ostentatious, and praising himself. He has combined three obscenities while supposing, in his ignorance, that he is among the righteous who abstain from backbiting.

Similarly, Satan plays with the ignorant when they occupy themselves with worship without knowledge. He tires them, nullifies their deeds with his ruses, then laughs at them and ridicules them.

And [a similar example is someone who] mentions the defect of a person and no one present pays any attention. But then he says, "Glory be to God, here is something amazing . . ." so that they listen to the backbiting and become aware of what he says. He mentions God تَعَالَىٰ and uses His name as an instrument to realize his maliciousness, and [thinks] in his ignorance and delusion that he is being gracious toward God عَزَّوَجَلَّ by mentioning Him!

Similarly, he might say, "I am so pained by the indignity that has befallen our companion. We ask God to grant him relief from it." [In this] he is lying by claiming to be saddened and by displaying his supplications [for his companion]. If his aim was really to supplicate for him, he should have done so privately at the end of his prayer. And if he was truly saddened by it, he should also be saddened to display what [his companion] would deplore [to have displayed].

Similarly, he might say, "That poor man! He is truly being put to the test by such a great bane! May God forgive us and him!" In all of that, he is displaying his supplication, but God knows the
517 maliciousness of his heart and his hidden aim. | In his ignorance, he does not perceive that he is subjecting himself to a detestation greater than what the ignorant subject themselves to when they speak aloud.

Similarly, listening to backbiting and [showing] amazement by what the backbiter says, encourages him and spurs him on to more, as if [the listener] were drawing the backbiting out of him by saying, "That is amazing! I did not know he was like that! I only knew what was good about him until now and I considered him different than this. May God spare us from His tribulations!" All this attests to the backbiter, and the attestation that backbiting is, itself, backbiting. Even the one who is quiet [while someone else backbites] shares in the [sin of] the backbiting.

The Messenger of God ﷺ said, "The listener is one of two backbiters."[40]

It was related about Abū Bakr and ʿUmar رَضِيَ ٱللَّهُ عَنْهُمَا that one of them said to the other, "So-and-so is [always] sleepy." Then they asked the Messenger of God ﷺ for a condiment to eat with their bread and he said to them ﷺ, "You have already had your condiment." They said, "Not that we know of." [The Prophet] said, "Yes, you have. You have eaten from the flesh of your brother!"[41] See how he combined the two of them even though one of them was speaking and the other was listening.

[The Prophet] said to the two men—one of whom said, | "That 518
man died quickly like a dog dies." [The Prophet said:] "Take a bite out of that corpse."[42] He combined [the two of them].

So the one who listens is not excluded from [that is, is included in] the sin of backbiting unless he verbally objects to it.

And if he fears [for his life, to do so openly], then [let him at least object] in his heart. And if it is possible for him to stand up [and leave] or to interrupt the talk by talking about something else, and he does not do so, then [the sin] remains with him.

And if he says with his tongue [to the other], "Be quiet!" but in his heart he actually wants to hear more, then he is a hypocrite. He does not escape the sin unless he deplores it with his heart.

And it is not enough, in this situation, just to gesture with his hand to be quiet, or gesture with his eyebrows and his forehead, since that only [amounts to] disdaining the victim [of backbiting].

40 Abū Nuʿaym, *Maʿrifat al-ṣaḥāba*, 6:3122.

41 Al-Kharāʾiṭī, *Masāwiʾ al-akhlāq*, 188.

42 Al-Ṭayālisī, *Musnad*, 2473; Abū Dāwūd, *Sunan*, 4428; and al-Nasāʾī, *Kitāb al-sunan al-kubrā*, 7128.

Rather, he needs to treat it [the sin] as grave and defend him [the victim] unequivocably (*ṣarīḥ*).

[The Prophet] صلى الله عليه وسلم said, "If a believer is humiliated in someone's presence and he fails to aid him while being able to aid him, God will humiliate him before all creatures on the day of resurrection."[43]

Abū l-Dardāʾ said, "The Prophet صلى الله عليه وسلم said, 'He who wards off [an attack on] the reputation of his brother in his absence, God will surely ward off [an attack on] his reputation on the day of resurrection.'"[44] |

519 [The Prophet] also said, "Whoever defends the reputation of his brother in his absence, God will surely emancipate him from the fire."[45]

Many sayings were narrated about aiding a Muslim in his absence and the merit of doing so, and since we quoted them in *The Book on the Proprieties of Friendship* [*and Brotherhood*] and the rights of Muslims,[46] we will not repeat them here. |

❁ ❁ ❁

520 An elucidation of the causes that motivate (*bāʿtha*) backbiting (*ghība*)

Know that the motivations for backbiting are many, but they can be reduced to eleven causes, eight of which [commonly] apply to laymen, and three of which specifically concern the people of *dīn* and the elect.

As for the eight, [they are as follows].

The first [motive] is to vent rage. This means that when something provokes a person's anger against another and that anger erupts, he

43 Ibn Ḥanbal, *Musnad*, 3:487; and al-Ṭabarānī, *al-Muʿjam al-kabīr*, 6:73.

44 Ibn Abī l-Dunyā, *al-Ghayba wa-l-namīma*, 103.

45 Ibn Ḥanbal, *Musnad*, 6:461; and al-Ṭabarānī, *al-Muʿjam al-kabīr*, 24:176.

46 Trans.: Book 15 of the *Revival of the Religious Sciences: The Proprieties of Friendship and Brotherhood* (*Kitāb ādāb al-ṣuḥba wa-l-maʿāshara maʿ aṣnāf al-khalaq*).

vents it by mentioning the other's evil deeds. Naturally the tongue rushes to [this], if there is not a *dīn* to impede [such a reaction] and bar [one from] venting [one's] rage when angry. But the anger builds up inside and turns into deep-seated malice, and this becomes an ongoing cause for mentioning [another's] evil deeds. Thus, malice and anger are two of the greatest motives for backbiting.

❁ ❁ ❁

The second [motive] is the approval of peers, to flatter friends, and to support them in what they are speaking about. If they amuse [themselves] by mentioning [someone's] reputation, and someone believes that if he disapproved of them or left the assembly, they would find him burdensome and abandon him, he supports them and sees it as part of good companionship and considers it [part of the] flattery of friendship. If his companions become angry, he too needs to become angry because of their anger to display his participation [with his companion] through thick and thin, and so he delves into mentioning [their] defects and evil deeds. |

❁ ❁ ❁

The third [motive] is that he senses that a person will pursue him and speak at length against him, or denounce him before a respected [authority], or bear witness against him in testimony, and so he hastens, before his condition is denounced, and attacks [this person] to nullify the effect of his testimony. Or he begins by mentioning something true about [this person] only to lie about him later, [thereby] promoting [his own] lie by means of the intitial truth and then citing it as [evidence], saying, "It is not my habit to lie. I informed you such-and-such about him, and he is as I said." 521

❁ ❁ ❁

The fourth [motive] is when he is accused [of something] and, to show his innocence, he names the one who did it. He is within his rights to declare that he himself is innocent but not to name the one who did it. He should not accuse anyone else [of the deed] nor mention anyone else as a partner in the deed in order to prepare an excuse for himself for his action.

❁ ❁ ❁

The fifth [motive] is [one's] will toward artificiality and boasting, that is, to elevate himself by diminishing another. So, he says, "So-and-so is ignorant, his understanding is feeble, and his speech is weak," [he says this] to assert his own superiority [by implication], and show others he is superior to the one [he is backbiting], or guard against [others] glorifying anyone like [his victim]. So, he maligns the other

❁ ❁ ❁

The sixth [motive] is envy. Someone may be envious of the commendations that people express for another and of how they love him and honor him. He wants to strip [that person] of that blessing and finds no other way to do it than by maligning him so that he is disgraced[47] before people and [people] cease honoring and com-
522 mending | him. For it weighs heavily on [the envier] to hear people commend and honor [the envied]. This is, in fact, the essence of envy and it is other than anger and malice, for those necessitate a crime [committed by] the one with whom one is angry, while envy may be toward a good friend or an agreeable relative.

❁ ❁ ❁

The seventh [motive] is play, foolishness, pleasantries, and passing the time with laughter. And so someone mentions another to make people laugh by way of imitation, [eliciting] amazement, and delight.

❁ ❁ ❁

47 Eds.: The Arabic, *yasquṭ māʾ wajhhi*, literally "the water falls from his face," refers to one who loses honor or is disgraced before people. See Wehr, *A Dictionary of Modern Written Arabic*, 932.

The eighth [motive] is ridicule and mockery in order to disdain [someone]. This can happen both in the presence [of that person] and in [his] absence. Its origin is arrogance and the belittlement of the one being mocked.

❁ ❁ ❁

As for the three causes that pertain to the elect, these are more obscure and subtle because they are evils that Satan has hidden among what appear to be good [deeds]. And [while] they contain good, Satan has tainted them with evil.

The first [of these causes] is motivated from the *dīn* [and] occasions amazement by disapproving of the wrong or the offense [committed] in the *dīn*. So he says, "How amazing is what I saw so-and-so [doing]!" The one who says this might truthfully be amazed by the wrong he saw. And while it is his right to be amazed, it is not his right to mention [the perpetrator's] name. Satan makes it easy for him to also mention the name of [the perpetrator] in the course of expressing his amazement, and thus he becomes a backbiter and a sinner without knowing it. |

For example, a man might say, "I am amazed at how much 523
so-and-so loves his maidservant even though she is repugnant," or "how he sits with so-and-so even though he is ignorant."[48]

The second [of these causes] is [expressing] compassion for [one who is] distressed about a tribulation [that person] is going through. So he says, "Poor so-and-so. I am saddened about his situation and the tribulations he faces." Though he is truthful in his claim to [feel] be saddened, the sadness distracts him from being careful to not mention the person's name, so he does [mention it] and thus becomes a backbiter. His sadness and compassion are good, and so is his amazement. But Satan leads him to evil from a direction he does not perceive. It is possible to feel compassion and sorrow without mentioning someone's name, but Satan incites him to mention the person's name to invalidate the reward for his sadness and compassion.

48 Eds.: That is, this *ghība* is against a maidservant and in the second case, against a scholar who is being called ignorant; al-Zabīdī, *Itḥāf*, 7:546.

The third [of these causes] is anger for [the sake of] God تَعَالَىٰ. One may be angered by some wrong that he sees or hears a person yield to, and he displays his anger and mentions [his] name. Even if it is mandatory that his anger be displayed [in the course of] commanding what is right and forbidding what is wrong (*amr bi-l-maʿrūf wa-nahī ʿan al-munkar*), this should not be displayed to anyone else, or if it is, then the name [of the person involved] should be covered and not mentioned as wicked.

These three [causes] are among [the concepts] that are difficult for the scholars, let alone laymen. For they [the scholars] assume that if amazement, compassion, and anger are for [the sake of] God تَعَالَىٰ, then it is [a valid] excuse to mention a person by name, but this is incorrect. Rather, the license to backbite is necessary in specific cases, when it is indispensable for him to mention the name [of the perpetrator] as we will mention later.

And it was related on the authority of ʿĀmir b. Wāthila that during the life of the Messenger of God صَلَّىٰ ٱللَّٰهُ عَلَيْهِ وَسَلَّمَ, a man came upon some people, greeted them, and they returned his greeting.
524 Then when he had passed them, | one of them said, "I loathe that [person] for [the sake of] God تَعَالَىٰ." The people who were sitting with him said, "What a terrible thing to say! By God, we are going to tell him!" Then they said to a man among them, "Get up and go tell him what this man said!" He caught up with the man [who was walking] and told him what [one of them] had said about him, and so the man went to the Messenger of God صَلَّىٰ ٱللَّٰهُ عَلَيْهِ وَسَلَّمَ and told him what was said about him. [The Prophet صَلَّىٰ ٱللَّٰهُ عَلَيْهِ وَسَلَّمَ] asked him to call [the man] and then [the person came] and [the Messenger] asked what [he had said] and he said, "Yes, I said that." The Messenger of God صَلَّىٰ ٱللَّٰهُ عَلَيْهِ وَسَلَّمَ [then] said, "Why do you loathe him?" [The man] answered, "I am his neighbor, I know him well, and by God, I have never seen him pray a prayer except the obligatory [lit., the ones written]." The [accused] man said [to the Prophet], "Ask him, O Messenger of God, if he has ever seen me once delay [the prayer] past its time or improperly [make] the ablution or the bowing and prostration." So [the Prophet] asked him [the accuser] and he said no. Then [the accuser] said, "By God, I have never seen him fast any other time except that month when both the pious and the

profligate fast."[49] [The accused man] said, "Ask him, O Messenger of God, if he has ever seen me break the fast [during that month, that is, Ramaḍān] or [be] deficient in any of its requirements." So he [the Prophet] asked him [the accuser], and the man said no. Then [the accuser] said, "By God, I have never seen him give to a beggar or a poor person, nor have I ever seen him give some of his wealth for the sake of God except the *zakāt* that both the pious and the profligate give." [The accused] said, "But ask him, O Messenger of God, if he has ever seen me deficient in [paying] any of it, or [seen me] withhold it from a petitioner asking for it." So [the Prophet] asked [the accuser] and [the accuser] said no. Then [the Prophet of God] صَلَّى ٱللَّهُ عَلَيْهِ وَسَلَّمَ said to the man [the accuser], "Stand up, for [the accused] may be better than you."[50] |

❁ ❁ ❁

An elucidation of the remedy for backbiting (*ghība*): restraining (*yumnaʿ*) the tongue 525

Know that all evil characteristics are treated by a combination of knowledge and actions and the treatment for any illness is countering its causes, so let us examine the cause [of backbiting].

The treatment for stopping the tongue from backbiting has two aspects, one general and the other particular.

The general [treatment] is to know that, when one backbites, he subjects himself to the wrath of God تَعَالَىٰ, as all these reports that we have related show. He [should also] know that it will make his good deeds futile on the day of resurrection and transfer his good deeds to the one he backbit, in exchange for what he ruined [of his victim's] reputation And if he has no good deeds, then the bad deeds of his victim will be transferred to him [that is, to his account]. And, he is subjected to the detestation of God عَزَّ وَجَلَّ and is comparable

49 Trans.: That is, fasting the month of Ramaḍān.
50 Ibn Ḥanbal, *Musnad*, 5:455.

to one who consumes a dead body. Indeed, a servant will enter hell because the side [of the scale] bearing his bad deeds outweighs the side of his good deeds, and perhaps a single bad deed by the one he backbites will be transferred to [his account] and will be enough to shift the balance and [thus he will] enter the fire. At the very least, the reward for his actions will be diminished, and that will come after the disputation and reparation, the questioning, answering, and the reckoning.[51] The Messenger ﷺ said, "Fire [consumes] dry [wood] no more rapidly than backbiting [consumes] the good deeds of a servant."[52] |

526 It was related that a man said to Ḥasan, "I heard that you backbit me." He said, "Your worth to me is not such that I would give you control over my good deeds."

So long as a servant believes in the reports about backbiting, he will not unleash his tongue out of fear [of the punishment mentioned in the reports].

It is also useful for him to contemplate his own soul. If he finds in it a defect, let him be occupied with his own defects [instead of others'] and remember the words of [the Prophet] ﷺ, "Blessed be whoever is occupied with his own defects rather than the defects of [other] people."[53]

Whenever he finds a defect [in himself], he should be too ashamed to abandon censuring himself to censure others. Further, he should realize that someone else's inability to overcome a defect is no different than his own inability to do the same. This is [the case when] a defect relates to his actions and choices.

If it is a matter of [finding fault with someone's] appearance, then censuring [their appearance] is censuring the Creater, for whoever censures the workmanship is censuring its Maker. A man said to a sage, "What an ugly face you have!" and [the sage] replied, "The creation of my face was not mine [to control, such that I could make it] more beautiful!"

51 Trans.: These events on the day of resurrection are explained in Book 40 of the *Revival of the Religious Sciences*. See Winter (trans.), *The Remembrance of Death*, 171ff.

52 Ibn Abī l-Dunyā, *al-Ṣamt wa-ādāb al-lisān*, 302.

53 Abū Nuʿaym, *Ḥilya*, 3:202; and al-Bayhaqī, *Shuʿab al-īmān*, 10079.

And if the servant does not find defects in his own soul, let him thank God تَعَالَىٰ and not sully himself with the worst of defects, for defaming people and eating the flesh of the dead is among the worst defects. [Rather] if he were just, he would realize that to assume that he is innocent of every defect is to be ignorant of his own soul, and that in itself is one of the worst defects. |

It would benefit him to know that the pain [he causes] another 527
by backbiting is like his pain if another backbit him. If he is not pleased for himself to be backbitten, then he should not be pleased for another [to experience] what he is not pleased with for himself.

These are the general treatments.

As for the specific [treatments], these consist of examining the causes that motivate someone to backbite; for the treatment of any illness is to eliminate its causes. We have presented these causes [above].

As for anger, its treatment is what will be described in *The Book on the Banes of Anger, [Malice, and Envy]*,[54] which is to say, "If I carry out my anger against him, then maybe God تَعَالَىٰ would carry out His anger against me because of [my] backbiting, for He forbade me from [backbiting] and yet I dared [to violate] what He forbade and took lightly His disapproval.

[The Prophet] صَلَّىٰ اللَّهُ عَلَيْهِ وَسَلَّمَ said, "Hell has a door that is entered only by those who vent their rage by disobeying God تَعَالَىٰ."[55]

And [the Prophet] صَلَّىٰ اللَّهُ عَلَيْهِ وَسَلَّمَ said, "Whoever fears his Lord, his tongue is wearied and he does not vent his rage."[56]

And [the Prophet] صَلَّىٰ اللَّهُ عَلَيْهِ وَسَلَّمَ said "Whoever suppresses his rage when he is able to carry it out will be called by God تَعَالَىٰ on the day of resurrection before all creatures [lit., over the heads of all creatures] so that he may choose [for himself] any *ḥūri* he wants."[57] |

In one of the books revealed to one of the prophets, [it is written], 528
"O child of Adam, remember Me when you are angered and I will

54 Trans.: Book 25 of the the *Revival of the Religious Sciences: The Banes of Anger, Malice, and Envy* (*Kitāb āfat al-ghaḍab al-ḥaqd wa-l-ḥasad*).

55 Al-Bazzār, *Musnad al-Bazzār*, 5180; Ibn ʿAdī, *al-Kāmil*, 6:51; and al-Bayhaqī, *Shuʿab al-īmān*, 7978.

56 Ibn Abī l-Dunyā, *al-Warʿa*, 104; and al-ʿUqaylī, *al-Ḍuʿafāʾ*, 2:734.

57 Abū Dāwūd, *Sunan*, 4777; al-Tirmidhī, *Sunan*, 2493; and Ibn Mājah, *Sunan*, 4186.

remember you when I am angered and not annihilate you among those whom I annihilate."[58]

As for the approval [of others], know that God تَعَالَىٰ will be angry with you if you seek His wrath to please His creatures. How can you be pleased with yourself if you revere someone else and disdain your Guardian, abandoning His pleasure for their pleasure? Your anger [is permitted] for [the sake of] God تَعَالَىٰ, but this does not mandate [you] to speak ill of one with whom you are angry. Rather, you must be angry for [the sake of] God [even] against your companions if they speak ill against [one who is absent], for [in doing that] they are disobeying your Lord with the most obscene of transgressions, backbiting.

As for exonerating yourself by attributing a crime to another when there is no need to mention him, the treatment for that is to know that to subject [yourself] to the detestation of the Creator is more severe than to subject [yourself] to the detestation of creatures, and by backbiting another, you are surely subjecting [yourself] to God's wrath. And you do not know if you can free [yourself] from people's wrath or not. And so you imagine that you free yourself in this world, but in reality you destroy yourself in the hereafter and lose your good deeds. While God's عَزَّوَجَلَّ censure of you is as certain as cash [in hand], expecting payment for censuring creatures is [as uncertain as being repaid] a long-term loan. Such is the height of ignorance and disappointment.

And as for your excuse, you say, "If I ate something unlawful, so-and-so also eats it," [or] "if I accepted money [from] the sultan, so-and-so did so as well . . . ," this is ignorance. For you are excusing yourself by [following] the example of someone whose example
529 [you are] | not allowed to [follow], for whoever violates God's تَعَالَىٰ command is not an exemplar, whoever he is. If another entered hell and you were able not to enter it, you do not go along with him; if you went along with him, [it would mean that] you had lost your mind. So what you cited [about the other person] is backbiting, and [this] is an additional disobedience you added to what you are excusing. By combining the two disobediences, you are on record [testifying to] your ignorance and your stupidity. Thus, you are like

58 Ibn Ḥanbal, *al-Zuhd*, 45; and Ibn Ḥibbān, *Rawḍat al-ʿuqalāʾ*, 50.

the ewe who sees the she-goat throw herself off a mountain peak and [then] throws herself off also. If she had a tongue that could speak, she would articulate her excuse, and say, "The she-goat is more clever than I am and she destroyed herself, so I will do the same!" You may laugh at her ignorance, but your situation is like her situation and you are not amazed, nor do you laugh at yourself.

As for your [backbiting] with the aim of boasting and praising oneself (*tazkiyat al-nafs*), [that is, implicitly] adding to your merit by maligning [the character of the other] you must know that by speaking [ill] against another, you invalidate any merit you have with God and other people's belief in your merit is in danger, for perhaps their belief about you would be diminished if they knew you defame people. Thus, you will have sold what is certain with the Creator for what you imagine exists with creatures. Even if they completely believe in [your] merit, still it would not benefit you in the least with God.

As for backbiting out of envy, this combines two punishments. For you envied another for some worldly blessing, and you were punished in [this] world [because of your] envy. But you were not satisfied with [this painful worldly punishment for envy] so you added to it punishment in the hereafter [for backbiting], thereby combining two exemplary punishments. You were a loser in [this] world and you become, additionally, a loser in the hereafter. Your aim was [to harm] the one you envied but you hit yourself instead and gifted him your good deeds. Thus, you are his friend but your own enemy. Your backbiting did not harm him but it harmed you 530
| and benefitted him since it transferred your good deeds to him or transferred to you his bad deeds and did not benefit you. And so you added to the maliciousness of envy the ignorance of the idiotic. Moreover, your envy and maligning [him] might even be the means of spreading the merit of the one you envied, as [a poet] said,[59]

> When God wants to proclaim a merit
> that was hidden, He does so with the tongue of an envier.

As for mockery, [if] your aim is to dishonor another before people, [you are doing so] at the expense of dishonoring yourself

59 This verse is by Abū Tammām, *Dīwān*, 1:397.

in the eyes of God تَعَالَىٰ, the angels, and the prophets عَلَيْهِمُ ٱلسَّلَامُ. If you were to reflect about your affliction, your crime, your indignity, and your dishonor on the day of resurrection, the day on which you will bear the bad deeds of the one you mocked, you will be dragged to the fire and it will shock you [from any thought] of dishonoring your companion. If you knew your state, [you would see that] you are the one most deserving of being laughed at, for you ridiculed someone before a small group of people but subjected yourself, on the day of resurrection, to being taken by the hand before a huge assembly of people, and being led to the fire, burdened [lit., under] by his bad deeds like a donkey. [All the while] he mocks you, happy at your dishonor, and delighted that God تَعَالَىٰ gave him triumph over you, and overpowered you with his revenge.

As for [expressing] compassion for one who sinned, that is good, but Iblīs envied you for it and misguided you into pronouncing [the name of the person you backbit] such that more of your good deeds were transferred to him than [the reward for] your compassion, because he—the one you had compassion for—is compensated for your sin [of backbiting]. [In fact,] he ceases to be the one [deserving of] compassion and inversely, you become the one deserving compassion—because your reward [for your compassion] was lost and your good deeds diminished. |

531 Similarly, anger for [the sake of] God عَزَّوَجَلَّ does not necessitate backbiting. It is Satan who makes backbiting beloved to you so that the reward of your [righteous] anger is futile and with backbiting you are subjected to the anger of God عَزَّوَجَلَّ.

As for the amazement that leads you to backbite, be amazed at yourself and how you destroyed yourself and your *dīn* because of another person's [practice of] *dīn* or [his] worldly [life]. With all this, you are not safe from worldly punishment if God تَعَالَىٰ uncovers His veil [over your sins], just as you uncovered the veil [protecting] your brother [because of your expression] of amazement.

Thus, the treatment for all this is simply knowledge and the verification of these matters that pertain to the degrees (*abwāb*) [lit., doors] of faith. Whoever strengthens his faith by [understanding] all of this, his tongue will undoubtedly stop backbiting. |

❁ ❁ ❁

An elucidation of the unlawfulness of backbiting (*ghība*) in the heart 532

Know that a wicked supposition (*sūʾ al-ẓann*) is as unlawful as a wicked statement. Just as it is unlawful (*ḥarām*) for you speak with your tongue about the evil [deeds] of another, so it is not for you to speak to yourself [and form] a wicked suspicion about your brother. And by this, I mean your heart's belief and judgment that someone is wicked. As for a passing thought or the murmurings of the soul, that is excused. Doubts are also excused. What is forbidden is supposition, and supposition is an expression of what the soul [believes is] reliable, and the heart inclines toward. God تَعَالَىٰ says, *O you who have believed, avoid much* [*negative*] *assumption* (*ẓann*). *Indeed, some assumption* (*ẓann*) *is sin* [Q. 49:12].

The reason for its unlawfulness is [because] the secrets of the hearts are known only to the Knower of the unseen [God], so it is not for you to believe in another's wickedness unless it is disclosed to you by observation and cannot be explained [away]. In that case you cannot but believe what you know and witness. But if what you have not witnessed with your own eyes nor heard with your own ears enters your heart, it is Satan who has cast it there and you must reject it, for he is the most corrupt of the corrupt. God تَعَالَىٰ said, *O you who have believed, if there comes to you a disobedient one* (*fāsiq*) *with information, investigate, lest you harm a people out of ignorance* [Q. 49:6]. [For these reasons,] it is not allowable to believe Iblīs.

And if some image [arising in your heart] indicates depravity and an alternative is possible, then it is not allowable to believe [the depravity]. The corrupt [person] may conceivably be truthful in his report, but it is not allowable for you to believe him. Thus, even if

someone has been examined and found to be smelling of wine, it is not allowable to [punish] him [by law] *ḥadd*, for it is said, "Perhaps he rinsed his mouth with wine and spit it out without drinking it,
533 or he was | forced to [drink] it. All of this evidence is absolutely possible. Therefore it is not allowable to believe this in the heart and [form] a wicked supposition of a Muslim.

[The Prophet] صَلَّى ٱللَّٰهُ عَلَيْهِ وَسَلَّمَ said, "God has made it unlawful [to take] a Muslim's blood and property and believe a wicked supposition about him."[60]

Suppositions of wickedness [of a Muslim] are only permissible [if his] property is permissible [to be seized, meaning], with a legally valid testimony or with legal evidence. Lacking that, if there occurs to you a wicked supposition [about another], then you should expel it from your heart and acknowledge that his inner heart is hidden from you like it was before [the suspicion] and that what you saw from him could be good or bad.

❁ ❁ ❁

If you said, "How can one recognize when a supposition is believed, doubts stir, and the soul has murmurings?"

I would say, the sign that the supposition is believed is having a change of heart toward [that person] such that you shun him in a certain manner, [find him] unbearable, and you are ambivalent about him, or [about] visiting him, or honoring him, or worrying about him. Such are the signs [that you] believe the supposition and affirm it. [The Prophet] صَلَّى ٱللَّٰهُ عَلَيْهِ وَسَلَّمَ said, "There are three [things that can afflict] the believer [but] from which he can escape, and his escape from wicked suppositions is by
534 not verifying it."[61] | That is, by not verifying it in himself in belief or deed, neither in his heart nor in his limbs. In his heart by

60 Al-Bayhaqī, *Shuʿab al-īmān*, 6280.

61 Al-Ṭabarānī, *al-Muʿjam al-kabīr*, 3:228, from a *ḥadīth* related by Ḥāritha b. al-Nuʿman رَضِيَ ٱللَّٰهُ عَنْهُ, "There are three things that will always be found in my community: portending [evil], envy, and wicked supposition." A man asked, "What gets rid of them, O Messenger of God, from one who has them?" He said, "If you envy, ask forgiveness from God. If you have a supposition do not verify it, and if you portended [something wicked, let it] pass.

changing, shunning, and deploring [that person]; and in his limbs by acting in accordance with [his heart]. Satan may settle in the heart, with the smallest illusion, the wickedness of people, and may cast [in your heart the idea] that such [an insight] is the fruit of your perceptiveness, acuity, and intelligence. The believer sees by the light of God تعالى,[62] whereas actually he sees through Satan's deception and his darkness.

If you are informed about [someone's wickedness] by an upright person, and your supposition is inclined to believe [the upright person], you are excused, because if you disbelieved him, you would be wronging this upright person by supposing he lied, and that is also a wicked supposition. Indeed, you should not believe [something] good of one person, and [form] a wicked [supposition] about another.

Yes, you should determine whether there is some enmity, envy, or quarrel between them that could have led to the reason for the accusation. For the law rejects the testimony of an upright father for his accused son just as it rejects the testimony of an enemy.[63] So for that, you should pause, and even if he is upright, neither believe nor disbelieve, rather say to yourself, "The state of the person mentioned [the accused person]—for me—is covered by God تعالى. His affair was hidden from me, and it remains so. Nothing of his affair was disclosed to me." |

It may [also] be that the man [who has related something to 535
you] is outwardly upright and there is no envy between him and the person mentioned [that is, the accused], but it is the habit [of this upright person] to meddle in people's affairs and mention their bad deeds. This kind [of person] may be supposed to be upright, but he is not upright. Rather, one who backbites is corrupt, and if that is his habit, his testimony is rejected. But because of peoples'

---

62 Trans.: This is a paraphrase of an oft-quoted *ḥadīth* found in al-Tirmidhī, *Sunan*, 3127, and elsewhere. It states, "Beware of the believer's intuition because he sees by the light of God."

63 Al-Tirmidhī, *Sunan*, 2298, records a *ḥadīth* related by ʿĀʾisha رضي الله عنها which says, "Inadmissible is the testimony of a traitor, man or woman; or one who has been flogged for a crime (*ḥadd*), man or woman; or one who harbors hatred toward his brother; or a professional witness; or someone who is supported by a family; or someone suspected of an allying with [a clan], or [family] relations."

habituation to [backbiting], they take the issue of backbiting lightly, and pay little heed to what harms peoples' reputations.

Whenever a wicked thought comes to mind about a Muslim, you should be more caring toward him and supplicate [God's] goodness for him, for that enrages Satan and repels him from you, such that he stops casting wicked thoughts [into your heart] out of fear that you will occupy yourself with supplications and caring [for others].

Whenever you know, with evidence, about the slip of a Muslim, counsel him in private and do not let Satan trick you by tempting you to backbite him. And when you admonish him, do not admonish him while delighting at learning of his shortcomings, such that he sees you as one to esteem or you see him as one to disdain, and you are raised above him by admonishing [him]. Rather, let your aim be to rid him of the sin while sorrowful, just as you would be sorrowful for yourself if a shortcoming came into your *dīn*.

If he gives up [a sin] without your advice, that should be preferable to you than if he gave it up [because of your] advice, and if you did that, you would have combined the reward of the admonishment, and the reward for concealing[64] his misfortune, and the reward for supporting him in his *dīn*.

Among the consequences of having wicked suppositions [about people] is spying. This is because the heart is not satisfied with [just] supposition—it seeks verification and so is occupied with spying, and
536 this is also forbidden, as God تعالى says: | *And do not spy* [Q. 49:12].
Thus, backbiting, [having] wicked suppositions about others, and spying are all forbidden in one verse.

Spying means not leaving the servants of God [undisturbed] beneath God's cover, [but rather] examining and tearing off the cover until it is disclosed to you what, if it had been hidden from you, would have been safer for your heart and your *dīn*. In the book

64 Or, being saddened at his misfortune.

on the *Commanding of Right* [*and the Forbidding of Wrong*],[65] we discussed the legal status of spying and its true nature. |

❁ ❁ ❁

An elucidation of the justifications that authorize backbiting (*ghība*) 537

Know that what is authorized of backbiting and mentioning the evil deeds of others is a sound objective according to the law, if it cannot be achieved otherwise. [In that case] the sin of backbiting is removed [lit., pushed away].

There are six matters [in which backbiting is authorized]:

The first: [Lodging] a complaint

Whoever accuses a judge of injustice, treachery, or taking bribes is [considered] a backbiter and a seditionist if he has not been wronged.

As for a person wronged by a judge, he should lodge his complaint with the sultan and accuse [that judge] of injustice, for [the wronged person] cannot fully receive his due right save through it [the complaint, which involves backbiting]. [The Prophet] صَلَّى ٱللَّٰهُ عَلَيْهِ وَسَلَّمَ said, "The one who has a right [should lodge] a complaint."[66]

And [the Prophet] صَلَّى ٱللَّٰهُ عَلَيْهِ وَسَلَّمَ said, "The delay [of payment] by the wealthy is an injustice."[67]

And [the Prophet] صَلَّى ٱللَّٰهُ عَلَيْهِ وَسَلَّمَ said, "The delay of the well-off [person makes it] lawful to [harm] his reputation and punish him."[68]

❁ ❁ ❁

65 Trans.: Book 19 of the *Revival of the Religious Sciences: The Commanding of Right and the Forbidding of Wrong* (*Kitāb al-amr bi-l-maʿrūf wa-l-nahī ʿan al-munkar*).

66 Al-Bukhārī, *Ṣaḥīḥ*, 2306; and Muslim, *Ṣaḥīḥ*, 1601.

67 Al-Bukhārī, *Ṣaḥīḥ*, 2287; and Muslim, *Ṣaḥīḥ*, 1564.

68 Abū Dāwūd, *Sunan*, 3628; al-Nasāʾī, *Sunan*, 7:316; and Ibn Mājah, *Sunan*, 2427.

538 **The second: Aiding [someone] to change a wrong and returning the disobedient [person] to the way of righteousness**

It has been related that ʿUmar passed by ʿUthmān—or by Ṭalḥa رَضِيَ ٱللَّهُ عَنْهُمْ [according to some narrations]—and greeted him, but he did not return his greeting. So he went to Abū Bakr رَضِيَ ٱللَّهُ عَنْهُ and mentioned this to him and Abū Bakr went to him [ʿUthman or Ṭalḥa] and reconciled them but they did not consider [ʿUmar's actions] backbiting.[69]

Similarly, when ʿUmar رَضِيَ ٱللَّهُ عَنْهُ learned that Abū Jandal had become addicted to wine in Shām, he wrote him [a letter with these verses]: *In the name of God, the All-Merciful, the All-Compassionate. Ḥā Mīm. The revelation of the Book is from God, the exalted in Might, the Knowing, the Forgiver of sin, Acceptor of repentance, severe in punishment, owner of abundance. There is no god except Him; to Him is the destination* [Q. 40:1–3] and [Abū Jandal] repented.[70] ʿUmar did not consider the one who had told him [about Abū Jandal] a backbiter because his aim was for ʿUmar to disapprove of what [Abū Jandal] was doing so that he could benefit by [ʿUmar's] advice in a way that no one else's advice could benefit him.

This is permissible for a sound aim; if that is not the aim, [then] it is unlawful.

❁ ❁ ❁

The third: [Seeking] a legal ruling

When a person says to a *muftī*, "My father . . . or my brother . . . or
539 my wife has wronged me, how do I proceed [to find] relief?" | The safest [way to communicate this] is by allusion. Ask [the *muftī*], "What would you say in the case of a man whose father or brother or wife wronged him?" It is permissible in these circumstances to speak of specific [people]. [This is based on] what was related about Hind bt. ʿUtba, that she said to the Prophet صَلَّى ٱللَّهُ عَلَيْهِ وَسَلَّمَ, "Abū Sufyān is a stingy man. He does not give me enough to support myself and

69 Ibn Ḥanbal, *Musnad*, 1:6. It has been said that ʿUthmān did not return the greeting because he was still in shock from the death of the Prophet صَلَّى ٱللَّهُ عَلَيْهِ وَسَلَّمَ.

70 ʿAbd al-Razzāq, *al-Muṣannaf*, 9:244.

my son. Should I take [money] without his knowing?"[71] And [the Prophet] صَلَّى ٱللَّهُ عَلَيْهِ وَسَلَّمَ said, "Take what will suffice you and your child fairly." Although she mentioned his stinginess and injustice toward her and her son, the Messenger of God صَلَّى ٱللَّهُ عَلَيْهِ وَسَلَّمَ did not rebuke her for that, because her aim was to seek a legal judgment.

❁ ❁ ❁

The fourth: Cautioning Muslims against evil

When you see a student of *fiqh* frequent a deviant or corrupt [person] and you fear that his deviancy or corruption will pass on to [the student], you are [allowed] to disclose [to the student] the deviance (*bidʿa*) and corruption of that person, as long as your only reason is the fear of the transmission of deviancy and corruption. And this is an occasion [fraught] with deception, because the [true] motivation might be envy. Satan may obscure [this true motive] by presenting it as benevolence to creatures.

Similarly, whoever bought a slave, and knew that the slave was a thief, or corrupt, or had another defect, you are obliged to mention this because by saying nothing, there is a harm to the buyer. [True,] in your mentioning [that], there may be harm for the slave [as well], but the buyer's right takes precedence.

Similarly, if someone is asked to vouch for a witness, he must impeach [that witness] if he knows [a reason] for his impeachment. |

Similarly, an adviser on the issue of marriage or the consignment 540
of a trust must state what he knows [about the person]. The aim is advising the advisee, not the aim of disparagement. If [the adviser] knows that [his advisee] will abandon [his pursuit of] the marriage if he simply tells him: "It will not be suitable for you," then it is mandatory [to say just that] and no more. But if [the adviser] knows that [his advisee] will not leave it unless the defects [of the person being sought in marriage] are declared, then he needs to clarify it.

The Messenger of God صَلَّى ٱللَّهُ عَلَيْهِ وَسَلَّمَ said, "Are you too scrupulous to mention [the faults] of the profligate? Expose him so that people

71 Al-Bukhārī, *Ṣaḥīḥ*, 2211; and Muslim, *Ṣaḥīḥ*, 1714.

may beware of him, mention what is in him until people are warned about him."[72]

They used to say, "There are three [types of people] about whom it is not [considered] backbiting [to mention their faults]: an oppressive leader, a deviant, and someone who flaunts his corruption."[73]

❁ ❁ ❁

The fifth: When a person is known by a nickname that refers to his disability

For example, the "lame" (*aʿraj*), or the "rheumy-eyed one" (*aʿmash*). It is not a sin to say, "Narrated by Abū l-Zanād, from al-Aʿraj [the Lame], and Sulaymān [narrates] from al-Aʿmash [the rheumy-eyed]," and other such examples. The scholars did this out of necessity, to identify [a person] and because the one [with such a name] became accustomed to it, does not deplore for it to be mentioned, and became well-known by it. |

541 Yes, if an alternative were found that enables [one to] know him by another formulation, [using] that is preferable. For example, saying of a blind person, the "insightful" (*baṣīr*), instead of the name of the disability.

❁ ❁ ❁

The sixth: [One who is] openly corrupt

For example, a brothel-keeper,[74] a bar owner, [someone who] drinks intoxicants openly, or one who takes property [with impunity]. These are people who are outwardly corrupt, have no objection to its

72 Ibn Abī l-Dunyā, *al-Ṣamt wa-ādāb al-lisān*, 221; and al-Ṭabarānī, *al-Muʿjam al-awsaṭ*, 4369.

73 Ibn Abī l-Dunyā, *al-Ṣamt wa-ādāb al-lisān*, 227.

74 Eds.: Here, the Arabic word, *mukhanith* is defined by Lane (*An Arabic-English Lexicon*, 814–), as one who does something excessively foul or obscene. Al-Zabīdī (*Itḥāf*, 7:557) states that a *mukhanith* refers to a pimp (*dayyūth*). Lane defines a *dayyūth* in the same way, and also as a man who has no jealousy (Lane, *An Arabic-English Lexicon*, 941). We have translated this as a brothel-keeper in keeping with al-Ghazālī's emphasis on polite speech, and because this is the work of a *dayyūth* and it follows

being known, and may even be proud of it, so if whatever he displays outwardly is spoken about, there is no sin in it. The Messenger of God صَلَّى ٱللَّهُ عَلَيْهِ وَسَلَّمَ said, "Whoever throws off the cloak of decency from his face, it is not backbiting [to speak against him]."[75]

And ʿUmar b. al-Khaṭṭāb رَضِيَ ٱللَّهُ عَنْهُ said, "A profligate has no inviolability,"[76] by which he meant someone who is corrupt openly rather than [the sinner] who conceals [his sins]. If they are concealed, then his inviolability should be observed.

Al-Ṣalt b. Ṭarīf said, "I said to Ḥasan [al-Baṣrī], 'If I speak badly of a profligate who is overt in his profligacy, is it backbiting?' He said, 'No, for he has no honor.'"[77]

And Ḥasan [al-Baṣrī] said, "There are three for whom there is no backbiting: a capricious [person], a corrupt [person] who is
overt in his | corruption, and an unjust leader."[78] These three are 542
mentioned together because all of them display [their sins] and may even be proud of them. Indeed, how could they deplore that [these be mentioned] when their aim is to display [their sins] outwardly?

Yes, if you were to mention something not displayed outwardly, it would be a sin.

ʿAwf [b. Abī Jamīla al-Aʿrabī l-Baṣrī] said, "I came to Ibn Sīrīn and talked to him about al-Ḥajjāj. [Ibn Sīrīn] said, "God is a just judge. He will punish anyone who backbites al-Ḥajjāj just as He will punish al-Ḥajjāj for anyone he wronged. As for you, if you were to meet God تَعَالَىٰ tomorrow, the smallest transgression you committed would be much worse for you than the greatest transgression committed by al-Ḥajjāj!"[79] |

❁ ❁ ❁

that one engaged in something foul or obscene, and a man without jealousy is the only sort of person who would run a brothel.

75 Ibn ʿAdī, *al-Kāmil*, 1:386; and al-Bayhaqī, *al-Sunan al-kubrā*, 10:210.

76 Ibn Abī l-Dunyā, *al-Ṣamt wa-ādāb al-lisān*, 233.

77 Ibn Abī l-Dunyā, *al-Ṣamt wa-ādāb al-lisān*, 232.

78 Ibn Abī l-Dunyā, *al-Ṣamt wa-ādāb al-lisān*, 235.

79 Al-Qushayrī, *al-Risāla*, 284, and with similar wording in Ibn Abī Shayba, *al-Muṣannaf*, 31226; and Abū Nuʿaym, *Ḥilya*, 2:270.

543
An elucidation of the expiation (*kaffāra*) for backbiting (*ghība*)

Know that it is mandatory for a backbiter to regret, to repent, and to be sorry for what he has done in order to release himself from the right of God سُبْحَانَهُ [on him], then to ask for pardon from [the person] he backbit in order to release himself from his wrongdoing. In asking for pardon,[80] he should do so with sadness, remorse, and regret for his deed, for someone who acts to be seen by others might seek pardon [from the person he wronged] just to make himself appear pious while inwardly he has no regrets, and [in doing this] he would be committing another disobedient act.

Ḥasan [al-Baṣrī][81] said, "It is enough to ask forgiveness [from God] rather than to seek pardon [from the victim, for backbiting]." Perhaps he was basing this on what was related by Anas b. Mālik who said the Messenger of God صَلَّى ٱللَّهُ عَلَيْهِ وَسَلَّمَ said, "Expiation from the [one who] was backbitten is to ask [God's] forgiveness for [the victim]."[82]

And Mujāhid said, "The expiation for eating the flesh of [that is, backbiting] your brother is commending him and supplicating for his welfare."[83]

ʿAṭāʾ b. Abī Rabāḥ was asked about repentance from *fariyya*[84]
544 and he said, "Go to | your companion and say, 'I lied in what I said [about you]; I was unjust and I was wrong. If you wish, claim your right [on me], and if you wish, pardon [me].'"[85]

This [last view] is the most correct.

One said—"there is no compensation for [damaged] reputation, so it is not mandatory to seek pardon from [the victim]; [this is] unlike [crimes against] property [which must be compensated]." This is a

80 Eds.: Ar., *istiḥalla* means asking for pardon from the victim of backbiting; see al-Zabīdī, *Itḥāf*, 7:558.

81 Eds.: Al-Zabīdī identifies him as Ḥasan al-Baṣrī (*Itḥāf*, 7:558).

82 Ibn Abī l-Dunyā, *al-Ṣamt wa-ādāb al-lisān*, 293; al-Kharāʾiṭī, *Masāwiʾ al-akhlāq*, 213; al-Bayhaqī, *Shuʿab al-īmān*, 6368; and al-Bayhaqī, *al-Daʿwāt al-kabīr*, 507.

83 Ibn Abī l-Dunyā, *al-Ṣamt wa-ādāb al-lisān*, 294.

84 Eds.: Ar., *fariyya* is a euphemism for backbiting; al-Zabīdī (*Itḥāf*, 7:559) says some copies of the *Iḥyāʾ* have *ghība* instead of *fariyyā*.

85 Ibn Abī l-Dunyā, *al-Ṣamt wa-ādāb al-lisān*, 295.

weak argument, since [damaging someone's] reputation mandates punishment (*ḥadd*) for defamation and it is valid to request [that this punishment be carried out].

[In fact,] in a sound *ḥadīth*, it was related that [the Prophet] صَلَّى ٱللَّٰهُ عَلَيْهِ وَسَلَّمَ said, "Let the one who has wronged his brother in respect to either his reputation, or his wealth [or property], ask him to exonerate him of [his misdeed] before the day when there will be no dinar nor dirham, for it will be taken from his good deeds, and if he has no good deeds [left], the bad deeds will be taken from the victim and added to his [the defamer's] bad deeds."[86]

And ʿĀʾisha رَضِيَ ٱللَّٰهُ عَنْهَا said to a woman who said to another, "This one's robe is trailing behind her."[87] You have backbitten about her. You should [ask her] to exonerate you."[88]

Thus, it is necessary [to ask the victim of backbiting] for exoneration if you are able. If that person is absent or dead, you should [ask] forgiveness for him, supplicate for him in abundance, and increase [your] good deeds. |

❁ ❁ ❁

If you were to say, "Is seeking pardon mandatory?" 545

I would say no, it is voluntary. What is voluntary has merit, but it is not mandatory, though it is preferred. And the way to ask [a person] to pardon you is to be effusive in commending him and showing him affection, and to continue in that way until his heart is pleased. But if his heart is not pleased, then the extent to which you sought his pardon and affection [will be] a good deed counted in your favor and on the day of resurrection it will counteract the bad deed of backbiting.

❁ ❁ ❁

86 Al-Bukhārī, *Ṣaḥīḥ*, 2449. Trans.: Ar., *Istiḥlāl* literally means "to consider something lawful (*ḥalāl*)." By extension, it is to ask someone to disregard a wrong committed against him or her.

87 FC: Ar., *ṭawīl al-dhayl* can also mean one is rich, proud, or conceited (see Lane, *An Arabic-English Lexicon*, 991).

88 Al-Kharāʾiṭī, *Masāwiʾ al-akhlāq*, 200.

There were certain of the Predecessors (Salaf) who would not pardon [others who spoke ill against them]. Saʿīd b. al-Musayyib said, "I do not pardon one who wronged me."[89]

And Ibn Sīrīn said, "I did not make [backbiting] unlawful for him, [such that I can] make it lawful for him. God is the one who made it unlawful for him to backbite, and it is not for me to ever make lawful what God has made unlawful."[90]

❁ ❁ ❁

And if you were to ask me, "Then what is the meaning of the Prophet's صَلَّىٱللَّهُعَلَيْهِوَسَلَّمَ saying, 'You should seek pardon' [because] making lawful what God تَعَالَىٰ has made unlawful is not possible."

We would answer that what [the Prophet] meant by [pardon] was [being] pardoned for the wrong, and not to invert an unlawful [act]
546 into something lawful. | What Ibn Sīrīn mentioned is correct [as it pertains to making] backbiting lawful before [it occurs], but indeed it is not allowable for him [that is, Ibn Sīrīn] to make backbiting lawful for others.

❁ ❁ ❁

And if you said, "And what is the meaning of the Prophet's صَلَّىٱللَّهُعَلَيْهِوَسَلَّمَ saying, 'Are any of you not able to be like Abū Ḍamḍam, who would say when he left his house, "O God, I have given my reputation in charity to people,"'[91] How can someone give his reputation in charity? And if someone does that, is it permissible to take his offer? And if it cannot be given in charity, why [did the Prophet صَلَّىٱللَّهُعَلَيْهِوَسَلَّمَ] encourage it?"

We would say it means, "on the [day of] resurrection, I will not seek [redress] from one who wronged me and I will not dispute with him." Nevertheless, backbiting [about this person] does not become lawful. Nor is the wrongful action against [the victim] void because it is a pre-emptive pardon. It is a promise—and he resolved

89 Ibn Saʿd, *Ṭabaqāt*, 7:127.

90 Al-Kharāʾiṭī, *Masāwiʾ al-akhlāq*, 190; and Abū Nuʿaym, *Ḥilya*, 2:263.

91 Al-Ṭabarānī, *Makārim al-akhlāq*, 53.

to keep it—not to dispute [with the one who wrongs him], but if he goes back [on what he said] and disputes it, then, by analogy, it is like any other right that he has. In fact, the jurists have clarified that [even] if someone permits defamation, his right to demand punishment is not voided [that is, it remains]. An injustice in the hereafter is like an injustice in [this] world. |

❁ ❁ ❁

In general, pardon is preferable. Ḥasan [al-Baṣrī] said, "When all the communities of people are kneeling before | God عَزَّوَجَلَّ on the 547
day of resurrection, a call will go out: 'let them stand, all those who asked for God's reward [in lieu of worldly reward], and none will stand except those who pardoned people in [this] world.'"[92]

And God تَعَالَىٰ said, *Be ready to pardon* (*ʿafū*) [*enjoin what is good, and turn away from the ignorant*] [Q. 7:199], and the Prophet صَلَّىٰٱللَّهُعَلَيْهِوَسَلَّمَ said, "O Gabriel, what is this [pardon]?" He said, "God commands you to pardon the one who wrongs you, to stay in contact with the one who cuts you off, and to give to the one who withholds from you."[93]

It was related from Ḥasan [al-Baṣrī] that a man said to him, "So-and-so backbites you." So [Ḥasan] sent him a plate of dates and said, "I have been told that you have given me some of your good deeds and I wanted to return the favor to you. But please excuse me, I cannot compensate you in full!"[94]

92 Al-Bayhaqī, *Shuʿab al-īmān*, 7960.

93 Abū Nuʿaym, *Maʿrifat al-ṣaḥāba*, 4:231; and Ibn Abī l-Dunyā, *Makārim al-akhlāq*, 25.

94 Al-Qushayrī, *al-Risāla*, 285.

[16]

548 ## The Sixteenth Bane: Gossip (*Namīma*)

God تَعَالَىٰ says, *A scorner, going about with malicious gossip* [Q. 68:11] and then He says, *Cruel, moreover, and an illegitimate pretender* (*zanīm*) [Q. 68:13].

ʿAbdallāh b. al-Mubārak said, the *zanīm* is one born of adultery (*zinā*) who does not conceal [private] speech.

And by that he meant that failing to conceal [private] speech and going around gossiping indicates that one was born out of wedlock (*zinā*) [that is, it betrays one's low birth]. Calling him "born out of wedlock" is derived from [God's] words عَزَّوَجَلَّ, *Cruel, moreover, and an illegitimate pretender*, and thus *zanīm* [means] "pretender" [that is, illegitimate].[1]

[God] تَعَالَىٰ said, *Woe to every scandal-monger* (*humaza*) *and mocker* [Q. 104:1], it is said that *humaza* means a gossiper.[2]

[God] تَعَالَىٰ said, *The carrier of firewood* [Q. 111:4], and it is said that [the woman referred to] was a gossiper who carried [private] speech [between people].[3]

[God] تَعَالَىٰ said, *They were under two of Our righteous servants but betrayed them, so they* [*those prophets*] *did not avail them from God at all* [Q. 66:10]. It is said that Lot's wife informed [the townspeople]

1 Eds.: *Zanīm* refers to one born out of wedlock. See Wehr, *A Dictionary of Modern Written Arabic*, 383; and Lane, *An Arabic-English Lexicon*, 885.

2 Ibn Abī l-Dunyā, *al-Ṣamt wa-ādāb al-lisān*, 264. Trans.: The person originally referred to was Arwa bt. Ḥarb, the wife of Abū Lahab. Eds.: A gossiper (*namīma*) is someone who goes about causing division between brothers and provoking enmity in the community.

3 Ibn Abī l-Dunyā, *al-Ṣamt wa-ādāb al-lisān*, 265.

on the guests and Noah's wife informed [the townspeople] that [Noah] was demented.[4] |

The Prophet ﷺ said, "A gossiper will not enter heaven."[5] 549

And in another *ḥadīth*, "A *qattāt* will not enter heaven."[6] *Qattāt* is another [word for a] gossiper.

Abū Hurayra said,

> The Messenger of God ﷺ said, "The most beloved of you to God are those with the best character, who tread gently, and who love to be with others as others love to be with them. And the most loathed of you in the [eyes of] God are those who go about gossiping, who cause division between brothers, and who look for the failings of the innocent."[7]

[The Prophet] ﷺ said, "Shall I not tell you who is most evil among you?" They answered, "By all means!" He said, "Those who go around spreading gossip, undermine what is between dear [friends], and want to see the innocent [suffer] hardship."[8]

Abū Dharr said, "The Messenger of God ﷺ said, 'he who loudly publicizes so much as a [single] word against a Muslim to disgrace him unjustly will be disgraced by God with the [same word] on the day of resurrection [as he is led to] the fire.'"[9]

Abū l-Dardā᾽ said,

> The Messenger of God ﷺ said, "Any man who circulates so much as a [single] word against a man to disgrace him in [this] world—while he is innocent of [the charge]—it
> is God's right on the day of resurrection | to melt him away 550
> with [that word] in the fire."[10]

Abū Hurayra said, "The Messenger of God ﷺ said, 'He who bears witness with a testimony he is not qualified to give [that is, false testimony] against a Muslim has prepared his place in the fire.'"[11]

---

4 Ibn Abī l-Dunyā, *al-Ṣamt wa-ādāb al-lisān*, 271.

5 Muslim, *Ṣaḥīḥ*, 105.

6 Al-Bukhārī, *Ṣaḥīḥ*, 6056.

7 Al-Ṭabarānī, *al-Muʿjam al-ṣaghīr*, 2:25; and Ibn Abī l-Dunyā, *Mudārāt al-nās*, 146.

8 Ibn Ḥanbal, *Musnad*, 6:459; and al-Ṭabarānī, *al-Muʿjam al-kabīr*, 24:167.

9 Ibn Abī l-Dunyā, *al-Ṣamt wa-ādāb al-lisān*, 258.

10 Ibn Abī l-Dunyā, *al-Ṣamt wa-ādāb al-lisān*, 259.

11 Ibn Ḥanbal, *Musnad*, 2:509; and Ibn Abī l-Dunyā, *al-Ṣamt wa-ādāb al-lisān*, 260.

And it was said that one-third of the punishment of the grave is due to gossip.[12]

> From Ibn ʿUmar [we learned that], the Prophet صَلَّى ٱللَّهُ عَلَيْهِ وَسَلَّمَ [said], When God created heaven, He said to it, "Speak!" and it said, "Felicitous is the one who enters me." Then the All-Mighty (al-Jabbār), exalted be His Majesty جَلَّ جَلَالُهُ, said, "By My Might and Majesty, eight types of people will not dwell in [heaven]: the one addicted to intoxicants, a persistent fornicator [that is, one who commits *zinā*], a *qattāt*—and that is a gossiper (*namām*)—a panderer, a [corrupt] law officer, a man [who assumes an aura of softness] (*mukhanith*), the one [who] cuts family ties, and the one who says, 'I vow to God that I will do this or that . . .' and then does not fulfill it."[13] |

551 Kaʿb al-Aḥbār related that a drought struck the children of Israel and Moses عَلَيْهِ ٱلسَّلَامُ [prayed] the prayer for rain (*istisqā*) numerous times but none came. Then God تَعَالَىٰ revealed, "I will not answer [your prayers] nor [prayers] of those who are with you when there is a gossiper among you who insists on [spreading] gossip." Moses said, "O Lord, who is he? Point me to him, so we may expel him from our midst." And God answered, "O Moses! Would I forbid you from gossip and then be a gossiper [Myself]?" So they all repented and it rained [lit., they were quenched].

It is said that a man followed a sage for seven hundred leagues[14] to ask him seven words. When he caught up to him, he asked,

> "I have come to you [to gain] some of the knowledge that God تَعَالَىٰ gave you. Tell me about the heavens and what is heavier than them, and about the earth and what is vaster

---

12 Ibn Abī l-Dunyā, *al-Ṣamt wa-ādāb al-lisān*, 190.

13 Al-Zabīdī (*Itḥāf*, 7:563) says al-ʿIrāqī notes, "I do not find this saying in its entirety." Ibn Ḥanbal (*Musnad*) relates the *ḥadīth*, "He who grieves for his parents and the panderer will not enter heaven." And in al-Nasāʾī, a *ḥadīth* related by Ibn ʿUmar states "He who recounts his favors to people, he who grieves his parents, and he who is addicted to wine will not enter heaven . . ." and in the two sound collections (that is, al-Bukhārī, *Ṣaḥīḥ*, and Muslim, *Ṣaḥīḥ*), it is, "One who cuts [ties] will not enter heaven . . ." Eds.: For kh-n-th see Lane, *An Arabic-English Lexicon*, 814.

14 FC: A league (*farsakh*, pl. *farāsakh*) is approximately 3 miles (Wehr, *A Dictionary of Modern Written Arabic*, 705; and Lane, *An Arabic-English Lexicon*, 2369).

than it, and about the stones and what is harder than them, and about the fire and what is hotter than it, and tell me about the bitter frost (*zamharīr*) and what is colder than it, and about the ocean and what is richer than it, and about the orphan and what is lowlier than he."

The sage answered him, "To falsely accuse the innocent is heavier than the heavens, the truth is vaster than the earth, the heart of a satisfied person is richer than the ocean, greed and envy are hotter than the fire, need that is nearby but unattainable is colder than a bitter frost, the heart of the disbeliever is harder than stone, and the gossiper, when his act is exposed, is lowlier [in status] than the orphan."[15] |

❁ ❁ ❁

An elucidation of the definition of gossip (*namīma*) and what is mandatory to counter it 552

Know that the noun gossip mostly refers to one who unleashes the statement of another person to the one who was spoken about. As when you say, "So-and-so was talking about you and said this or that . . ." But gossip is not limited to that. Its [precise] definition is disclosing what [others] would deplore to have disclosed, regardless of whether it is deplored by the person who it is related about, or by the person it is related to, or deplored by a third [party]; [the word applies] regardless of whether it is disclosed in words, writing, symbols, or mimicry; [the word applies] regardless of whether what is related is in actions or speech; and regardless of whether or not [what is disclosed] is a defect or deficiency in the person it is related about. Indeed, the reality of gossip is divulging what is secret, tearing off the cover from what [someone would] deplore to have revealed. Rather, all of what a person sees of the states

15 Al-Dīnawarī, *al-Majālasa wa-jawāhir al-ʿilm*, 470.

of people that are deplored, one must remain quiet about, unless speaking about it benefits a Muslim or repels a disobedience. For example, if someone saw a person taking another person's property, he must testify about it to protect the rights of the one for whom he is testifying [that is, the one whose property was taken]. But if he saw him hiding his own wealth, then speaking about it would be gossip and divulging what is secret.

And if what he is gossiping about is a deficiency or defect of the one he is speaking about, then he has combined backbiting and gossip.

The motivation for gossip is wishing ill for the one about whom he is speaking, or [he wants] to show his love for the one to whom he is speaking, or [wants] to entertain others with talk, or [wants] to delve into needless, baseless [talk].

Anyone to whom gossip is said, "So-and-so said such-and-such
553 about you, | or did such-and-such against you," or "... is planning to undermine you," or "is in collaboration with your enemy," or "portrays you as repugnant," or anything like this, should observe six principles:

First, he should not be believed because a gossiper is corrupt and his testimony is inadmissible. God تَعَالَىٰ says, *O you who have believed, if there comes to you a disobedient (fāsiq) one with information, investigate, lest you harm a people out of ignorance* [Q. 49:6].

Second, he should forbid him from that, counsel him, and denounce his deed as repugnant. God تَعَالَىٰ says, *Enjoin what is right, forbid what is wrong* [Q. 31:17].

Third, he should loathe him for [the sake of] God تَعَالَىٰ, because he is loathed by God تَعَالَىٰ, and he must loathe what God تَعَالَىٰ loathes.

Fourth, he should not suspect ill of his brother in his absence, like God تَعَالَىٰ says, [*O you who have believed*], *avoid much* [*negative*] *assumption* (*ẓann*). *Indeed, some assumption* (*ẓann*) *is sin* [Q. 49:12].

Fifth, he should not let what has been related to him lead him to spying in order to verify it, as in the words of [God] تَعَالَىٰ, *And do not spy* [Q. 49:12].

Sixth, you should not accept for yourself what you have forbidden to the gossiper. That is, you should not relate his gossip, saying, "So-and-so told me such-and-such," for in doing so you [yourself] become a gossiper, a backbiter, and someone who does what he forbids others to do.

It was related that a man came to ʿUmar b. ʿAbd al-ʿAzīz رَضِوَاللَّهُعَنْهُ and began to say something to him about another man. ʿUmar said,

> If you wish, we will look into your situation and if you are lying, then you are among those to whom this verse refers: [*O you who have believed,*] *if there comes to you a disobedient one with information, investigate* [Q. 49:6]. And if | you 554
> are truthful, then you are among those to whom this verse refers: . . . *A scorner, going about with malicious gossip* (*namīma*) [Q. 68:11]. And if you wish, we will pardon you.
>
> He said, "Pardon me, O Commander of the Faithful. I will not repeat it ever again."

And it was mentioned that one of the sages was visited by one of his brothers who conveyed to him news about one of his friends. The sage said, "You have not visited for a long time, and you have come to me with three crimes: you have made my brother loathesome in my eyes, you have occupied my heart that was empty [of gossip], and you accused your trustworthy soul [lit., brought transgressions against your own soul]."

And it was related that Sulaymān b. ʿAbd al-Malik was sitting with al-Zuhrī when a man came to him. Sulaymān said,

> "I heard that you have been attacking me, saying such-and-such a thing."
>
> The man said, "I have not done or said [anything]."
>
> Sulaymān said, "The one who told me this is truthful."
>
> Al-Zuhrī said to him, "A gossiper cannot be truthful."
>
> Sulaymān replied, "What you said is true," and then said to the man, "Go in peace."

Ḥasan [al-Baṣrī] said, "Whoever gossips about someone [in your presence] will gossip about you [in someone else's presence]."

This indicates that one should loathe a gossiper and should not put faith in his words or his friendship. How could you not loathe him when he does not desist from lying and backbiting, treachery and betrayal, spite, envy, and hypocrisy, from undermining what is between people, and deception, and he is one who strives to sever what God has ordered to be joined, as God تَعَالَىٰ said: *And they sever that which God has ordered to be joined and cause corruption on earth* [Q. 2:27]. |

555 And [God] تَعَالَىٰ says, *The cause is only against the ones who wrong the people and tyrannize* [*those*] *upon the earth without right* [Q. 42:42], and the gossiper is among them.

And [the Prophet] صَلَّىٰ ٱللَّهُ عَلَيْهِ وَسَلَّمَ said, "Among the most evil of people is [one whose] evil people must beware"[16] and the gossiper is among them.

And [صَلَّىٰ ٱللَّهُ عَلَيْهِ وَسَلَّمَ] said, "One who cuts [ties] will not enter heaven."[17] It was said that "one who cuts [ties] between people," is the gossiper. And it was said that [this refers to] one who cuts family [ties].

And it was related from ʿAlī رَضِيَ ٱللَّهُ عَنْهُ that a man came to him about another man [gossiping], and [ʿAlī] said to him, "O you, we are asking you what you said. If you are truthful, we find you detestable, and if you are lying, we will penalize you, and if you wish for us to exempt you, we will exempt you." He said, "Exempt me, O Commander of the Faithful."

It was said to Muḥammad b. Kaʿb al-Quraẓī, "Which quality of the believer most debases him?" He answered, "Speaking too much, divulging what is secret, and accepting the statements of everyone."[18]

A man said to ʿAbdallāh b. ʿĀmir when he was a commander [of Basra], "I have heard that so-and-so reported to the commander that I spoke ill of him."

[ʿAbdallāh b. ʿĀmir] said, "That is true."

[The man] said, "So tell me what he said to you so I can make apparent his lie to you."

[ʿAbdallāh b. ʿĀmir] said, "I do not want to vilify myself with
556 my tongue. It is enough for me that I did not | believe what he said and that I do not sever relations with you."

[The issue of] slander (*siʿāya*) was mentioned in the presence of one of the righteous and he said, "What do you think of a

16 Al-Bukhārī, *Ṣaḥīḥ*, 6032; and Muslim, *Ṣaḥīḥ*, 2591.

17 Al-Bukhārī, *Ṣaḥīḥ*, 5984; and Muslim, *Ṣaḥīḥ*, 2556.

18 Al-Khaṭṭābī, *al-ʿUzla*, 71.

group—when veracity from every level of people is praised except theirs [that is, the slanderers]?"

Muṣʿab b. al-Zubayr said,

> We hold that accepting slander is more evil than [the act of] slandering. Slander amounts to tendering [some news] and accepting [it] amounts to an endorsement [of it; lit., allowing it]. One who points something out, and thus informs [others] of it, is not like someone who accepts and endorses it. So beware of the slanderer. If he is truthful in what he says, he is still inquitous in his truthfulness, because he did not protect the sanctity [of another] and did not cover the faults.[19]

Slander amounts to gossip unless it is [conveyed] to someone who is feared, then it is called "slander." [The Prophet] صَلَّى ٱللَّهُ عَلَيْهِ وَسَلَّمَ said, "The one who slanders one people to another people is like [someone] without guidance," meaning, not a legitimate child.[20]

A man came to Sulaymān b. ʿAbd al-Malik, asked him for permission to speak, and said,

> "I have come to you, O Commander of the Faithful, with words that you should bear even if you deplore them because after them will be something you love if you accept it."
>
> He said, "Speak."
>
> The man said, "O Commander of the Faithful, all around you are men who have sold their *dīn* for what you have in [this] world, [who seek] to gain your pleasure by the wrath of their Lord. They fear you for the sake of God but do not fear God for your sake. Do not trust them with what God has entrusted to you and do not listen to them about what God has put under your protection, for they will not stop until they degrade the community and lose the trusts | and sever 557
> and violate [people's] reputations. The best of their deeds is tyranny and gossip and their greatest means [of accomplishing this] is backbiting and disparagement. You are responsible for what they commit while they are not responsible for what

19 There is a saying attributed to Imām al-Shāfiʿī with similar wording; reported in Abū Nuʿaym, *Ḥilya*, 9:122.

20 Al-Ḥākim al-Nīsābūrī, *al-Mustadrak*, 4:103. Eds.: This is not meant to imply that an illegitimate child is inherently bad, rather it refers to the parents who committed grave offenses that led to his circumstances, his upbringing, and the consequences for society.

> you commit. So do not better their worldly [state] by ruining your hereafter, for the most gullible person is someone who sells his hereafter for someone else's worldly [life]."[21]

A man slandered Ziyād al-Aʿjam to Sulaymān b. ʿAbd al-Malik, so he [Sulaymān] brought them together for reconciliation and Ziyād turned to the man and said [in verse]:

> Either I have trusted you like a close friend and you have betrayed me
> Or you have spoken of something without knowledge.
>
> And thus you are—in this matter between us—
> In a place between treachery and sin.

A man said to ʿAmr b. ʿUbayd, "al-Uswārī continues to tell evil stories about you." ʿAmr said to him,

> O you, you did not observe the proper etiquette of social intercourse with the man when you conveyed to us what he said, nor did you respect my right when you conveyed to me, concerning my brother, what would make me deplore him. But convey to him that death will overtake us all, the grave will enclose us, resurrection will gather us, and God تَعَالَىٰ will judge between us—and He is best of judges.[22] |

558 Some slanderers delivered a piece of paper to al-Ṣāḥib b. ʿAbbād on which [they] alerted him to some wealth [left to] an orphan and encouraged him to seize it because of how much it was. [Al-Ṣāḥib] wrote on the other side:

> Slander is repugnant even if it is true. If you intended it as advice, then your loss from it is better than profiting from it. I seek refuge in God from accepting [the advice of] one who has disgraced (*mahtūk*) [himself] regarding one who is blameless (*mastūr*) [that is, the orphan].[23] If it were not for

---

21 Al-Dīnawarī, *al-Mujālasa wa-jawāhir al-ʿilm*, 105; and Ibn ʿAsākir, *Tārīkh madīnat Dimashq*, 68:174.

22 Al-ʿAskarī, *Jamharat al-amthāl*, 2:269.

23 Eds.: Here al-Ghazālī includes a play on words: one who disgraces (*mahtūk*) [himself] is one who is uncovered, and one who is blameless (*mastūr*), is one who is covered, or protected.

your old age, I would confront you with what your action warrants for someone like you. O cursed one, beware of [this] defect, truly God knows best the hidden. May God have mercy on the dead, may God console the orphan, may God make fruitful the wealth [he was left], and may God curse the slanderer.

Luqmān said to his son,

O my son, I enjoin on you these properties—if you cling to them, you will always be noble. Manifest your [noble] character to both relatives and strangers, withhold your ignorance from the honorable and iniquitous, protect your brother, maintain contact with your relations and keep them secure from accepting the word of a slanderer, or from listening to an unjust person who desires to undermine you and seeks to deceive you, and let your brothers be those who, when you are apart from them or they from you, you do not find fault with them nor they with you.[24]

One of them [that is, a man] said, "gossip is built on lying, envy, and hypocrisy, and those are the trivets[25] of humiliation."

And one of them said, "If what a gossiper conveys to you is true, it means that he is bold enough to vilify you [to your face], in which case the one from whom he conveyed [it] is more deserving of your clemency, because he did not vilify you to your face."

In general, the evil of the gossiper is great and we should beware of him. |

Ḥammād b. Salama said, 559

A man sold a slave and said to the buyer, "He has no defects except gossiping."

The man said, "I accept [him]." So he bought the slave and after a few days with him the slave said to the man's wife, "Your husband does not love you. He plans to take a concubine. If you take a razor and while he is asleep cut some hair from the

24 Ibn Abī l-Dunyā, *al-Ḥilm*, 50.

25 Trans.: *Uthfiyy* (pl. *athāfin*) refers to the three stones used to support a cooking vessel over a fire, perhaps similar to a trivet.

> top of his head, I can use it in magic that will return his love to you." Following that, he spoke to the husband and said, "Your wife has taken a lover and wants to kill you. Pretend to her that you are sleeping so that you can find out for yourself." So he pretended to be asleep and his wife approached him with a razor [to cut some hair], but he thought she wanted to kill him, so he jumped up and killed her [instead]. After this, the wife's family came and killed the husband, and a feud arose between the two tribes that went on for years.[26]

We ask God for the best of success.

26 Ibn Abī l-Dunyā, *al-Ṣamt wa-ādāb al-lisān*, 270; and Ibn Ḥibbān, *Rawḍat al-ʿuqalā*, 179.

[17]

The Seventeenth Bane: The Speech of [One with] Two Tongues, [Someone] Who Goes Back and Forth between Two Adversaries and Says What Is Agreeable to Each of Them 560

RARELY can someone who is in the presence of two adversaries avoid doing this, and it is the essence of hypocrisy (*nifāq*). ʿAmmār b. Yāsir said, "The Messenger of God ﷺ said, 'He who has two faces in this world will have two tongues of fire on the day of resurrection.'"[1]

Abū Hurayra said, "The Messenger of God ﷺ said, 'You will find among the most evil of God's servants on the day of resurrection [a man] with two faces, who comes to these with what those have said, and comes to those with that these have said.'"

And in another version, "[a man] who comes to these with one face and those with [another] face."[2]

And Abū Hurayra said, "A person with two faces is not trustworthy in [the eyes of] God."[3]

And Mālik b. Dīnār said, "I read in the Torah, 'Invalid is the trust of a man who [converses] with his | companion with two 561
conflicting lips. On the day of resurrection God تَعَالَىٰ will destroy all [those with] conflicting lips.'"[4]

---

1 Abū Dāwūd, *Sunan*, 4873; and al-Kharāʾiṭī, *Masāwiʾ al-akhlāq*, 292.

2 Al-Bukhārī, *Ṣaḥīḥ*, 3494, 6058; Muslim, *Ṣaḥīḥ*, 2526; and with wording similar to al-Ghazālī's in Ibn Abī l-Dunyā, *al-Ṣamt wa-ādāb al-lisān*, 277, 278.

3 Ibn Ḥanbal, *Musnad*, 2:289; and Ibn Abī l-Dunyā, *al-Ṣamt wa-ādāb al-lisān*, 283.

4 Al-Kharāʾiṭī, *Masāwiʾ al-akhlāq*, 291.

And the Messenger of God ﷺ said,

> The most loathed of God's creatures on the day of resurrection are the liars, the arrogant, and those who loathe their brothers in their breasts but who, when they meet them, speak to them flatteringly, and those who, when they are called to God and His Messenger, are slow [to respond], but when they are called to Satan and his affairs, come quickly.[5]

Ibn Masʿūd said, "Do not by any means let yourselves become an *immaʿat*." They said, "What is *immaʿat*?" He said, "Someone who turns with every wind"[6] [i.e., fickle].

[The learned] agreed that whoever meets two people with two faces is a hypocrite, and hypocrisy has many signs and this is one of them.

It was related that a man from the Companions of the Prophet ﷺ died and Ḥudhayfa[7] did not join [the funeral] prayers for him. ʿUmar said to him, "A man from among the Companions of the Messenger ﷺ died and you did not pray [the funeral prayer] for him?" He answered, "O Commander of the Faithful, he was one of them." ʿUmar said, "I ask you, by God: am I one of them or not?" He said, "By God, no, but I cannot guarantee that anyone after you is safe from it [hypocrisy]."[8] |

❁ ❁ ❁

562 And if you were to ask, "How does a man come to have two tongues and what is the definition of that?"

I would answer that if he comes between two adversaries and treats each of them courteously and is sincere in this, he is not a

5 Al-Kharāʾiṭī, *Masāwiʾ al-akhlāq*, 299.

6 Al-Kharāʾiṭī, *Masāwiʾ al-akhlāq*, 301. Trans.: It appears that the word *immaʿat* was unfamiliar to those with whom Ibn Masʿūd was speaking. It is defined as "a characterless person, an opportunist." See Wehr, *A Dictionary of Modern Written Arabic*, 28.

7 Eds.: Ḥudhāyfa was entrusted with knowledge of the names of the hypocrites, but the Prophet instructed him not to reveal their names while they were alive; when they died and Ḥudhāyfa did not attend their funeral prayers, it was understood that they were among the hypocrites.

8 Al-Kharāʾiṭī, *Masāwiʾ al-akhlāq*, 311

hypocrite nor is he two-tongued, for one can be friendly to two adversaries. But his friendship is weak and does not reach the level of brotherhood, because if it were true friendship, it would result in [feeling] enmity toward [his brother's] adversaries, as we have mentioned in *The Book on the Proprieties of Friendship and Brotherhood*.[9]

And if he conveys the speech of each one of them to the other, he has two tongues, and that is worse than gossip. Gossip means conveying something from only one of the two sides, but conveying [speech] from both [adversaries to each another] is more evil than the gossiper.

And if he does not convey speech but advocates each one of the two [adversaries] for their enmity against the other, then he has two tongues.

Similarly, if he promises each one of them that he will support him against the other, or commends each one of them for his enmity [against the other], or if he commends one of them [to his face] but speaks ill of him in his absence—in all that, he has two tongues.

Instead, he should remain quiet or commend the deserving adversary in his presence, in his absence, and in the presence of his adversary.

It was said to Ibn ʿUmar رَضِيَ ٱللَّٰهُ عَنْهُمَا, "When we go before our rulers, we say one thing, and after we leave, we say something else." He said, "In the time of the Messenger of God صَلَّى ٱللَّٰهُ عَلَيْهِ وَسَلَّمَ, we considered that hypocrisy."[10] |

This is hypocrisy even if one has no [real] need to go before the 563
ruler and glorify him. If he has no need to go [before the *amīr*], but if he goes and fears *not* to glorify him, that is hypocrisy. The one who convinces himself that he needs [to go before a ruler], when [in truth] he has no such need, if he were satisfied with little and able to forego property and rank, and he goes before [the ruler] needing rank and wealth and glorifies [the ruler], then he is a hypocrite.

---

9 Trans.: Book 15 of the *Revival of the Religious Sciences*: *The Proprieties of Friendship and Brotherhood* (*Kitāb ādāb al-ṣuḥba wa-l-maʿāshara maʿ aṣnāf al-khalaq*).

10 Al-Kharāʾiṭī, *Masāwiʾ al-akhlāq*, 302.

This is the meaning of [the Prophet's] صَلَّىٱللَّهُعَلَيْهِوَسَلَّمَ statement, "The love of property and rank causes hypocrisy to grow in the heart like water [facilitates] growth of greenery." This is because [love of wealth and rank] compels one to [seek out] rulers, to defer to them, and be seen with them.

But if someone is tested by necessity and fears not glorifying [a ruler], then he is excused, for it is allowable to take precaution against evil. Abū l-Dardāʾ رَضِيَٱللَّهُعَنْهُ said, "We grin in the faces of [certain] groups while in our hearts, we loathe them."[11]

And ʿĀʾisha رَضِيَٱللَّهُعَنْهَا said,

> A man asked permission to see the Messenger of God صَلَّىٱللَّهُعَلَيْهِوَسَلَّمَ and he said, "Permit him—[he is] an evil man of his clan." But when he entered, [the Messenger صَلَّىٱللَّهُعَلَيْهِوَسَلَّمَ] spoke gently to him. After he left, I said, "O Messenger of God, you said about him what you said, but then you spoke gently with him?" He صَلَّىٱللَّهُعَلَيْهِوَسَلَّمَ said, "O ʿĀʾisha! The most evil of people are those who are treated honorably out of precaution of [their] obscenity."[12] |

564 This was conveyed about receiving a visitor with a grimace or a smile.[13] As for commending [the person], that is evident lying, and is not allowed except in [cases of] necessity or compulsion. It is permissible to lie in the situations we have mentioned in [the section on] the bane of lying. [Otherwise], it is not allowable to commend, attest, or even nod one's head in assemblies[14] confirming false declarations. One who does so is a hypocrite. Rather, he should deny [in speech what is being said], and if he is not able, his tongue should remain quiet and [he should] deny it in his heart.

---

11 Al-Bukhārī, *Ṣaḥīḥ*, 6131; al-Bayhaqī, *Shuʿab al-īmān*, 7749; and Abū Nuʿaym, *Ḥilya*, 1:222.

12 Al-Bukhārī, *Ṣaḥīḥ*, 6054; and Muslim, *Ṣaḥīḥ*, 2591, with similar wording.

13 Eds.: A grimace (*kashr*) is forced, while a smile (*tabasūm*) is genuine; see Wehr, *A Dictionary of Modern Written Arabic*, 828.

14 Eds.: For example, when a tyrant gathers people together to confirm his decisions or statements.

[18]

The Eighteenth Bane: Praise (*Madḥ*) 565

[PRAISE] is forbidden in certain circumstances. As for the censure [of praise], it is [because it can involve] backbiting and disparagement, and we have mentioned their ruling.

Six banes enter into praise: four pertain [to the one who] praises and two [to the one who] is praised.

As for [the one who] praises:

First, he may become excessive [in his praise] and excess ends in lying.

Khālid b. Maʿdān said, "Whoever, in the presence of witnesses, praises a leader or anyone else for [qualities] they do not have, will be raised up by God on the day of resurrection tripping over his own tongue."[1]

Second, he may become ostentatious. Praising someone expresses love, but it may be that he does not [really] harbor [love] for [the one he is praising], and does not believe everything he says, and so he becomes ostentatious and hypocritical.

Third, it may be that he says something that he has not verified and has no way of knowing. It was related that a man praised [another] man in the presence of the Prophet صَلَّى ٱللَّهُ عَلَيْهِ وَسَلَّمَ and he said, "Woe to you! You have cut the neck of your companion.[2] If he heard it . . . he would not succeed." Then he [صَلَّى ٱللَّهُ عَلَيْهِ وَسَلَّمَ] said, "If one of you must praise his brother, just say . . . 'I consider that so-and-so [is good]';

1 Ibn Abī l-Dunyā, *al-Ṣamt wa-ādāb al-lisān*, 603.

2 Eds.: Here the reference to cutting his neck implies that this praise will go to his head, leading him to think that he has done enough good deeds, and can cease doing any additional good.

566 | no one but God can [truly] vouch for someone. God is his reckoner, and sees if he [that is, that person] is like that."[3]

This bane applies to praise of someone with general attributes that are known through proof, as when one says, "He is pious, scrupulous, ascetic, excellent," and the like.

As for [when] one says, "I saw him praying [that is, superogatory prayers] at night, giving in charity, making the pilgrimage . . ." these are matters that are certain.

> A similar statement [might be], "He is just and agreeable," but [this statement] is about hidden [matters], about which no statement can be settled [authoritatively], except after internal experience. ʿUmar رَضِيَ اللَّهُ عَنْهُ heard a man commend another man and [ʿUmar] asked him, "Have you traveled with him?"
>
> He said, "No."
>
> [ʿUmar] asked, "Have you been involved with him in financial transactions and dealings [lit., buying and selling]?"
>
> He said, "No."
>
> [ʿUmar] said, "Then are you his neighbor [such that you see him every] morning and evening?"
>
> He said, "No."
>
> [ʿUmar] said, "Then by God, the one beside whom there is no god except Him, I do not consider you [one who] knows him."[4]

The fourth [bane] is that [he may] please the one who is being praised, but that one [being praised] is a tyrant or corrupt, and [praising him] is not permissible. The Messenger of God صَلَّى اللَّهُ عَلَيْهِ وَسَلَّمَ said, "Verily, God تَعَالَى is angered when a corrupt person is praised."[5] |

567 And Ḥasan said, "He who supplicates for a tyrant to have a long life is one that loves for God تَعَالَى to be disobeyed on His earth."[6]

---

3 Al-Bukhārī, *Ṣaḥīḥ*, 6061; Muslim, *Ṣaḥīḥ*, 3000; Ibn Abī l-Dunyā, *al-Ṣamt wa-ādāb al-lisān*, 597; and Ibn Ḥanbal, *Musnad*, 5:51.

4 Ibn Abī l-Dunyā, *al-Ṣamt wa-ādāb al-lisān*, 607.

5 Ibn Abī l-Dunyā, *al-Ṣamt wa-ādāb al-lisān*, 229; and al-Bayhaqī, *Shuʿab al-īmān*, 4543.

6 Ibn Abī l-Dunyā, *al-Ṣamt wa-ādāb al-lisān*, 231; and al-Bayhaqī, *Shuʿab al-īmān*, 8986.

A corrupt tyrant should be censured so he is sorrowful, not praised so he is happy.

❁ ❁ ❁

As for the one [who is] praised, it harms him in two ways. First, it produces in him arrogance and conceit, which are destructive. Ḥasan رَضِيَ ٱللَّٰهُ عَنْهُ said,

> ʿUmar رَضِيَ ٱللَّٰهُ عَنْهُ was holding a small leather whip and people were sitting around him when al-Jārūd b. al-Mundhir approached. A man among them said, "This is the chief of the Rabīʿa [clan]!" in a way that ʿUmar, the people sitting around him, and al-Jārūd could hear. When [al-Jārūd] was near him, [ʿUmar] hit him with the whip. He said, "What have I done wrong to you, O Commander of the Faithful?" [ʿUmar] answered, "What have you done wrong? Did you not hear [what was] said?"
>
> He answered, "I heard it, so?"
>
> [ʿUmar] said, "I feared that some of it would mix with your heart, and I wanted to help you be rid of it."[7]

Second, if [the one praised] is commended for his goodness, he is happy about it, slackens [in his efforts], and is pleased with himself. Whoever is conceited about himself reduces his efforts, while whoever [increases] his efforts [lit., rolls up his sleeves to work] sees himself as falling short. So when tongues are unleashed in commending him, he believes he has attained [perfection]. And | 568
the Prophet صَلَّى ٱللَّٰهُ عَلَيْهِ وَسَلَّمَ said, " . . . You have cut the neck of your companion. If he heard it, he would not succeed."[8]

And, [the Prophet] صَلَّى ٱللَّٰهُ عَلَيْهِ وَسَلَّمَ said, "If you extol your brother to his face, it is as if you passed over his throat with a sharp blade."[9]

---

7 Ibn Abī l-Dunyā, *al-Ṣamt wa-ādāb al-lisān*, 605.

8 Ibn Ḥanbal, *Musnad*, 5:51. It is also found in al-Bukhārī, *Ṣaḥīḥ*, 2662; and Muslim, *Ṣaḥīḥ*, 3000, without the phrase, "If he heard it, he will not succeed."

9 Ibn al-Mubārak, *Zuhd*, 52.

And [the Prophet صَلَّى ٱللَّهُ عَلَيْهِ وَسَلَّمَ] also said to someone who had extolled a man, "You have wounded that man—may God wound you."[10]

Muṭarrif said, "Whenever I hear myself being commended or extolled, I feel small [lit., my soul is decreased]." And Yazīd b. Abī Muslim said, "No one hears himself commended or extolled except that Satan puts ostentation [in his heart], but the believer recovers from it."[11] Ibn al-Mubārak said, "Both of them were correct in what they said, but Yazīd spoke about the hearts of the laymen (*ᶜawāmm*) while Muṭarrif spoke about the hearts of the elect (*khawāṣṣ*)."[12]

And [the Prophet] صَلَّى ٱللَّهُ عَلَيْهِ وَسَلَّمَ said, "If one man came at another
569 with a sharpened knife, | it would be better than commending him to his face."[13]

ᶜUmar رَضِيَ ٱللَّهُ عَنْهُ said, "To extol is to slay,"[14] because the one who is slain is the one who slackens in his [good] deeds. Extolment brings slackness [to his work], and extolment brings arrogance and conceit, and both of these are destructive, like slaughter, and that is why he compared it to that.

If extolment is free from these banes that effect the one who extols and the one who is extolled, not only is there nothing wrong with it, but it is recommended. Thus, the Messenger of God صَلَّى ٱللَّهُ عَلَيْهِ وَسَلَّمَ commended the Companions, saying "If the faith of Abū Bakr were weighed against the faith of the entire world, his would be weightier," and he said to ᶜUmar, "If I had not been sent [as a messenger], you would have been sent, O ᶜUmar." What commendation could be higher than this? But when [the Prophet] صَلَّى ٱللَّهُ عَلَيْهِ وَسَلَّمَ said it, he did so with truthfulness and insight, and they themselves رَضِيَ ٱللَّهُ عَنْهُمْ were at too high a [spiritual] level for [such praise] to produce in them arrogance, conceit, or slackness.

Moreover, a man [who] extols himself is repugnant because it
570 expresses arrogance and boasting, [the Prophet] صَلَّى ٱللَّهُ عَلَيْهِ وَسَلَّمَ said, | "I am the [most] noble of the children of Adam and [I say this] without

10 Al-Bukhārī, *al-Adab al-mufrad*, 335.

11 Ibn al-Mubārak, *Zuhd*, 213

12 Al-Muḥāsibī, *Ādāb al-nufūs*, 73.

13 Al-Muḥāsibī, *Ādāb al-nufūs*, 100.

14 Ibn Abī Shayba, *al-Muṣannaf*, 26788. Lit., *al-madḥ huwa al-dhabiḥ*.

boasting."[15] That is, "What I say is not boasting about myself as people are wont to do when they commend themselves." Rather, his boasting was of God and of his proximity to God, not of his being preferred to all the children of Adam, just as someone who is favored by the king [has been given] a great favor and boasts of [the king's] favor and is happy because of [the king's] approval of him, not because of his being preferred over some of [the king's] other subjects.

By [looking at] these banes in detail, you can see how extolling [someone] can be both censured and encouraged. [The Prophet] صَلَّى ٱللَّهُ عَلَيْهِ وَسَلَّمَ said, "It has become mandatory" to commend certain people who died.[16]

And Mujāhid said,

> There is an assembly of angels for the children of Adam, and whenever a man among them mentions good about his Muslim brother, the angels say, "And for you the same!" and whenever he speaks ill of [his brother], the angels say, "O child of Adam whose faults are hidden! Moderate yourself [before you speak of your brother's faults], and praise God who has covered your faults."[17]

These, then, are the banes of praise. |

❁ ❁ ❁

An elucidation on what is incumbent on the [one who] is extolled (*mamdūḥ*) 571

Know that [someone who is] extolled needs to take the strictest precautions against the banes of arrogance, conceit, and slackness. No one is safe from these except one who knows himself, who has reflected on the dangers of the end [of life], on the subtleties of

---

15 Ibn Mājah, *Sunan*, 4308; and Muslim, *Ṣaḥīḥ*, 2278 with a different wording.
16 Al-Bukhārī, *Ṣaḥīḥ*, 1367; and Muslim, *Ṣaḥīḥ*, 949.
17 Ibn Abī l-Dunyā, *al-Ṣamt wa-ādāb al-lisān*, 615.

ostentation and the banes of [one's] deeds; for he knows [things] about himself that the one who extolled him does not know. If his secrets and the thoughts that pass through his mind were all disclosed, the one extolling him would stop extolling him.

[Someone being praised] should display his aversion to extolment by humiliating the [one] extolling him. Indicative of this are [the Prophet's] words صَلَّى ٱللَّهُ عَلَيْهِ وَسَلَّمَ, "Cast dust into the faces of those who extol [others]."[18]

Sufyān b. ʿUyayna said, "Being extolled will not harm the one who knows himself."[19]

A man from among the righteous ones was commended and said, "O God, they do not know me, You know me."[20]

And another of them said, on being commended, "O God, this servant of Yours wishes to be nearer to me by way of something that You detest, and I bear witness that I detest it as well."[21] |

572 ʿAlī [b. Abī Ṭālib] رَضِيَ ٱللَّهُ عَنْهُ said when he was commended, "O God, forgive me for what they do not know, do not take me [to task] for what they say, and make me better than what they assume."[22]

A man commended ʿUmar [b. al-Khaṭṭāb] رَضِيَ ٱللَّهُ عَنْهُ; he said, "Do you [wish to] destroy me and destroy yourself?"[23]

A man commended ʿAlī [b. Abī Ṭālib] رَضِيَ ٱللَّهُ عَنْهُ to his face—and [news] reached [ʿAlī] that [this same man] had disparaged him [in his absence]—so ʿAlī said to him, "I am less than what you said and greater than what is in you [that is, what you really think of me]."[24]

18 Muslim, *Ṣaḥīḥ*, 3002.

19 Ibn Abī l-Dunyā, *al-Ṣamt wa-ādāb al-lisān*, 608.

20 Ibn Abī l-Dunyā, *al-Ṣamt wa-ādāb al-lisān*, 601.

21 Ibn Abī l-Dunyā, *al-Ṣamt wa-ādāb al-lisān*, 602.

22 Ibn ʿAsākir, *Tārīkh madīnat Dimashq*, 30:332.

23 Ibn Abī l-Dunyā, *al-Ṣamt wa-ādāb al-lisān*, 610.

24 Ibn Abī l-Dunyā, *al-Ṣamt wa-ādāb al-lisān*, 611.

[19]

The Nineteenth Bane: Heedlessness (*Ghafla*) about Subtle Errors (*Khaṭāʾ*) in the Meaning[s] of Speech 573

[Heedlessness about subtle errors applies] especially to what concerns God and His attributes, and what is related to matters of *dīn*. No one is able to speak correctly about matters of *dīn* except the eloquent scholars. Thus, if someone is lacking in knowledge or eloquence, his speech will not be free of oversights, but God تعالى will pardon him for his ignorance.

An example [of these kinds of errors] is what Ḥudhayfa said the Prophet صلى الله عليه وسلم said, "Let none of you say, 'What God and you will' (*mā shāʾ Allāh wa-shiʾta*), but rather say, 'What God wills and then what you will.'"[1]

This is because in an unrestricted conjunction (*ʿaṭf muṭlaq*) [between the will of God and the will of a creature, there is an aspect of] association and equivalence and that is incongruent with the reverence [due to God].

Ibn ʿAbbās رضي الله عنهما said, "A man came to the Prophet صلى الله عليه وسلم and spoke to him about a certain matter, saying [in the course of it], 'What God and you will' and | [the Prophet] صلى الله عليه وسلم said to 574
him, 'Did you put me on the same level as God? Rather, [say] what God alone wills.'"[2]

A man was speaking in the presence of the Messenger of God صلى الله عليه وسلم and said,

---

1 Ibn Mājah, *Sunan*, 2117, and with similar wording in Ibn Abī l-Dunyā, *al-Ṣamt wa-ādāb al-lisān*, 344; and Abū Dāwūd, *Sunan*, 4980.

2 Al-Nasāʾī, al-*Sunan al-kubrā*, 10759.

> He who obeys God and His Messenger is guided, and he who disobeys the two of them (*himā*)[3] is misguided. [Hearing this,] he [صَلَّىٰ ٱللَّٰهُ عَلَيْهِ وَسَلَّمَ] said, "Say, 'he who disobeys God and His Messenger is misguided.'" That is, the Messenger of God صَلَّىٰ ٱللَّٰهُ عَلَيْهِ وَسَلَّمَ deplored one saying "whoever disobeys [the two of] them," for this is an equivalence and a union [between God and the Messenger].[4]

Ibrāhīm used to deplore a man's saying, "I seek refuge in God and in you," but would allow one to say, "I seek refuge in God and then in you." And he would [allow] someone to say, "Were it not for God and then so-and-so . . . ," but not for him to say "Were it not for God and so-and-so . . ."[5]

Some of them would deplore [peoples'] saying, "O God, liberate us from the fire," saying, "Liberation is after entering it." They would ask for protection from the fire and would seek refuge [in God] from the fire.[6] |

575 A man said, "O God, make me among those reached by the intercession of Muḥammad صَلَّىٰ ٱللَّٰهُ عَلَيْهِ وَسَلَّمَ!" Ḥudhayfa said, "Verily, God relieves the believers [of the need for] the intercession of Muḥammad. [Muḥammad's] intercession will be for the transgressors among the Muslims."[7]

And Ibrāhīm said, "If a man says to another man, 'O you donkey! O you swine,' it will be said to him on the day of resurrection, 'Did you see Me create him as donkey? Did you see Me create him as a swine?'"[8]

---

3 Muslim, *Ṣaḥīḥ*, 870. Trans.: That is, he disliked the man's use of the dual pronoun *himā*.

4 Al-Zabīdī, *Itḥāf*, 7:575. This was at the beginning of Islam. After it had become well-known and spread, and the light of faith was established, this manner of speaking was allowed, as the commentator on *al-Shifāʾ* mentions. And perhaps what is meant is that using two nouns (e.g., God and His Messenger) is preferrable to using a dual pronoun (e.g., *himā*). For example, the phrases . . . *And whoever obeys God and His Messenger*, and *whoever disobeys God and His messenger* occur frequently in the Qurʾān.

5 Ibn Abī l-Dunyā, *al-Ṣamt wa-ādāb al-lisān*, 347.

6 Ibn Abī l-Dunyā, *al-Ṣamt wa-ādāb al-lisān*, 348.

7 Ibn Abī l-Dunyā, *al-Ṣamt wa-ādāb al-lisān*, 349. Eds.: The transgressors are those Muslims who commit major sins.

8 Ibn Abī l-Dunyā, *al-Ṣamt wa-ādāb al-lisān*, 353.

And it was related that Ibn ʿAbbās رَضِيَ ٱللَّهُ عَنْهُمَا said, "One of you attributes partners [to God] even including a dog, when he says, 'If it had not been [for that dog], we would have been robbed last night!'"[9]

ʿUmar [b. al-Khaṭṭāb] رَضِيَ ٱللَّهُ عَنْهُ said, "The Messenger of God صَلَّى ٱللَّهُ عَلَيْهِ وَسَلَّمَ said, 'Verily, God تَعَالَىٰ forbids you from swearing oaths by your parents. If someone swears, let him swear by God or be silent.'" ʿUmar رَضِيَ ٱللَّهُ عَنْهُ added, "By God, I have not sworn by [my parents] since I heard this."[10]

And [the Prophet] صَلَّى ٱللَّهُ عَلَيْهِ وَسَلَّمَ said, "Do not call grapes *karm*, for *karm* is the Muslim man."[11]

Abū Hurayra said,

> The Messenger of God صَلَّى ٱللَّهُ عَلَيْهِ وَسَلَّمَ said, "Let none of you say 'my male slave' (*ʿabdī*) or 'my female slave' (*amatī*), for all of you are God's slaves and all of your women are God's slaves. Rather | say, 'My boy (*ghulām*) and my girl (*jāriya*),' and 'my young man (*fatāy*) and my young woman (*fatātī*).' And let 576
> not the slave say, my lord or my lady but rather, my master or my mistress. For all of you are slaves of God and the Lord (al-Rabb) is God سُبْحَانَهُ وَتَعَالَىٰ."[12]

And [the Prophet] صَلَّى ٱللَّهُ عَلَيْهِ وَسَلَّمَ said, "Do not say to a hypocrite, 'our master' (*sayyidnā*), for if he were your master it would [bring on] the wrath of your Lord."[13]

And [the Prophet] صَلَّى ٱللَّهُ عَلَيْهِ وَسَلَّمَ said, "If someone says, 'I have nothing to do with Islam,' and he is telling the truth, then it will be as he says, and if he is lying, then he will not return to Islam untainted.'"[14]

These and similar examples [show how subtle errors] can enter into one's speech; it would be impossible to list them all.

---

9 Ibn Abī l-Dunyā, *al-Ṣamt wa-ādāb al-lisān*, 360.

10 Al-Bukhārī, *Ṣaḥīḥ*, 6647; and Muslim, *Ṣaḥīḥ*, 1646.

11 Al-Bukhārī, *Ṣaḥīḥ*, 6183; and Muslim, *Ṣaḥīḥ*, 2247. Eds.: The word *karm* (pl. *kurūm*), refers to grapes, while *karam* means one with a noble nature; see Wehr, *A Dictionary of Modern Written Arabic*, 821.

12 Al-Bukhārī, *Ṣaḥīḥ*, 2552; Muslim, *Ṣaḥīḥ*, 2249; and Ibn Abī l-Dunyā, *al-Ṣamt wa-ādāb al-lisān*, 365.

13 Abū Dāwūd, *Sunan*, 4977; and Ibn Abī l-Dunyā, *al-Ṣamt wa-ādāb al-lisān*, 367.

14 Abū Dāwūd, *Sunan*, 3258; al-Nasāʾī, *Sunan*, 7:6; and Ibn Mājah, *Sunan*, 2100.

And if someone reflects deeply on all that we have presented about the banes of the tongue, he will know that when he unleashes his tongue he is not safe and then he will know the secret of his statement ﷺ, "Whoever is silent is saved,"[15] for all these banes are destructive and ruinous [pitfalls] that lie on the path of one who speaks. |

577 If he says nothing, he is safe from all [the banes], and if he articulates and speaks, he himself is in danger—unless he has been granted an eloquent tongue, ample knowledge, protective scruples, constant vigilance, and he reduces his speech. In such a case, he may be safe, but even with all that, he will not be beyond danger. So if you are not able to be one of those who speaks and profits, then [at least] be among those who say nothing and are thereby safe, for safety is one of the two profits.

15 Al-Tirmidhī, *Sunan*, 2501.

[20]

The Twentieth Bane: Questions from Laymen about God's تَعَالَىٰ Attributes, His Speech, and the Letters [of His Speech] and Whether His [Speech or Attributes] Are Eternal or Created 578

THE duty [of laymen] is to put into practice [the commandments and prohibitions] in the Qurʾān, but that can weigh heavily on the soul, while curiosity is light on the heart. Thus, the layman (*ʿāmmī*) is happy to delve into [the realm of] knowledge because Satan causes him to imagine, "You are one of the scholars and the people of virtue."

[Satan] continues to urge him in that [direction] until he starts talking about knowledge in a way that is [actually] disbelief, while he is unaware.

Any major [sin] that a layman might commit is safer for him than his speaking about knowledge [that he does not know], especially when it concerns God and His attributes. Indeed, the job of
laymen is to occupy themselves with worship, believe in what the | 579
Qurʾān conveys, and accept what the messengers brought without investigating it [deeply].

Their questions about anything except what is related to worship is impropriety on their part, merits the detestation of God عَزَّوَجَلَّ, and exposes them to the danger of disbelief. It is akin to stablemen asking about the secrets of kings, for which penalties are mandated. Anyone who asks about some obscure science, but whose understanding is not at the degree [required], is censured, and this is in addition to his being a layman.[1] Thus the Messenger of God ﷺ said, "Leave me [and be content] with what I have left you.[2] Those who came before you were destroyed because of their many questions and disagreements with their prophets. Avoid what I have forbidden for you, and accomplish as much as you can of what I have commanded from you."[3]

And Anas said,

> People asked the Messenger of God ﷺ one day so much [that] they angered him. So he mounted the *minbar* and said, "Ask me. About anything you ask me, I will inform you."
>
> So a man stood up and said, "O Messenger of God, who is my father?"
>
> He answered, "Your father is Ḥudhāfa."
>
> Then two youths who were brothers stood up and said, "O Messenger of God, who is our father?"
>
> He answered, "Your father is the one whom you are called after."
>
> Then another man stood up and asked, "O Messenger of God, am I in heaven or the fire?"
>
> He answered, "You are in the fire."
>
> When people saw that they were angering the Messenger of God ﷺ, they refrained [from asking questions]. Then ʿUmar رَضِيَ ٱللَّهُ عَنْهُ stood up and said, "We are satisfied with God as our Lord, with Islam as our *dīn*, and with Muḥammad ﷺ as our Messenger."
>
> [The Prophet] said, "Sit down, O ʿUmar, and may God be merciful toward you. You have truly been [granted] what I know to be [God's] accord.[4] |

---

1 Eds.: That is, one is not blamed for being a layman without knowledge, rather this indicates that it is not his place to involve himself in such matters.

2 Trans.: That is, do not ask about things I have not spoken to you about.

3 Al-Bukhārī, *Ṣaḥīḥ*, 7288; and Muslim, *Ṣaḥīḥ*, 1327.

4 Al-Bukhārī, *Ṣaḥīḥ*, 93; and Muslim, *Ṣaḥīḥ*, 2359.

And in a *ḥadīth*, the Messenger of God ﷺ forbade "it was said, it was said" [that is, gossip], wasting money, and asking too many questions.[5] 580

And [the Prophet] ﷺ said,

> It has almost reached the point that people ask one another, "God created the world, but who created God?" If they say that, say to them, *Say, "He is God, One. God, the Eternal Refuge [He neither begets nor is born, nor is there to Him any equivalent]"* [112:1–4] until you finish the *sūra*, then spit to the left three times and seek refuge in God from Satan the accursed.[6]

And Jābir said, "The verse of cursing (*āyat al-talāʿun*) was only revealed [because people asked] too many questions."[7]

In the story of Moses and al-Khiḍr, عَلَيْهِمَا السَّلَامُ, there is a warning about asking questions before their proper time, as when [al-Khiḍr] said, *"Then if you follow me, do not ask me about anything until I mention it to you"* [Q. 18:70]. Then, when he asked about [sinking] the boat, [al-Khiḍr] disapproved, until [Moses] apologized, and said, "*Do not blame me for what I forgot and do not overwhelm me in my matter with difficulty*" [Q. 18:73]. But he [Moses] could not be patient, and when he asked a third question, [al-Khiḍr] said, *"This is parting between me and you"* [Q. 18:78], and he parted [ways] with him.

The questions of the laymen about obscure issues of the *dīn*
is one of the great banes and an agent | of tribulations. So they 581
should be censured and barred from that. Their delving into the letters of the Qurʾān is akin to the case of a man to whom the king writes a letter in which he describes [many] matters, but the man pays no attention to [what is in the letter] and instead wastes his time in questions, about whether the paper on which it is written is ancient or modern. Such [behavior] surely merits a penalty, and similarly, the laymen neglects the limits [enjoined by] the Qurʾān and becomes preoccupied [in questions] of whether [God's] letters

---

5 Al-Bukhārī, *Ṣaḥīḥ*, 1477; and Muslim, *Ṣaḥīḥ*, 593.

6 Abū Dāwūd, *Sunan*, 4722; and with similar wording in al-Bukhārī, *Ṣaḥīḥ*, 7296; and Muslim, *Ṣaḥīḥ*, 134.

7 Al-Khaṭīb al-Baghdādī, *al-Asmāʾ al-mubhama*, 481. Trans.: The verse containing God's curse is 24:6–9. It is also referred to as the verse of the curse (*āyat al-laʿn*).

are created or eternal, and similarly for all the rest of the attributes of God سُبْحَانَهُ وَتَعَالَىٰ, and God تَعَالَىٰ knows best.

❁ ❁ ❁

Here ends *The Book on the Banes of the Tongue*, the fourth
book in the Quarter of Perils from the books of the
Revival of the Religious Sciences. Praise be to God,
Lord of the worlds, praise that is eternal,
bountiful, blessed, and pure, and
may God shower blessings on
our master Muḥammad,
the Arab prophet,
the one chosen
from among
the best
of His creation,
may salutations of peace
in abundance be on him and
his family and Companions.
Here follows [the book on]
The Banes of Anger,
Malice, and
Envy.

Bibliography

Works in Western Languages

al-Ghazālī, Abū Ḥāmid. *Al-Ghazālī on the Condemnation of Pride and Self-Admiration: Book XXIX of the Revival of the Religious Sciences (Iḥyāʾ ʿulūm al-dīn)*. Translated by Mohammed Rustom. Cambridge: Islamic Texts Society, 2018.

——. *The Remembrance of Death and the Afterlife*. Translated by T. J. Winter. Cambridge: Islamic Texts Society, 1989.

——. *The Revival of the Religious Sciences: The Banes of Anger, Malice, and Envy*. Translated by Omar Edaibat. Louisville, KY: Fons Vitae: forthcoming.

——. *The Revival of the Religious Sciences: The Commanding of Right and the Forbidding of Wrong*. Translated by J. Pavlin. Louisville, KY: Fons Vitae, forthcoming.

——. *The Revival of the Religious Sciences: The Proprieties of Friendship and Brotherhood*. Translated by M. Holland and J. Pavlin. Louisville, KY: Fons Vitae, forthcoming.

Lane, E. W. *An Arabic-English Lexicon*. 8 vols. Beirut: Librairie du Liban, 1968.

Wehr, Hans, *A Dictionary of Modern Written Arabic*. Edited by J. Milton Cowan. Ithaca, NY: Cornell University Press, 1961.

Works in Arabic

ʿAbd al-Razzāq b. Hammām al-Ṣanʿānī. *al-Muṣannaf*. Edited by Ḥabīb al-Raḥmān al-ʿAẓamī. 12 vols. Beirut: al-Maktab al-Islāmī, 1983.

Abū Dāwūd, Sulaymān b. al-Ashaʿth al-Sijistānī. *al-Murāsil*. Edited by ʿAbdallāh Musāʿid al-Zaharānī. Riyadh: Dār al-Ṣumayʿī, 2001.

——. *Sunan Abū Dāwūd*. Edited by ʿIzzat ʿAbīd al-Daʿās and ʿĀdil al-Sayyid. Beirut: Dār Ibn Ḥazm, 1997.

Abū Nuʿaym al-Iṣbahānī, Aḥmad b. ʿAbdallāh. *Ḥilyat al-awliyāʾ wa-ṭabaqāt al-aṣfiyāʾ*. 11 vols. Cairo: Maṭbaʿāt al-Saʿāda wa-l-Khānijī, 1357/1938; repr. Beirut: Dār al-Kitāb al-ʿArabī, 1987.

——. *Maʿrifat al-ṣaḥāba*. 6 vols. Saudi Arabia: Dār al-Waṭan, 1998.

Abū Ṭālib al-Makkī, Muḥammad b. ʿAlī. *Qūt al-qulūb*. Edited by Muḥammad al-Zaharī al-Ghumurāwī. 2 vols. Cairo: al-Maṭbaʿat al-Mayymaniyya, 1310/1893; repr. Beirut: Dār Ṣādir/Dār al-Fikr, n.d.

Abū Tammām Tayy. *Dīwān Abī Tamām bi sharḥ al-Khaṭīb al-Tabrīzī*. Edited by Muḥammad ʿAbdu ʿAzzām. 4 vols. Cairo: Dār al-Maʿārif, 2009.

Abū Yaʿlā, Aḥmad b. ʿAlī. *Musnad Abū Yaʿlā l-Mawṣūlī*. Edited by Ḥusayn Salīm Asad al-Dārānī. Damascus: Dār al-Maʾmūn li-l-Turāth and Dār al-Thaqāfa al-ʿArabiyya, 1989.

Aḥmad b. Ḥanbal. *See under* Ibn Ḥanbal.

al-ʿAskarī, Abū Hilal al-ʿAskarī. *Jamharat al-amthāl*. Edited by Aḥmad ʿAbd al-Salām and Muḥammad Saʿīd b. Bassiyūnī Zaghlūl. 2 vols. Beirut: Dār al-Kutub al-ʿIlmiyya, 1988.

al-Bayhaqī, Aḥmad b. al-Ḥusayn. *Dalāʾil al-nubuwwa wa-maʿrifa aḥwāl ṣāḥib al-sharīʿa*. Edited by ʿAbd al-Muʿṭī Qalʿajī. Cairo: Dār al-Rayyān, 1988.

———. *al-Daʿwāt al-kabīr*. Edited by Badr b. ʿAbdallāh al-Badr. Kuwait: Dār Gharās, 2009.

———. *al-Madkhal ilā l-sunan al-kubrā*. Edited by Muḥammad Ḍiyāʾ al-Raḥmān al-ʿĀẓamī. Medina: Dār Aḍwāʾ al-Salaf, 1420/1999.

———. *al-Jāmiʿ al-Shuʿab al-īmān*. Edited by ʿAbd al-ʿAlī ʿAbd al-Ḥamīd Ḥāmid. 14 vols. Riyadh: Maktabat al-Rushd, 2004.

———. *al-Sunan al-kubrā*. Beirut: Dār al-Maʿrifa, 1356/1937.

———. *al-Zuhd al-kabīr*. Edited by ʿĀmir Aḥmad Ḥaydar. Lebanon: Muʾassasat al-Kutub al-Thaqāfiyya, 1996.

al-Bukhārī, Muḥammad b. Ismāʿīl. *al-Adab al-mufrad*. Edited by Muḥammad Fūʾad ʿAbd al-Bāqī. Cairo: al-Maktab al-Salafiyya, 1997.

———. *Ṣaḥīḥ al-Bukhārī*. 9 vols. Būlāq, 1311–13; repr. Beirut: Dār Ṭawq al-Najāt, 1422/2001.

al-Bazzār, Abū Bakr b. Aḥmad b. ʿAmr. *al-Baḥr al-zakhkhār* (known as *Musnad al-Bazzār*). Edited by Maḥfūẓ al-Raḥmān Zayn Allāh. 20 vols. Medina: Maktabat al-ʿUlūm wa-l-Ḥikam, 1988.

al-Dārimī, ʿAbdallāh b. ʿAbd al-Raḥmān. *Musnad al-Dārimī = Sunan*. Edited by Ḥusayn Salīm Asad al-Dārānī. Riyadh: Dār al-Mughnī, 2000.

al-Daylamī, Shīrawayh b. Shahdār. *al-Firdaws bi-maʾthūr al-khiṭṭāb = Musnad al-firdaws*. Edited by Saʿīd b. Basyūnī Zaghlūl. 6 vols. Beirut: Dār al-Kutub al-ʿIlmiyya, 1986.

al-Dīnawarī, Aḥmad b. Marwān b. Muḥammad. *al-Majālasa wa-jawāhir al-ʿilm*. Beirut: Dār Ibn Ḥazm, 2002.

al-Ghazālī, Abū Ḥāmid. *Iḥyāʾ ʿulūm al-dīn*. 9 vols. Jedda: Dār al-Minhāj, 2011.

al-Ḥākim al-Nīsābūrī, Muḥammad b. ʿAbdallāh. *al-Mustadrak ʿalā l-Ṣaḥiḥayn*. 5 vols. Hyderabad: Dāʾirat al-Maʿārif al-Niẓāmiyya, 1335/1917; repr. Beirut: Dār al-Maʿrifa, n.d.

Hannād b. al-Sirrī b. Mūsā l-Dārimī l-Kūfī. *al-Zuhd*. Edited by ʿAbd al-Raḥmān b. ʿAbd al-Jabbār al-Firiyawāʾī. Kuwait: Dār al-Khulafāʾ li-l-Kitāb al-Islāmī, 1406/1986.

al-Haythamī, Nūr al-Dīn. *Majmaʿ al-zawāʾid wa-manbaʿ al-fawāʾid*. 10 vols. in 5. Beirut: Dār al-Maʿrifa, 1986.

Ibn ʿAbd al-Barr, Yūsuf b. ʿAbdallāh. *al-Istīʿāb fī maʿrifat al-aṣḥāb*. Edited by ʿĀdil Murshid. Amman: Dār al-Aʿlām, 2002.

———. *al-Tamhīd*. Casablanca: Wizārat al-Awqāf, 1967.

Ibn Abī ʿĀṣam, Aḥmad b. ʿAmr. *al-Zuhd*. Edited by ʿAbd al-ʿĀlī ʿAbd al-Ḥamīd Ḥāmid. Cairo: Dār al-Rayyān li-l-Turāth, 1408/1988.

Ibn Abī l-Dunyā, ʿAbdallāh b. Muḥammad al-Qurashī. *al-Ghayba wa-l-namīma*. Edited by Muṣṭafā ʿAbd al-Qādir ʿAṭā. Beirut: Muʾassasat al-Kutub al-Thaqāfiyya, 1993.

———. *al-Ḥilm wa-yalīhi Kitāb al-tawwakul ʿalā Allah*. Edited by Majdī l-Sayyid Ibrāhīm. Egypt: Maktabat al-Qurʾān, n.d.

———. *al-ʿIyyāl*. Edited by Najm ʿAbd al-Raḥmān Khalaf. Mansoura, Egypt: Dār al-Wafāʾ, 1997.

———. *Mudārāt al-nās*. Edited by Muḥammad Khayr Ramaḍān Yūsuf. Beirut: Dār Ibn Ḥazm, 1998.

———. *Makārim al-akhlāq*. Edited by Majdī l-Sayyid Ibrāhīm. Cairo: Maktabat al-Qurʾān, n.d.

———. *Qiṣar al-amal*. Edited by Muḥammad Khayr Ramaḍān Yūsuf. Beirut: Dār Ibn Ḥazm, 1995.

———. *al-Ṣamt wa-ādāb al-lisān*. Edited by Najm ʿAbd al-Raḥmān Khalaf. Beirut: Dār al-Gharb al-Islāmī, 1986.

———. *al-Shukr*. Edited by Aḥmad Muḥammad Ṭāḥūn. Saudi Arabia: N.p., n.d.

———. *al-Warʿa*. Edited by Bassām ʿAbd al-Wahhāb al-Jābbī. Beirut: Dār Ibn Ḥazm, 2002.

Ibn Abī Shayba, ʿAbdallāh b. Muḥammad. *al-Muṣannaf*. Edited by Muḥammad ʿAwāmma. 26 vols. Jedda: Dār al-Minhāj, 2006.

Ibn ʿAdī = ʿAbdallāh b. ʿAdī l-Jurjānī. *al-Kāmil fī ḍuʿafāʾ al-rijāl*. Edited by Suhayl Zakkār and Yaḥyā Mukhtār Ghazāwī. 7 vols. Beirut: Dār al-Fikr, 1988.

Ibn ʿAsākir, ʿAlī b. al-Ḥasan. *Tārīkh madīnat Dimashq*. Edited by Muḥibb al-Dīn ʿUmar b. Gharāma al-ʿUmrāwī. 80 vols. Beirut: Dār al-Fikr, 1995.

Ibn al-Ḍarīs, Muḥammad b. Ayyūb. *Faḍāʾil al-Qurʾān*. Edited by Misfir b. Saʿīd al-Ghāmidī. Riyadh: Dār Ḥāfiẓ, 1988.

Ibn Ḥanbal = Aḥmad b. Ḥanbal. *Musnad al-Imām Aḥmad b. Ḥanbal*. Edited by Shuʿayb al-Arnāʾūṭ. 50 vols. Beirut: Muʾassasat al-Risāla, 1995.

———. *al-Zuhd*. Edited by Muḥammad ʿAbd al-Salam Shāhīn. Beirut: Dār al-Kutub al-ʿIlmiyya, 1999.

Ibn Ḥibbān = Muḥammad b. Ḥibbān al-Bustī. *Rawḍat al-ʿuqalāʾ*. Edited by ʿAbd al-ʿAlīm Muḥammad al-Darwīsh. Damascus: al-Hayʾa al-ʿĀmma al-Sūriyya li-l-Kitāb, 2009.

Ibn al-Jawzī, ʿAbd al-Raḥmān b. ʿAlī b. Muḥammad. *al-Adhkiyāʾ*. Edited by Muḥammad ʿAbd al-Karīm al-Nimrī. Beirut: Dār al-Kutub al-ʿIlmiyya, 2001.

——. *al-Mudhish*. Edited by ʿAbd al-Karīm Muḥammad Munīr Tattān and Khaldūn ʿAbd al-ʿAzīz Makhlūṭa. 2 vols. Damascus: Dār al-Qalam, 2014.

Ibn Mājah, Muḥammad b. Yazīd. *Sunan Ibn Mājah*. Edited by Muḥammad Fuʾād ʿAbd al-Bāqī. 2 vols. Cairo: Dār Iḥyāʾ al-Kutub al-ʿArabiyya, 1954.

Ibn al-Mubārak, ʿAbdallāh. *Zuhd wa-l-raqāʾiq*. Edited by Ḥabīb al-Raḥmān al-ʿAẓamī. Beirut: Dār al-Kutub al-ʿIlmiyya, n.d.

Ibn Saʿd = Muḥammad b. Saʿd al-Baṣrī. *Ṭabaqāt al-kabīr*. Edited by ʿAlī Muḥammad ʿUmar. 11 vols. Cairo: Maktabat al-Khānjī, 2001.

Ibn Wahhab = ʿAbdallāh b. Wahhab al-Qurayshī. *al-Jāmiʿ fī l-ḥadīth*. Edited by Muṣṭafā Ḥasan Abū l-Khayr. Jedda: Dār Ibn al-Jawzī, 1996.

al-Jurjānī, Ḥamza b. Yūsuf b. Ibrāhīm. *Tārīkh Jurjān*. Edited by Muḥammad b. ʿAbd al-Muʿīn Khān. Beirut: ʿĀlam al-Kutub, 1981.

al-Kharāʾiṭī, Muḥammad b. Jaʿfar. *Masāwiʾ al-akhlāq wa-ṭarāʾiq makrūhihā*. Edited by Muṣṭafā ʿAṭā. Beirut: Muʾassasat al-Kutub al-Thaqāfiyya, 1993.

al-Khaṭīb al-Baghdādī, Aḥmad b. ʿAlī. *al-Asmāʾ al-mubhama fī l-anbiyāʾ al-muḥkama*. Edited by ʿAzz al-Dīn ʿAlī l-Sayyid. Cairo: Maktabat al-Khānjī, 1984.

——. *al-Faqīh wa-l-mutafaqqih*. Edited by ʿĀdil Yūsuf al-ʿAzāzī. Riyadh: Dār Ibn al-Jawzī, 1421/2000.

——. *Tārīkh Baghdād*. Edited by Muṣṭafā ʿAbd al-Qādir ʿAṭā. 24 vols. Beirut: Dār al-Kutub al-ʿIlmiyya, 1997.

al-Khaṭṭābī, Abū Sulaymān Ḥamd b. Muḥammad. *al-ʿUzla*. Edited by Yāsīn Muḥammad al-Saʿʿās. Beirut: Dār Ibn Kathīr, 1410/1990.

al-Makkī, Abū Ṭālib. *See under* Abū Ṭālib al-Makkī.

Mālik b. Anas. *al-Muwaṭṭaʾ*. Edited by Muḥammad Fuʾād ʿAbd al-Bāqī. 2 vols. Cairo: Dār Iḥyāʾ al-Kutub al-ʿArabiyya, n.d.

al-Marūzī, Muḥammad b. Nāṣr. *Taʿẓīm qadr al-ṣalāt*. Edited by Aḥmad Abū l-Majd. Cairo: Dār al-ʿAqīda, 2003.

al-Muḥāsibī, al-Ḥārith b. Asad. *Ādāb al-Nufūs*. Edited by ʿAbd al-Qādir Aḥmad ʿAṭā. Beirut: Muʾasassat al-Kutub al-Thaqāfiyya, 1991.

Muslim b. al-Ḥajjāj al-Qushayrī l-Nīsābūrī. *al-Jāmiʿ al-ṣaḥīḥ = Ṣaḥīḥ Muslim*. Edited by Muḥammad Fuʾād ʿAbd al-Bāqī. 5 vols. Cairo and Beirut: Dār Iḥyāʾ al-Kutub al-ʿArabiyya, 1954.

al-Nasāʾī, Aḥmad b. Shuʿayb. *Kitāb al-sunan al-kubrā*. Edited by Shuʿayb al-Arnāʾūt and Ḥasan ʿAbd al-Munʿim al-Salbī. 12 vols. Beirut: Muʾassasat al-Risāla, 2001.

al-Quḍāʿī, Muḥammad b. Salāma. *Musnad al-shihāb*. Edited by Ḥamdī ʿAbd al-Majīd al-Salafī. Beirut: Muʾassasat al-Risāla, 1985.

al-Qushayrī, ʿAbd al-Karīm. *al-Risāla al-Qushayriyya*. Edited by ʿAbd al-Ḥalīm Maḥmūd and Maḥmūd b. al-Sharīf. Cairo: Dār al-Shaʿab, 1989.

al-Ṭabarānī, Sulaymān b. Aḥmad. *Makārim al-akhlāq*. Beirut: Dār al-Mashārīʿ, 2007.

——. *al-Muʿjam al-awsaṭ*. Edited by Maḥmūd al-Ṭaḥḥān. Riyadh [?]: Maktabat al-Maʿārif, 1985.

———. *al-Muʿjam al-kabīr*. Edited by Ḥamdī ʿAbd al-Majīd al-Salafī. 25 vols. Beirut: Dār Iḥyāʾ al-Turāth al-ʿArabī, n.d.

———. *al-Muʿjam al-ṣaghīr*. 2 vols. Beirut: Dār al-Kutub al-ʿIlmiyya, 1983 [repr.].

al-Ṭaḥāwī, Aḥmad b. Muḥammad b. Salāma. *Sharḥ muskhil al-āthār*. Edited by Shuʿayb al-Arnāʾūṭ. Beirut: Muʾassassat al-Risāla, 1994.

al-Ṭayālisī, Sulaymān b. Dāwūd. *Musnad Abī Dāwūd al-Ṭayālisī*. Beirut: Dār al-Maʿrifa, 1321/1903.

al-Tirmidhī, Muḥammad b. ʿĪsā. *Sunan al-Tirmidhī = al-Jāmiʿ al-ṣaḥīḥ*. Edited by Aḥmad Shākir, Muḥammad Fuʾād ʿAbd al-Bāqī, and Ibrāhīm ʿAṭwa. 5 vols. Beirut: Dār Iḥyāʾ al-Turāth al-ʿArabī, n.d.; repr. Cairo, 1938.

———. *al-Shamāʾil al-Muḥammadiyya*. Beirut: Muḥammad ʿAwwāma, 2001.

al-ʿUqaylī, Muḥammad b. ʿAmr. *al-Ḍuʿafāʾ*. Edited by Ḥamdī ʿAbd al-Majīd al-Salafī. Riyadh: Dār al-Ṣamīʿī, 2000.

al-Zabīdī, Muḥammad Murtaḍā, *Itḥāf al-sadā al-muttaqīn bi-sharḥ Iḥyāʾ ʿulūm al-dīn*. 10 vols. [Cairo]: al-Maṭbaʿ al-Maymūniyya, 1311/1894.

———. *Tāj al-ʿarūs min jawāhir al-Qāmūs*. Edited by ʿAbd al-ʿAlīm al-Ṭaḥāwī. 40 vols. Kuwait: Maṭbaʿat Ḥukūmat al-Kūwayt, 1987.

Index of Qurʾānic Verses

Index of *Ḥadīth*

A servant does not have complete faith until . . . , 97
A servant tells a lie that drives the angel [recording his deeds] a mile away from him because of its stench, 84
The servant who continually lies and is intent on lying will be written, before God, as a liar, 81
The servant will not reach the reality of faith until he is able to give up arguing even when he is right, 29
Shall I not inform you of the easiest worship and the one that is most effortless for the body? Silence and good character, 8
"Shall I not inform you of the gravest of the major [sins]? . . . saying deceitful [words]," 83–84
"Shall I not teach you a practice that is light on the body but heavy in the balance?" . . . He said, "Silence, good character, and leaving what does not concern you," 17
"Shall I not tell you who is most evil among you?" . . . He said, "Those who go around spreading gossip . . . ," 139
A sign of the hypocrite . . . , 80 n.2
Silence is wisdom but few practice it; that is, it is wisdom and resoluteness, 5
The [single] dirham that a man gets from usury is a greater offense before God . . . but [attacking] the reputation of a Muslim is an even greater [offense] than usury, 104
Six things show [that a person] has reached the reality of faith . . . leaving an argument even when he is right, 29
In some poetry there is wisdom, 58
Stand up, for [the accused] may be better than you, 119
Stop his tongue against me, 59

Take everything off that camel and set it free, for it has been cursed, 48
There are four [traits] that, if you have them, anything you lose . . . in this world will not harm you, 85–86
There are three [things that can afflict] the believer [but] from which he can escape, and his escape from wicked suppositions is by not verifying it, 126
There are three things that will always be found in my community: portending [evil], envy, and wicked supposition, 126 n.61
There are three to whom God will not speak, nor look at, nor praise, 83
There are three [types of] individuals to whom God will not speak on the day of resurrection nor look upon . . . , 81
There are three whom God loves: a man who [fights] in a force, his chest thrust forward . . . , 82
There is no one who does not have white in their eyes!, 66
There is not a camel except that it is the offspring [lit., son of] a camel, 66
There is nothing in the body that does not complain to God about the tongue, 8
There was no characteristic more intense for the Companions of the Messenger of God صَلَّى ٱللَّٰهُ عَلَيْهِ وَسَلَّمَ than lying, 85

There will come a time when people will ruminate on their words like a cow ruminates on her grass, 41
These two are being punished, but not for major [sins]. One them used to backbite against people, 104
They said, "O Messenger of God! [That she-camel] threw off the Bedouin and killed him!" He said, "Yes, and your mouths are full of his blood," 63–64
Those of you who are most loathed to me . . . will be the prattlers, the long-winded [people], and those who are pompous in their speech, 40
Those who came before you were destroyed because of their many questions and disagreements with their prophets, 164
Those who curse [others] will not be intercessors nor witnesses on the day of resurrection, 49
Three [traits] are in a hypocrite . . . when he speaks, he lies; when he promises [something], he breaks it; and when he is given a trust, he betrays it, 77
The tongue of the believer is behind his heart . . . The tongue of the hypocrite, however, is in front of his heart . . . , 10
Truly, lying is a gate from [among] the gates of hypocrisy, 80
Truly, someone who does not show mercy will not be shown mercy, 68
Truly, the pedants are ruined! And he repeated this three times, 40
Truly, you promised me [something], O Messenger of God, 78
Two people insulting one another are two devils, 47

Verily, God forbids you from swearing oaths by your parents. If someone swears, let him swear by God or be silent, 161
Verily, God is angered when a corrupt person is praised, 154
Verily, in heaven there are rooms . . . which God has prepared for those who feed the hungry and are soothing in their speech, 38
Verily, merchants are profligates, 81
Verily, my Lord commanded that my speech be remembrance, my silence [be] reflection . . . , 15 n.4
Verily, throughout the days of your life, your Lord has breezes of the spirit. So be open to them, 14 n.2
Vulgarity and elucidation are two prongs of hypocrisy, 44
Vulgar [speech] is surely an iniquity, 43

We are going to mount you on a son of a camel, 97
"What do you fear most for me?" And he took hold of his own tongue and said, "This," 7
"What do you want to give him?" . . . He said, "[Know] that if you do not do it, it is written against you as a lie," 83
. . . what gives me most hope with God is that I keep my breast [that is, heart] sound and leave what does not concern me, 16
What is the matter with groups (*aqwām*) who do this or that?, 111

Index of People and Places

Subject Index

defects, 71, 73, 80, 121, 131, 141–142, 147. *See also* deficiencies; disabilities
occupying oneself with one's own, 106, 120
of others, 111–112, 115, 120
physical, 46
defending (one's brother), 114
deficiencies, 31–32, 71, 110, 119, 141–142. *See also* defects; disabilities
delight, 36, 116
by one's speech, 24
at others in joking, 97, 116
at shortcomings of others, 128
denouncing, 115
deeds as repugnant, 142
deplore/deploring, 38, 113
seeing someone, 96, 127
sins, 113
superfluous speech, 21
that something be mentioned, 31, 90, 107–109, 112, 141–142, 145–146, 160
that something be used to identify someone, 110, 132
what someone did, 111
depravity/depraved, 45, 50, 125
descent, falsely claiming, 100. *See also* lineage
detestable/detestation, 112, 144
of God/Creator, 119, 122, 163
deviancy (*bid*ʿ*a*), 33, 49–50, 53, 131
deviants, 50–51, 131–132
dignity/dignified, 9, 12
loss of, 62, 64
diminishment/diminishing, 123. *See also* belittling
of faith, 97
of good deeds/rewards, 120, 124
of oneself/one's provision, 17, 81
others, 32, 36, 62, 116
dīn, 1, 11, 21, 36, 107, 114–115, 117, 124, 164
and backbiting, 106, 108
and disputation, 29, 35
matters/questions of, 3, 25, 29 n.11, 31, 44, 159, 165
shortcomings in, 128
sold for this world, 145
disabilities, 110, 132. *See also* defects
disappointment, 122
disbelief (*kufr*), 2, 49, 51, 163
accusing others of, 53
dying in, 50–52, 55
and fighting a believer, 47
repenting of, 54
disbelievers, 7, 51–53, 54, 58
curse of God is on, 49–50
heart of, 141
disdain (*istiḥiqār*), 18–19, 35, 71–72, 117, 128. *See also* scorn(ful)
of God/your Guardian, 122
of victim of backbiting, 113
disgrace, 88, 139, 146
of others, 116
dishonoring (oneself), 123–124
disobedience, 2, 19, 25, 32, 94, 108, 122, 125, 134
to God, 26, 121
repelling, 142
disobedient (*fāsiq*), 48, 125, 130, 142–143
disparagement, 131, 145, 153, 158
disputation (*khuṣūma*), 3, 12, 35–37, 39, 120
consequences of, 38
dīn as object of, 29
insolence in, 78
distress, 17, 72, 117. *See also* harm/hurt
division (between brothers), 138 n.2, 139
divorce (by *khal*ʿ), 90
doubts, 44, 92, 125–126
dreams, 82, 100
drunkenness, 69. *See also* intoxicants; wine drinking
duplicity, 93

ear(s), 2

whoever is, is saved (*najā*), 5, 13
silent, 161, 162
silliness, 68. *See also* foolishness
singing (*ghināʾ*), 3, 57
sin(s), xxi, 15, 18–19, 21, 38, 81, 90 n.53, 93 n.61, 95, 100, 146
of accusing a Muslim of major, 53
of arguing, 30
of assumption (*ẓann*), 125, 142
of backbiting, 113–114, 117, 124, 129
displayed, *vs.* concealed, 133
gravest/greatest, 47, 83
and lying, 91, 97–98
major, 53–54, 65, 160 n.7, 163
minor, 65, 71
ridding brother of, 128
and swearing oaths, 85
of tongue, xxi–xxii
of usury, 104
slacken/slackness, 155–156, 157
slander (*siʿāya*), 144–146
slanderers, 144–147
slaves, 49, 131, 147
of God, 161
sleep, 84, 108
smile/smiling, 58 n.6, 60, 63, 65, 68, 71, 152
sociability, 20
social (intercourse)/sociability, 20, 146
sorrow(ful), 14 n.2, 72, 117, 128, 155
soul, 8, 23, 30, 33, 103, 163
characteristics of, xx
contemplation of one's, 120–121
decreased, 156
murmurings of, 125–126
trustworthy, 143
sound (*sālim*), 9, 16, 91, 94, 129–130
speaking/saying
about what does not concern one, 3, 14–15, 17–19, 24–25
excessively, 10, 23–25, 144
explicitly, 46
ill of someone, 107, 109, 123, 142, 151, 157
insistently, 35
manner of, 160 n.4
nothing (*sakata*), 9–10, 55, 162
only what is good, 8–9
refraining/keeping from, 10, 33
with rhymed prose, 41
with two tongues (*lisānayn*), 3, 151
speech, xxii, 9, 11–12, 15 n.4, 107, 116, 141
abounding in/abundant, 23–24
aim of, 41, 88
all-inclusive, 13
allusive (*maʿārīḍ*), 95, 97
backbiting in, 110
faculty of, as gift, xxi
of God, 3, 163
as good or repugnant, 57
limit/reduce one's, 25, 162
lying in, 3, 80
needless (*fuḍūl al-kalām*), 3
of others, attacking, 31
oversights/errors entering into, 159, 161
pleasant/soothing, 38–39
polite, 132 n.74
pompous in, 40, 42
pretentiousness in, 3, 40
private, concealing, 138
and ridicule, 71
superfluous (*fuḍūl al-kalām*), 13, 21–24
truthfulness in, 85–87
vulgar/malicious/obscene, 43–44, 46
spite, 143. *See also* envy
spoils (of battle), 59, 78
spouses, 20 n.23, 90 n.52, 91 n.55
spying, 128–129, 142
states (of people), xx, 14, 22, 51, 124, 141–142
change, 51
covered by God, 127

About the Translators

Michael Abdurrahman Fitzgerald, originally from California, and his wife migrated to Morocco in the late 1970s. Since that time, he has been involved in education and the study of Arabic, Islam, and Sufism. He is the co-translator of *Ibn al-Qayyim on the Invocation of God* (Islamic Texts Society, 2000) and, along with Fouad Aresmouk, translated *The Immense Ocean*, a section of Ibn ʿAjība's Qurʾānic commentary; *The Book of Ascension*, Ibn ʿAjība's spiritual glossary; four other books from al-Ghazālī's *Iḥyāʾ* series; and most recently he translated an additional section of Ibn ʿAjība's Qurʾānic commentary, *The Chapters of Mary and Ṭā Hā* (Fons Vitae, 2021). Abdurrahman holds degrees from the University of California and Shenandoah University, Virginia, and is co-founder and senior consultant of the Center for Language and Culture, Marrakesh.

Mohamed Fouad Aresmouk grew up in a traditional Marrakesh family, the son of an Arabic teacher in the public school system and grandson of one of the most renowned Qurʾān teachers in Marrakesh and *muqaddam* for the Tijānī Sufi order. Fouad completed his degree in Islamic Studies and Arabic at Cadi Ayyad University, Marrakesh, while at the same time plunging into a personal study of Sufism in Morocco that continues to this day. He is the author of *al-Rashād fī zabdat al-awrād*, a commentary (*sharḥ*) on the litany of the Ḥabībiyya Sufi order of Morocco; co-translator of four other books of *Iḥyāʾ* series; and he translated a number of other works from the Moroccan Sufi tradition. In addition to scholarly pursuits, he is co-founder and human resources manager of the Center for Language and Culture in Marrakesh and a husband and father of two.

About the Reviewer

Faris Casewit is an American scholar and translator in the field of Islamic Studies. He was born in Egypt and raised in Morocco. He received his PhD in Islamic Studies from Harvard University in 2019. His areas of research include mystical Qurʾānic exegesis, Sufi hermeneutics, and thirteenth-century North Africa and the Middle East. His dissertation, "Harmonizing Discursive Worlds: The Life and Times of Abū al-Ḥasan al-Ḥarrālī," explores the intellectual and spiritual legacy and biography of Abū al-Ḥasan al-Ḥarrālī (d. 638/1241), a Sufi-oriented polymath from the Maghrib. Casewit has expertise in Arabic to English translation, making a range of medieval to modern Arabic texts accessible to Western audiences. Casewit lives in northern Virginia with his wife and son.

About the Author

Abū Ḥāmid Muḥammad al-Ghazālī (d. 1111) was a leading jurist, theologian, and spiritual master of the golden age of Islam, and he remains its truest advocate in modern times. As a teacher of both the inward and outward aspects of faith, he systematized these practical teachings with eloquence and precision in his forty-book compendium of Islamic knowledge. Imām al-Ghazālī is the author of two hundred seventy-three works that span many disciplines such as, jurisprudence and legal theory; logic and philosophy; theology; ethics and educational theory; spirituality and Sufism; Qurʾānic studies; and political statecraft. See pp. xiii–xviii for a detailed biography and chronology of his life.

This publication was made possible through the generous support of Ikbal and Ercument Tokat and SufiCorner. May God reward them and their family.